New Address:

The Princeton Computer Group, Inc.
109 Princeton Avenue
Providence, RI 02907

P9-DFJ-644

Million Dollar Consulting

The Professional's Guide to Growing a Practice

Alan Weiss

McGraw-Hill, Inc.

New York   St. Louis   San Francisco   Auckland   Bogotá
Caracas   Lisbon   London   Madrid   Mexico   Milan
Montreal   New Delhi   Paris   San Juan   São Paulo
Singapore   Sydney   Tokyo   Toronto

Library of Congress Cataloging-in-Publication Data

Weiss, Alan.
    Million dollar consulting : the professional's guide to growing a
practice / Alan Weiss.
        p.   cm.
    Includes index.
    ISBN 0-07-069102-9
    1. Consultants—Marketing.   I. Title.
HD69.C6W46   1992
001'.068'8—dc20   92-6613
                                                            CIP

Copyright © 1992 by Alan Weiss. All rights reserved. Printed in the
United States of America. Except as permitted under the United States
Copyright Act of 1976, no part of this publication may be reproduced or
distributed in any form or by any means, or stored in a data base or
retrieval system, without the prior written permission of the publisher.

1 2 3 4 5 6 7 8 9 0   DOC/DOC   9 8 7 6 5 4 3 2

ISBN   0-07-069102-9

*The sponsoring editor for this book was Betsy N. Brown, the editing supervisor
was Ann A. Craig, and the production supervisor was Donald F. Schmidt. It
was set in Baskerville by McGraw-Hill's Professional Book Group composition
unit.*

Printed and bound by R. R. Donnelley & Sons Company.

This book is dedicated to educators everywhere.
Theirs is the noblest of all callings.

Contents

Preface   ix
Acknowledgments   xiii

Part 1. Strategy: Establishing Your View of the Profession   1

1. The State of the Art: Most Art Is in the Eye of the Beholder   3

What a Consultant Is and Is Not   3
How Organizations Choose Consulting Help   8
Emphasizing Results, Not Tasks   13
Trends and Likelihoods for the Coming Decade   17

2. The Right State of Mind: Rudderless Ships Are Only Good at Drifting   23

How Jobs Get in the Way of Careers   23
Will Growth Cut You Down to Size?   28
Abandoning Clients Gracefully   30
Business You Should Abandon   31
Establishing the Ideal Goals   32
As in Show Business, Timing Is Everything   36

3. Prerequisites for Growth: Expanding the Envelope   41

The Success Trap   41
Establishing the Firm's Image   45

Abandoning the Past   50
Accepting Prudent Risk   54

4. Breaking Paradigms: The Worst Piece of Advice I've Ever Received   59

A Surefire Strategy for Growing Your Firm   59
Fine-Tuning the Strategy   63
Ten Ways to Develop Breakthrough Relationships   67
The Core Value of Your Firm's Success   71

5. Turning the Corner: The Light at the End of the Tunnel   77

Surviving Transition Periods   77
Eight Secrets for Retaining Key Personal Business   81
Raising Capital   85
The Ten Basic Principles of Million Dollar Consulting   90

Part 2. Tactics: Implementing Your Vision of Your Firm   93

6. The Look of the Business: Prospects Believe What They See and Hear   95

Memberships, Networks, and Affiliations   95
Promotion and Publicity   100
Personal Conduct   108
Facing Up to the Challenge   110

7. Acquiring People: Practicing What You Preach Could Save Your Life   115

Options for Participation.   115
Where to Find Good People and How to Recognize Them   121
How to Reward Collaboration: The Revenue-Sharing Formula   124
The First Rule of Leverage: Don't Give Up the Ship   129

8. Establishing Fees: If You're Charging a Per Diem, You're Still Just Practicing   135

Formulaic Methods to Establish Per Diem Fees   135
Market Demand Methods for Establishing Fees   140
Perceived Value as a Basis on Which to Establish Fees   143
Establishing the Value of a Client's Investment   147
When to Raise Your Fees and What Will Always Happen   150

Other Reasons for Raising Fees   151

9. Investing in Success: Absence Doesn't Make the Heart Grow Fonder—It Weakens the Memory   **155**

Periodic Client Communications   155
Publishing Options   160
The Speaking Circuit   165
Pro Bono Work   169

10. Turning Change into Opportunity: Bad Times Can Be Good Times If You Play Your Cards Right   **173**

Early Warning Signs of Business Decline   173
Avoiding Down Times: The Five Up-Time Rules   176
Contrarian Consulting: Swimming against the Current   180
The Myth of Cutting Expenses (Don't Sell the Conference Table)   184

Part 3. Success: Achieving Self-Realization   **189**

11. Managing Capital: Borrow $1000 and They Own You, but Borrow $1 Million and...   **191**

Establishing Credit Lines   191
The Rules of Incoming Cashflow   197
Collecting Receivables   198
Ten Expense-Management Tactics   202

12. Accelerating Growth: Growth Does Not Always Equal Expansion   **209**

Seven Techniques for Intensifying the Firm's Profile   209
Intensifying Your Personal Profile   217
Becoming a Star: The Camera Calls   222

13. The Ultimate Relationships: When Clients Call *You*   **227**

Long-Term Contracts   227
Client Advisory Groups and Conferences   231
The Value-Added Discounting Principle of Never Losing Clients   235

14. Beyond Success: Money Is Only a Means to an End   **243**

Ethical Issues   243

Expanding Internationally   251
Designing the Future   254

Annotated Resources   259
Index   271

Preface

Those who can, do..Those who can't do, teach.
Those who can't teach, consult.
— CITED BY AN EXECUTIVE WHO HAD POOR
RESULTS WITH CONSULTANTS

Somehow, I think there's more to the craft than that. In the pages ahead, I intend to demonstrate how to be excellent and successful in this wonderful and unique profession.

A couple of years back, Bob Ingram — who was then president of Merck Frosst Canada and is now with Glaxo Pharmaceuticals — introduced me as the after-dinner speaker at his annual sales awards banquet in this manner:

> Alan Weiss is with us today, and he is a consultant. You all know what a consultant is, of course. He's someone who knows 40 ways to make love, but doesn't know any women.

As I ascended to the lectern, the place was in an uproar. One hundred people anxiously awaited whatever it was I could possibly say to regain control. And so I said the only thing that could logically follow:

> Well, I guess the first thing I'd like to do is to introduce myself to the women in the audience...

The recording of that introduction and speech is part of one of my cassette albums, and is very popular. In fact, it has continually helped me to obtain new clients. One of the reasons, I believe — aside from the repartee — is that the incident represents what it means to be a successful consultant:

- First, you have to retain your sense of humor and perspective at all times.
- Second, your relationship with the client has to be solid enough and close enough to make you part of the family. (People don't take the time to kid people they don't like.)
- Third, you can never take *anything* for granted, not even an introduction. You must be alert and ready to respond to all kinds of interference and static.
- Fourth, you have to see all the twists and turns as *opportunities*, not threats, and learn to exploit them, not flee from them.
- Fifth, you have to be confident about who you are, what you are doing, and why you are doing it. Self-esteem is not a function of win or lose; it's the result of knowing that you're prepared, qualified, and doing your absolute best, cognizant of the fact that, on occasion, even your best won't be enough.

Bob Ingram also mentioned, in a more sober part of his introduction, that I was one of the most highly regarded consultants in the world, and that Merck and I had a long-standing, extremely beneficial relationship. As a matter of fact, for the past seven years I have been one of the principal external consultants to Merck and Co., the pharmaceutical giant which has been named "America's Most Admired Company" for an unprecedented six years in a row by the annual *Fortune* magazine poll. My "small" firm, Summit Consulting Group, Inc., is certainly not in the same league as McKinsey and Co., Booz Allen, Boston Consulting Group, Bain, or a hundred others of their ilk. But we do consult with Mercedes-Benz, the New York Times, the British Standards Institute, BusinessWeek, Hewlett-Packard, GTE, GE, the American Institute of Architects, Marine Midland Bank, and scores of others. Yet I only started "doing my own thing" nine years ago.

I've been able to accomplish what I have by listening to some good advice, ignoring a lot of bad advice, and not allowing the thinking blinders — the "paradigms," if you're into buzzwords — of the profession to limit me. It is said that, aerodynamically speaking, there is no way that a bumblebee should be able to fly. No one has yet found a way to communicate that to bumblebees. Sometimes you're better off if you don't know what you don't know.

One such thinking blinder is that all consulting work must follow models and matrices, rational approaches and strict methodologies. But fortunately for my clients and my business, I've learned that intuition, randomness, and pure folly can all play an important role. "There are two equally dangerous extremes," said Blaise Pascal, "to shut reason out and to let nothing else in." In a famous experiment, a researcher filled a bottle with flies and bees, and placed the closed end of the bottle against a window pane. Knowing that bees are much smarter than flies, he waited to see how the bees would reason their way out of the enclosure. However, the bees flew toward the light from the window and remained there until they all died. The flies, pursuing random flight patterns within the bottle, eventually found the opening at the other end, and all escaped. Life, business, and consulting are not subject merely to formulaic approaches; if they were, everyone would be good at them and, in reality, very few are.

A second thinking blinder is an old rubric which states that a "lone wolf" (read: individual practitioner, whether working alone or employed by others) cannot generate over $300,000 in revenue as a consultant. This is the figurative equivalent of the runner's "wall," or the test aircraft's "envelope." Well, we know that every human race event has produced new records over the past decade, and test pilots are paid to test the envelope on a regular basis. A superb consultant can make a million dollars or more a year and, in so doing, help others to the extent that they are convinced that they've received value worth many times what they paid as a fee. If you settle for the paradigm, you can make about $300,000 a year. If you believe that consulting is a craft that is based on value, not hours, you can make a million dollars.

If you'd like to know where the $700,000 difference is, read on.

Alan Weiss

Acknowledgments

I am indebted to the many clients of Summit Consulting Group, Inc., who, over the past nine years, have allowed me to practice, develop, and hone my craft. Their trust at first amazed me and now exhilarates me.

In particular I want to thank Fred Kerst at Calgon, Rick Haugen at Allergan Optical, and Mike Magsig of Cologne Reinsurance, three of the finest CEOs I've had the pleasure to work with and learn from. I also very much appreciate the long-standing working relationship I've enjoyed with Del Macpherson, Jim Jones, and George Rizk of Merck, who know how to work hard and laugh harder. All three are admirable people in America's "Most Admired Company."

I owe a great deal to Ben Tregoe for giving me 11 years of fine (and not so fine) tuning all over the world. Ben cofounded Kepner-Tregoe in a garage and built it into a business staple. To this day, his remains the best mind I've encountered in this business.

My thanks go to Bill Howe, principal of Kenny, Kindler, Hunt, and Howe for ten years of irregular lunches in the finest restaurants in New York and ten years of regular commonsense "smacks in the head" that kept my ego from becoming an entry in the Rose Bowl Parade.

Finally, common sense *is* hereditary, and I inherited 100 percent of mine from my wife, Maria, and from Danielle and Jason, who claim to be my kids. I am humbled by the fact that, although they have seen my act many times, they continue to tolerate it and help me to improve it. And for the second consecutive book, my appreciation goes to L. T. Weiss for his unerring editorial assistance and judgment.

About the Author

Alan Weiss, Ph.D., is an internationally recognized consultant, author, and speaker. He is founder and president of Summit Consulting Group, Inc., East Greenwich, Rhode Island, an organization and management development firm whose clients include Merck, GE, Hewlett-Packard, Mercedes-Benz, and The New York Times, among many others. He is the author of *Making It Work* and *Managing for Peak Performance* and the coauthor of *The Innovation Formula*.

PART 1

Strategy: Establishing Your View of the Profession

Do not seek to follow in the footsteps of the men of old; seek what they sought.

— MATSUO BASHO (1644–1694)

1
The State of the Art

Most Art Is in the Eye of the Beholder

What a Consultant Is and Is Not

An attorney is a person who has been graduated from an accredited school of law, passes a bar exam in the state in question, and deals with matters requiring legal opinions and actions. A doctor is a person who has been graduated from an accredited medical school, passes state exams in appropriate areas of expertise, and is licensed to practice medicine in conformance with certain regulatory laws and ethical practices. A certified public accountant is a person who...

You get the idea. Most professions have a clear definition. They require formal certifications and have specific, enforceable limitations. A teacher needs education courses and a college degree. A bus driver needs a driver's license. A manicurist must be state certified to work on your nails in a salon. But there are no such constraints on the consultant. Anyone, at any time, and virtually anywhere, can be a consultant. There is only one other calling I know of that exerts as much influence over the public and requires as few formal qualifications, and that's astrology. (However, I tend to think that it is tougher to get into astrology than into consulting, so my apologies are hereby proffered to any stargazers I've antagonized.)

Yet consulting is a profession that can earn its practitioners wealth far in excess of what can be earned in fields with such tight qualifying criteria. And that wealth isn't only in the form of financial success. It includes a dramatic learning curve, experiences of a broad and diverse nature, and the potential to provide value to clients that can have an impact on tens of thousands of people at any given moment. In view of this peculiar situation, I'd like to begin by establishing a definition of a consultant.

Now this isn't a definition for the ages, nor one that will be acceptable to everybody. But it is sufficient to serve as a working definition for the remaining chapters, and it serves to establish what a consultant *is* and what a consultant *is not*.

> **A consultant is someone who provides a specialized expertise, content, behavior, skill or other resource to assist a client in improving the status quo. This intervention focuses on a specific client need.**

Consultants may be internal—working for the organization full-time—or external. The latter group is hired on a situational basis. Those situations may last for a day or a year, but most are (and should be) of fairly brief duration. There will be more about timing in later chapters.

The most important part of my definition for those of you seeking to build consulting practices is the notion of bringing something of value to the equation that justifies a fee above and beyond the client's normal business investment.

Consulting is not synonymous with implementing, delivering, instructing, or executing, although consulting may include any of these activities.

A client who hires an outside instructor to conduct programs that the client has developed or purchased elsewhere has no more hired a training consultant than the client who hires part-time office help has hired a typing consultant. A great deal of the confusion that exists in the marketplace and among consultants ourselves is caused by an overly encompassing use of terms. Some trainers are *also* consultants, and some professional speakers *also* consult, just as some computer programmers *also* consult on programming applications. But merely being a programmer or speaker or trainer does not, de facto, make one a consultant, any more than being a consultant makes one a trainer or speaker or programmer.

There are many large training firms that have not been successful in crossing over into consulting, and many large consulting firms that have not been able to develop a training function. Although compatible, these are two separate disciplines, requiring separate skills. So try as they might, with advertising, promotion and attempts to manage public perception, training firms such as Wilson Learning, Forum, Kepner-Tregoe, and dozens of others have had little success as consulting firms, and consulting organizations such as Boston Consulting Group, McKinsey and A. D. Little have not become well known as training firms.

The fact is, consultants must deliver value-added to the client in one or more of the areas illustrated in Figure 1-1.

If the consultant isn't bringing anything to the endeavor that the client doesn't already possess, then why make the investment? The value-added that the consultant brings to bear usually falls into one of six basic categories:

1. *Content.* This is the most common consulting value, largely because most people enter consulting in a field they already know well. Their comfort, experience, and relationships usually lie within such a field. Consequently, there are retail-store display consultants, textile consultants, shrink-wrap packaging consultants (whose job, no doubt, is to ensure that no one opens a package of batteries or paper clips without dislocating a finger), and a plethora of similar content experts. Whatever the industry or pursuit, its work, or *content,* provides the basis for someone to consult in it. Although content

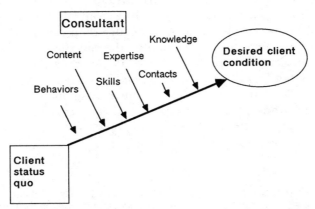

Figure 1-1. What the consultant brings to the client engagement.

consulting is often the province of those who break from organizational life to go out on their own, it is also the realm of very large
firms. For example, Kurt Salmon and Associates has always been regarded as the ne plus ultra of textile consulting whenever I've heard
a mutual client refer to it.

2. *Expertise.* Many consultants have a particular expertise that transcends industries and is applicable to a wide variety of environments.
For example, Bain & Co. tends to specialize in strategic planning. Its
clients are diverse, having only one thing necessarily in common: the
value-added they are seeking is help with strategic planning. Bain
can adapt its approaches to various areas of content. Similarly,
Braxton Associates has expertise in helping a firm determine appropriate courses of action according to a projection of shareholder
value. The type of firm doesn't matter. Braxton can apply its expertise and formulas equally well to any type, whatever the exact nature
of the client's business. Many consultants who strike out on their own
after working for a larger consulting firm often include expertise as
their value-added because they have been so intimately exposed to
those areas of expertise during the course of their work. (No, this is
not illegal, unethical, or even uncomfortable. Ideas cannot be pat-
ented and, indeed, there *is* nothing new under the sun. The basic
analytic problem-solving skills we all use today were first postulated
by the Greeks two millennia ago.)

3. *Knowledge.* In my definition, knowledge is largely experiential.
These are the people who have "been there before." A bank board
on which I served chose to hire a former regulator as a consultant
because he had vast knowledge of the rules and procedures the
regulators would be enforcing in a stricter banking environment.[1]
Engineering consultants are often hired out of this same need. In
general, knowledge is a broader category than expertise, just as engineering is a broader discipline than the specific pursuit of calculations of projected shareholder value. Moreover, knowledge includes
an understanding of *process, as opposed to content.* That is, the consultant understands the process of time management, irrespective of
content, or the process of decision making, regardless of the environment. This is often referred to as *process consultation.* It involves
form as well as substance.

---

[1]Note that these terms have considerable overlap. The former regulator could be seen
as a content expert or a contact expert. The key point, and the reason for the separations,
is that the client's perception of what he or she is hiring and the consultant's perception of
what is being offered are both critical to successful marketing.

4. *Behavior.* The value-added in this case is interpersonal. These consultants may facilitate groups to achieve conflict resolution, or teach others how to make presentations and interact with an audience. These consultants are virtually never behind-the-scenes as the others may be, but are hired specifically to be on stage. They possess a set of interpersonal competencies that enable them to resolve conflict, enhance brainstorming and creativity, focus on critical issues, listen to customer or employee feedback, and so on. Their utility is in the overt role they play, which, for any number of reasons, management itself cannot assume. Sometimes an objective third party is required, and sometimes specific behaviors must be applied. Many people specializing in these areas have found themselves naturally drawn to them because of previous successes in dealing with such issues. Mediators and arbitrators come to mind as consultants in this field.

5. *Special skills.* Some people have highly developed, well-defined skills that can be in great demand. These are often talents and innate abilities. For example, image consultants, who are able to improve one's wardrobe and grooming, bring to bear an instinctive sense of style and impact. (Contrast this with the shareholder value specialists, whose approach can be reduced to formulas, matrices, and calculations.) An image consultant might know nothing of the content of the client's work, may not have precise expertise or knowledge (i.e., about where to get the best buy on clothes, or how to arrange one's closet) but nonetheless has a talent for creating a certain look. Consultants in this area have a gift, or specialized talent, the client usually cannot acquire independently, or finds cost prohibitive to acquire. "We are translating this program into French-Canadian. Find someone who knows the particular idioms and cultural norms, and who can put it into conversational language that doesn't appear to be an insensitive translation from English."

6. *Contacts.* Basically, consultants called in to help because of their contacts are lobbyists of one stripe or another. Whether they are truly consultants is a question I don't propose to debate here. I've included the category primarily because a great many people entering consulting do so on the basis of being able to introduce clients to key contacts in public or private life. While consulting fees are paid for this work, it is the role least able to fulfill the definition I've provided above. Those entering the field as so-called introducers are advised to broaden their scope into the other areas fairly rapidly if they are serious about making it big as a consultant. Gerald Ford has always struck me as a good example of someone in this capacity who never chose to, or could not, leave it. He is hired for name value

only, and his appearance at events or on boards has never been dictated by any intrinsic expertise or ability other than having been the president. Calling him a consultant is courtesy, not accuracy.

Consultants bring one or more (and in more cases than you would suspect, *all*) of these competencies to bear to help a client move from the status quo to an improved position. If I were moving an operation to South America for the first time, I might need *content* to understand the nature of the competition for my goods and services in the new locale; *expertise* to provide the requisite language skills to my transferring managers; *knowledge* to gain the proper licenses and tax permits; *behavior* to help with the advance work in preparation for our arrival and in dealing with the local press; *skills* to assist in the acculturation process of what we should do to assimilate as rapidly as possible; and *contacts* to build relationships with local governmental and business leaders.

There are, I am told by professors who track such things, over several hundred thousand[2] independent consultants in the United States. In addition, there are thousands of consulting organizations, from tiny practices to the Arthur Andersens and McKinsey & Companys of the world. It is folly to attempt to make sense of that panoply in any conventional manner, since huge organizations such as IBM and GE often prefer to use the lone wolf for one assignment and Booz Allen for another just down the hall. Consequently, it's probably more useful to view the market in terms of the values the consultant brings to the client, rather than in terms of arbitrary category or size.

How Organizations Choose Consulting Help

There is more logic in the National Basketball Association play-off system, or in the myriad pieces of billing information you get from the phone company, or in any Rube Goldberg invention for catching a mouse, than there is in the selection process for consulting help.[3] Consequently, it is difficult and even foolhardy to try to market against a consistent buying habit, unless you are in a highly specialized area such

---

[2]The figure is given as 140,000—doing a $13 billion business in the United States and $9 billion overseas—in *Consultants News*, "How Big Is Consulting?" March 1991.

[3]We are dealing with *new* business, not the continuation of existing business or the expansion of current business within existing clients. The notion of repeat business will be dealt with in Chapter 4.

as government, in which requests for proposals (RFPs) are uniform and the only way in which the customer will do business.[4]

These are the major ways in which organizations go about securing the services of outside consultants:

1. *Word-of-mouth.* This is probably the most comfortable method for many buyers, particularly at middle-to-upper management levels. If a trusted colleague can endorse someone who's done the job for him or her, the client saves a great deal of time and minimizes the risk. If the colleague is in the same industry—even as a competitor—so much the better. (I've received hundreds of calls from potential buyers who have been referred to me by satisfied clients.) This technique is what I call passive marketing, since it is out of your hands. However, deliberately gathering the names of a client's colleagues and obtaining permission to use the client as a reference, can help you respond much more effectively to some of the other selection methods used by prospective buyers.

> **After successful engagements, million dollar consultants always ask the client two things. First: What other people do you know who can use these same services and approaches? Second: May I use you personally as a reference?**

2. *Repute.* This is slightly different from the first method, in that the potential buyer might not have actually spoken to anyone familiar with your work, but might have heard of you through a third party, publicity, or casual conversation. This method is often—and unfortunately—popular with top executives, who feel safer acquiring the services of a "name" firm or individual so as to justify the investment (and not have to think too analytically about the actual intervention). Reputation in this business is like reputation in the entertainment business: sometimes the biggest stars are the biggest flops, living on repute and little else, and sometimes the biggest unknowns are powerful surprises, living on talent and little else.

3. *Professional affiliations.* Clients often review basic consultant listings to establish a list of firms dealing in their area of need, be it stra-

---

[4]And even here there are exceptions. For example, if you can qualify as a sole source of a particular service, you can circumvent the entire competitive bidding process.

tegic planning or new-hire orientation. These listings appear in the *Who's Who of the American Society for Training and Development,* the *Buyer's Guide of Training Magazine,* recommendations by *Consultants News,* the membership of consulting associations such as ACME, and similar one-stop shopping alternatives. Typically, clients request information from all firms listed in certain areas of need, qualifying the search with criteria such as location, types of intervention, and methods of delivery.

4. *Internal data.*   In some cases, clients maintain a file of consultant capabilities that they review whenever appropriate. I've received many inquiries from firms that requested information years prior but did not see fit to follow up at that time. Toward this end, I maintain a mailing list of everyone who requests any type of information from our firm, and mail literature to them twice a year without fail. This periodic presence enables the prospect to update the files on you and continues a familiarity between your two organizations.

5. *Advertising.*   Some clients request proposals based on advertising when the ads focus on the client's need (or when free literature is offered). In my experience, advertising is not very conducive to securing consulting contracts (it works better for training and workshop alternatives), since its main appeal is to fairly low-level managers who are not in a position to purchase consulting help. Although they can be recommenders, the ultimate buyer usually relies on one of the first four methods.

6. *Personal contact.*   Occasionally, you will meet a potential buyer at a business meeting, through a third-party introduction, or at some other random event. Cards will be exchanged and information sent. The less effective consultants immediately record a probable deal on their business forecasts, while the more realistic simply add another name to their regular mailing list. *People you meet on airplanes, no matter how cordial or at what level, virtually never hire you.* And most association meetings I've attended involve precious few buyers. (At many conventions, I find consultants pitching to other consultants, which is roughly akin to trying to sell stamps to the post office.)

The exact people doing the selecting can vary, from the CEO personally to a task force formed to review proposals. But whether through one person or a crowd, and whether through one decision or a series, you will be known to the decision makers via one of the six routes above. From the point of requesting information or a meeting, you will be judged on form as well as substance. That is, the prospect is seeking a professional alternative to meet given needs and objectives. Figure 1-2 lists some of the all-star gaffes I've seen committed by consultants dur-

- No answer at the consultant's phone number
- An answering machine at the consultant's phone number
- Having to receive faxes through a local travel agent
- Lack of letterhead, envelopes, and/or business cards
- No brochure, company descriptive material, and/or press kit
- A brochure that fits in a #10 envelope
- Proposals with typos, poor grammar, and misused words
- Being late and/or unprepared for initial meetings
- Talking instead of listening
- Charging expenses to the client for phone calls and postage

Figure 1-2. How to shoot oneself in both feet simultaneously.

ing the selection process. I've seen people rack up all 10 of these without much effort because they are the result of not much effort!

> *Every interaction with a prospect should be seen as a personal moment of truth, and the consultant should always be thinking about the fourth sale, not the immediate one.*

We'll discuss what a consultant requires to present a professional image and the confidence of a solid, successful firm for clients in later chapters. But for now, bear in mind that it is extremely difficult to acquire clients, extremely lucrative to maintain long-standing client relationships, and extremely difficult to lose a happy client. Since most readers are probably not CEOs of the largest consulting firms, it's useful to remember that acquisition of clients is the bedrock of success, and that such acquisition will probably originate in the first four areas listed above, once you are established, but only in the third and fourth areas (professional affiliations and internal data) when you are establishing your practice. Consequently, stack the deck in your favor and be prepared to deal with *any* lead (I've received scraps of paper written in haste) in an assertive, timely, and professional manner.

This is how I obtained my largest contracts over the past year:

- An ongoing pharmaceutical client of seven years' standing requested an extension of one project and the beginning of another. Originally, this client had come on board when an internal buyer, having remembered me as a contact in a training firm I was once with, began hunting for me after I had moved out of state. The old firm passed on my new address, and I was asked if I'd be interested in what became a $14,000-project that the client believed I was suited for. Since then, I've completed $530,000 worth of projects and had the opportunity to bid on several others that went elsewhere. Next year alone has over $200,000 in potential business.

- A buyer at a banking client departed to become CEO of another organization. He promptly requested my assistance. The original client, for whom I had completed three projects over the past seven years, was generated by a 56-cent mailing to an individual recommended by a mutual professional acquaintance. The mailing was handed down two levels and finally came to rest on the desk of someone with a particular need (itch) that my literature addressed (scratched).

- An executive with an insurance client who had used my services on a very small contract left to become CEO of another firm. I updated my mailing list and sent him a series of items. About a year later, he contacted me for a major strategy project, and asked that I serve on his informal kitchen cabinet of consultants. The original client had come on board as the result of a recommendation by the president of another consulting firm who chose not to undertake such a small project within his organization. (This client will surface again on a fishing boat in Chapter 14.)

- A midlevel manager at an aerospace client for whom we did a small amount of work was laid off. I remained in touch and provided contacts and career advice as best I could. She obtained a management position with a large eye care firm and recommended me for a succession planning project, which led to a concurrent project for the president. She has since been promoted. My original association with her dates back to a collaboration with a training firm for which I designed and helped to implement workshops. She was not successful in implementing the workshops, but was impressed by my approaches and participation.

- I had done a small amount of business with a major telecommunications firm nine years ago, but a job change for the original recommender resulted in my abrupt dismissal—the new man wanted his own consultants on the job. I remained in contact with his boss through periodic mailings, and was asked to stop in on two occasions simply to discuss what I was doing in the field. About six months after the second such meeting, a new recommender selected me for a series of assignments.

There have been times when those contacts that have seemed most solid and well intentioned have gone absolutely nowhere despite my visits to the prospect and guarantees of my suitability. There have been many more times when a call out of the blue has resulted in a long-term, dramatic engagement. But even those occasions weren't as random as I once believed. They were the result of my having sown the seeds for my work in the first four areas above and having successfully avoided shooting myself in either foot.

Emphasizing Results, Not Tasks

We've already differentiated between a contractor and a consultant. The former is hired to implement specific work and to perform designated tasks. The latter is hired to provide unique abilities and talents that will improve the client condition, and constitutes a value-added component which the client doesn't already possess. The average consultant, however, tends to categorize the involvement by describing the tasks to be performed. *Million dollar consultants, by contrast, tend to describe results.* The difference is between input and output, task and results, activity and outcome. In assessing the value-added (which we'll be discussing in relation to fees in Chapter 8), which of the following is a client likely to perceive as most valuable and unique in contribution, and most meriting of a larger fee?

Task	Result
Survey all employees	Provide recommendations to improve morale
Visit field service units	Identify specific service gaps
Design training program	Improve delegation skills
Observe meetings	Enhance meeting productivity and time use
Reorganize the division	Optimize use of employee skills and talents

Interventions should be based on results and outcomes, not activities and tasks. The more the consultant emphasizes the latter, the more he or she becomes a *doer* whose progress and worth is assessed in terms of how much is *done*. Moreover, the consultant's time use becomes scrutinized (How long will it take you to conduct the survey? How many meetings do you have to observe?) and the alternatives become subject to debate (Why can't we have a two-day training program, instead of a three-day approach? Let us determine which field sites you should visit.). The more the results are emphasized, the more the consultant is free to pick and choose alternatives and to be flexible in abandoning certain approaches and beginning more fruitful ones.

Any intervention should be based on objectives, so that consultant and client are in agreement on the end results of the engagement and the consultant is free to employ a variety of techniques and use time to best advantage. The more the engagement is based on alternatives, the more the consultant becomes just another hired hand.

There are a variety of ways to view interventions, or *contracts*, as they are often called (that is, the contract with the client regarding responsibilities, not the legal contract that one signs).[5] But virtually all of them take a fairly limited view. For example, the consultant may be a backstage counselor who never appears to the organization in general, but rather concentrates on helping a single individual who interacts with others. Or the consultant may be a coach who is regularly seen on the sidelines sending in advice to the players. Or the consultant may be the front person who actually takes the lead role in running the meeting or leading the project.

However, these types of categories can be self-limiting, and are too often dictated more by what the consultant feels comfortable with, than by what the client needs. In other words, superb consultants tailor their roles—and vary them—according to the precise client needs that have engendered the presence of the consultant. The mere act of helping the client determine the appropriate range of pragmatic interventions is the initial consulting contribution. This determination should be collaborative, explicit, comfortable, and in conformance with the end results required.

At one end of the range of potential interventions shown in Figure 1-3 are those that resolve a client need and/or improve a client position.

---

[5]For example, see Peter Block, *Flawless Consulting*, Learning Concepts, Austin, 1981 and Robert R. Blake and Jane Srygley Mouton, *Consultation*, Addison-Wesley, Reading, Mass., 1976. These are older works, but they're all you need on the subject of establishing the type of intervention as a contract.

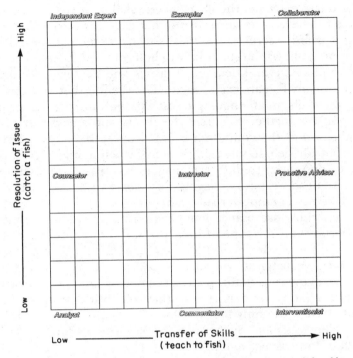

Figure 1-3. The range of potential consultant interventions as defined by client need.

In other words, the client is hungry and the consultant must catch a fish for dinner lest the client starve. At the other end of the range are interventions that educate the client so that such needs can be met self-sufficiently in the future. In other words, the client learns how to catch a fish without help.

In some extreme and valid cases, the client has no need to master the consultant's skills and approaches and simply requires situational, one-time expertise. This is an occasion for "the consultant-as-expert," in which the consultant brings the fishing gear, determines the best spot in the stream, catches the fish, cooks it, packs the tent, and departs. The client is responsible only for consumption and cleanup. The evaluation of the consultant is based upon the quantity and quality of the fish caught and whether or not they have sated the client's hunger at that moment. A consultant helping with an acquisition might well serve in this capacity. I've designed downsizing programs for organizations in this capacity.

In the other extreme, the client needs skills transferred as the end result itself. There is no larger issue that requires reconciliation or, if there is, it is also useful as the means to help transfer the skills. The interventionist shows the client how to hold the rod, how to cast, where to stand, and so on, and demands practice and performance improvements before any fish are even caught. The client is then responsible for utilizing the skills on an ongoing basis, although the consultant may be called upon for further comment, feedback, and analysis of progress. The evaluation of the consultant is based upon the client's decreasing need for outside help to sate hunger at any given moment. A consultant helping to design and educate managers in creative problem solving might serve in this capacity. Playing this role, I've worked with managers on processes to empower subordinates.

There's nothing sacrosanct about the terms provided in Figure 1-3. The importance of this type of breakdown, however, is that it is based on the client's needs for consulting help, and should be used as a template to decide collaboratively what the consultant's role should be. Unfortunately, many consultants picture themselves as experts, instructors, or facilitators and never depart from that role. But as Abraham Maslow observed, "When the only tool you have is a hammer, you tend to see every problem as a nail." Such categorization severely limits the value of a consultant to prospective (and current) clients.

I have a good friend who is perceived as an instructor in telemarketing. He is excellent at what he does, but he finds it extraordinarily difficult to enlarge client engagements beyond telemarketing. Yet when he works with me as an associate, he is involved in a wide variety of roles and areas. Unfortunately, he has restricted his considerable talents, not only by focusing on one content area—telemarketing—but even more so by concentrating on one type of intervention—running training programs. I pointed out that his preparation work for the training involved lengthy observations on the clients' sites and evaluation of strengths and weaknesses, which constitutes the core of an excellent needs analysis. That, in itself, is an analyst role on my chart, and one that he should consider as a separate value for the client, irrespective of whether he ever runs a training program. In other words, he is already utilizing other interventions, and is adept at them, but subordinates them to his preconceived role as an instructor. When I introduce him as an associate within my clients, his role is determined by the client's need and not his own, standard one, broadening the value he brings to the situation. He has since embarked on a plan to create an identical dynamic within his own client base. (This is very difficult, once the client has typecast you. The key is to avoid a predefined role with prospects, so that new clients never identify you with a single type of intervention.)

Figure 1-3 represents what I call the "pragmatic range of interventions" because they are based on client need and the combination of doing *for* the client and helping the client to become self-sufficient—both legitimate goals. The remainder of this book will assume that the consultant is willing to embrace a variety of practical interventions. That willingness is the first major step toward exponential growth in business.

Trends and Likelihoods for the Coming Decade

Consulting is a growing profession, both for good reasons and for spurious ones. The good reasons include these:

- Reduced staffing results in the need for outside specialized help.
- Increasing complexity and change taxes daily management.
- Growing diversity in the work force demands new approaches.
- Increasing internationalization creates new rules and opportunities.
- Baby boomers are moving into senior positions and experiment more.
- Customers and shareholders increasingly demand high performance.
- Emerging nations begin dynamic management modernization.
- Organizations require outside validation to monitor performance.
- Demographic shifts radically change markets.
- Trends (like customer service) continue to drive performance goals.

The spurious reasons include these:

- There continue to be no licensing or certification requirements.
- Consulting is seen as a way to make money with low overhead and tax demands.
- Consulting skills can be appropriated from books, courses, and tapes.
- Fads (like left brain/right brain learning) intrigue company trainers.
- Management prefers to use outsiders rather than face unpleasant jobs.
- Desperate organizations seek help too late.
- The nature of the role continues to be confused with implementors.

Unfortunately, consulting will continue to be a profession that readily grows in quantity but not as readily in quality. The good news, of course, is that those of us providing professional, quality services will continue to grow rich. But just as the average attorney earns far less than the heroes of "LA Law" (in fact, I was told by an acquaintance at the American Bar Association that the average general practice attorney earns below $80,000 a year), the average consultant will neither achieve great wealth nor establish a sound enough business to survive down times.[6] Many consultants are retired people seeking to use specific expertise or contacts to remain active, and many more are people holding down full-time jobs who consult on the side to earn extra income. (All too often that work on the side is at the expense of the regular employer's expertise, time, and/or materials. I call it "white-collar moonlighting," and it is a problem in all organizations that do not fully absorb the professional talents and interests of their managers.)

Overall, consulting work has tended to be reactive, rather than proactive, responding to the trends, fads, and whims of the marketplace. Sometimes those who merely respond fastest are seen as innovators, but in reality there are very few who provide new approaches proactively. For example, once *In Search of Excellence*[7] became a hit, there followed a plethora of consultants, trainers, and preachers who espoused "management by wandering around" and "sticking to the knitting" as though these were mantras whose very intonation would improve the operation. In actuality, most managers I observed wandering around under such guidance only managed to get in the way and generally had no idea what to do while they were wandering. One training firm, Zenger-Miller, actually purchased the rights to use the book's premises as the core of a training program, rolled out with very expensive fanfare. Today, that program no longer exists, though I suspect that managers continue to wander rather than manage. In what might be the apotheosis of consulting as a bizarre activity, there are those today who counsel organizations on how to apply for and try to win quality awards like the Baldrige, Deming or Nikkei prizes. Funny, I thought those awards recognized quality in products, services, and customer re-

---

[6]The late consulting guru Howard Shenson claimed in his advertisements that there are over 400,000 people engaged in the profession, of whom only 11 percent earn over $50,000 per year. He cited IRS figures as his source. A number in the "hundreds of thousands" is also supported by a prepublication reviewer of one of my manuscripts, John Young, Director of the University of Colorado Executive Programs.

[7]Thomas J. Peters and Robert H. Waterman, Jr., *In Search of Excellence: Lessons from America's Best-Run Companies*, Harper & Row, New York, 1982.

lations. But sometimes the pursuit of such recognition is at the cost of tending to business.[8]

Excellent consultants will explore with clients those results that actually constitute improvements in performance, service, and quality, and how well business goals are being met. That is, they will help establish the *objectives* to be attained, not merely the *alternatives* to measure progress. For the remainder of the 1990s we will see an increasingly sophisticated consumer in an increasingly complex international economy. (That does not apply only to large organizations. Local jewelry distributors in Rhode Island, for example, purchase goods in the Philippines and Korea, then use immigrant help from Portugal to assemble and ship the merchandise, which is ultimately sold in New York to Japanese tourists.) The need for consulting help will indeed grow because the marketplace will require it. The good reasons for growth listed above are largely *market-driven*, while the spurious reasons are largely *consultant-driven*.

My belief is that those consultants who are able to deal with high degrees of ambiguity, and who can offer a variety of the intervention roles described in Figure 1-3 (often shifting roles within the context of a single assignment) will best be able to provide the unique, value-added talents that meet client needs. The tolerance for ambiguity is necessary because fewer client needs will be cut-and-dried and simple to embrace.

One of my clients asked me to work with a newly appointed division president to enhance his ability to delegate. The parent group president had identified this lack as a potentially severe problem, since the individual would now be leading former peers. It would have been easy to have listed the various alternatives to improve delegation skills, and to provide the client with options for implementing them. However, I've long since learned that few things in this business are as they first appear, and that three things always jointly influence behavior: individual predispositions, environment, and interactions with others.

When I met with the president to explore whether we would work together, I didn't approach the conversation as one which would help

[8]Florida Power and Light recently disbanded its quality teams after winning the Baldrige Award because management felt that the focus was more on compliance with the team regulations than on results for the customer. And Cadillac won the award in 1990 even though its quality is below competitors' because it made such dramatic *improvements* in quality. In other words, if you let things slip long enough, you look good when you finally do something about it, and if you're attentive every day you don't have room for dramatic improvement. For a further discussion of ends-and-means confusion, see "Author Disputes Quality of Baldrige Awards," Associated Press report, *Providence Journal*, April 20, 1991, pages D1–D2; "Is the Baldrige Overblown?" *Fortune*, July 1, 1991, page 63; and "Florida Power and Light Eliminates 1,500 Jobs," *Wall Street Journal*, July 10, 1991, page A7.

me to understand a delegation problem. Instead, I spent the morning learning about the president's predispositions, his environment, and his interactions with others. I began to realize that the president's ability to delegate wasn't only a factor of his personal skills, but also of his team's willingness to accept delegation; that there were environmental factors—turf battles, outmoded procedures, confusion over mission—that had to be reconciled; and that there were doubts about whether all of the current players in their current positions were appropriate. We spent the morning determining at what level the organization should be performing if it were ideally successful, and what role the president would be playing in that performance. What had appeared on the surface to be a counselor's role, in actuality demanded skills ranging from analyst to collaborator. This has become one of my most successful client interventions ever. The client has retained me for two years thus far, and the organization has just completed its two finest consecutive years in recent memory. I'm convinced that the key to my ability to help that client demonstrably lay in refusing to allow myself to fall into a single preconceived role based on what I'd been told. Rather, *I listened, validated, and joined the client in establishing results that were to be achieved by any number of activities.* By moving among a variety of roles, I was able to:

- Provide facilitation sessions to top management to enhance execution
- Work one-on-one with senior managers on *accepting* delegation
- Visit customers to determine their perceptions of the client's services
- Analyze the business and contribute to strategic mission statements
- Develop the CEO's personal skills and interpersonal abilities

---

The best, longest-lived, most rewarding client relationships are those based on conceptual agreement of what is to be accomplished. The how is subordinated to the end result.

Consulting throughout the remainder of this decade will be most profitably based on helping the client to establish need and providing the flexibility in intervention roles to meet a wide variety of needs. This is as proactive as one can reasonably expect to be, and avoids the twin pitfalls of attempting to be a seer of issues over the horizon and being the knee-jerk responder to every capricious walk-over-hot-coals-while-surviving-in-the-wilderness fad that comes down the pike.

This has been a general view of the lay of the land. Let's move on to what's between the ears.

2

The Right
State of Mind

Rudderless Ships Are Only
Good at Drifting

How Jobs Get in the
Way of Careers

In the midst of a consulting assignment at Marine Midland Bank in Buffalo, my client was trying to explain why my help was needed in trying to align human resource strategies with the organization's business strategies.

"Throughout the bank," she reported, "there are talented people who are spinning their wheels too frequently, working hard to get things done that make sense at the moment, but aren't bona fide contributors to the bank's goals. We're no different within human resources, and we've got to be the ones to serve as an example to others in our consulting work and course offerings."

"Well," I responded (always a tremendously safe reply from a consultant), "if people are *too* focused on the details of the job at hand, what do we want them to shift their focus to? It's easy to say 'strategic goals,' but that's notoriously hard to do when you're a middle manager whose phone is ringing every three minutes."

"We all should realize that the current job is just one aspect of a full career within the organization. We need to take a longer-term view of our work. In fact," she concluded, "we criticize senior management when they focus only on short-term issues, allowing quarterly results to interfere with longer-term developmental needs. We should be equally tough on ourselves when we allow our jobs to get in the way of our careers."

And so a new concept was born — at least so far as I knew — and a fundamental goal was established for our project. *People had to stop allowing their jobs to interfere with their careers.* It was catchy, succinct, and increasingly clear as we demonstrated the difference between working hard and working smart, between aiming for short-term, temporary respite and going for long-term enduring achievement.

I've never forgotten that lesson and how well it applies to consulting work. It's very simple for a consultant to allow the daily travails of the job to become the entire raison d'être for the practice, and once that happens — consciously or subconsciously — time becomes scarce due to establishing work schedules, arranging for flights, grinding out reports, attending meetings, generating publicity, and so on. The conventional wisdom has us believe that the major impediment to exceeding a particular sales figure as a consultant (as established earlier, usually stated as $300,000) is the impossibility of being in two places at once: If you are marketing, then you can't be delivering; if you are at client A, you can't be at client B; if you are perceived as a counselor, you can't be perceived as a collaborator. But that particular paradigm is easily shattered once you view your work as a career that is fulfilled by generating a series of client results, and not as a succession of jobs or assignments that usurp time until their completion.

Here's a specific example of such lofty notions. Bob Janson is a good friend of mine who is the president of Roy Walters & Associates in New Jersey. His firm focuses on self-directed work teams and on empowering workers throughout the organization. (Hence, their value-added is expertise, using the parameters of Chapter 1.) He has consistently referred work to my firm, and we've collaborated on several projects over the years. During one such collaboration, I innocently asked him whose responsibility the final report would be. I, of course, was thinking it would be his firm or mine, and I was ardently hoping that it would be his, since reports take up *time*. His response floored me.

"It's the client's responsibility, naturally. Don't tell me that you usually generate the reports!"

Oh, oh. What had I been missing...

"Don't you see," he continued, "this client hasn't *asked* for any written report. He wants a system to improve communications, he needs help in implementing it, and he'll want us to keep him fully briefed on our progress and plans. But he never asked for a report. If he wants one, then we'll give the basic information to whomever he designates and the report can be created by his own people, in whatever style and format he prefers."

This was a very existential moment, one that I categorize as CBT (conceptual breakthrough time). I always had done reports because I regarded reports as a job which had to be undertaken to demonstrate tangible completion of certain aspects of the assignment. If the client didn't request one, I made sure that I volunteered one. Bob, on the other hand, *never* did reports because he was focused on the end results that he had agreed upon with the client, and a report is, with rare exception, never an end result in and of itself. If the client wanted one, Bob had no objection, so long as it was clear that it was the client's responsibility to generate it. Bob isn't in the business of creating reports — he is in the business of enhancing client results.

That's when I began to scrutinize my interactions with clients to determine the extent to which my job was interfering with my career. All of us can use more time, and that's understandable. What isn't understandable is the wasting of already scarce time on jobs that we make for ourselves which have no real, enduring impact on the results being sought for the client. My list of jobs that can get in the way of careers is compiled in Figure 2-1. It's amazing how much of our time can be dictated by conventional wisdom[1]!

One of my consulting colleagues once told me that he was weary of being on 12 airplanes a month just to attend meetings with a single client organization. "The meetings really are unimportant in terms of the quality of the project," he confided, "but the client has come to expect them."

Ah, but who set those expectations?

Consulting is one of the very few professions I know of in which the practitioner learns from virtually *every* assignment, and that learning is carried to the next assignment and the next client to enhance the value-added still further. In other words, each client is paying you to learn, and while the client's bank check is a nonrenewable resource you cash and spend, the learning is infinitely renewable and applicable. Imagine — a professional calling in which each client interaction makes you more valuable to prospective clients! I don't believe that a surgeon necessarily learns a great deal from each appendectomy, or that a classroom teacher learns a great deal more from the fortieth explication of the causes of the French Revolution, or that a soccer goalkeeper learns new techniques after several years on the job. Now, don't

[1]"Conventional wisdom," as far as I've ever been able to determine, isn't conventional and isn't really wisdom. It is actually a description of tired clichés intended to explain away failure before it occurs.

- Regularly scheduled meetings to "keep in touch"
- Periodic written reports and updates
- Physical trips to the client site when phone calls would suffice
- Needs analyses—when what's wrong is as obvious as a ham sandwich
- Presentations of interim results to various groups
- Extensive research when the issue is situational and unique
- Meals and entertaining—the world's most abused consulting habit
- Spending excessive time on unimportant calls
- Seeking ego strokes
- Responses to irrelevant issues and peripheral interests
- Telephone calls to "keep in touch," with no other agenda
- Paperwork and record keeping that contribute nothing to performance
- Overinvestigating without deciding: "analysis paralysis"

Figure 2-1. Thirteen ways to let a job get in the way of a career.

misunderstand: all these people can and do learn a great deal, through private study, practice, talks with colleagues, and so on. *But very few people have the opportunity to continually learn on the job as a condition of their employment.* In fact, all too often we hear of seasoned pros in various fields whose claim to fame is that "he's seen it all before" or that "nothing surprises her." But these are hardly indications of having reached the heights. Usually, they're indications of the depths of the ruts in which they are wallowing.

The learning I'm talking about isn't merely *content learning.* It's mainly *process learning,* in terms of the what, why, and how of my craft and my clients' needs. (It's true that, at this point in the game, I can accurately describe a paper machine's workings, credibly discuss the role of enzyme-blockers in pharmaceutical research, and pontificate on the marketplace for work stations versus personal computers. But I hardly consider such abilities of great worth in what I'm able to bring to the next client.)

Early in my career I was across the desk from the vice president of worldwide personnel for Merck & Co., Steve Darien. It appeared that I was well on my way to nailing down a key project when Steve asked how I would go about gathering some of the data required. Thinking that I had the perfect response, I coolly intoned, "Well, there are three options for doing that." (These I proceeded to describe.) "Which do you prefer?"

To my amazement, and as a fundamental contribution toward my lifelong learning curve, Steve said, "That's what you should be telling us. That's why you're here." Steve didn't need collaboration on the technique, he wanted an expert who could recommend precise courses of action and clarify exactly what would occur. To this day, whenever a client asks how something should be accomplished, I always provide options, together with the pros and cons of each, *and* my recommendation for which makes the most sense from my perspective. I learned that from a 30-second exchange with Steve in 1986, and I've used it to excellent advantage hundreds of times since.

> *No successful consultant will ever have the same year of experience twice. In fact, no successful consultant will ever have the same experience twice.*

The surest route to maximizing learning and enhancing your value-added potential, is to focus on the results the client requires and to prevent jobs and tasks from receiving undue attention and time. Every project requires a certain degree of "small picture" attention: follow-through, coordination, checks for accuracy, validation, and more. But these are truly ancillary chores.

Similarly, your career as a consultant should not revolve around numbers of client engagements (in fact, sometimes quantity is the poorest measure you can apply), numbers of prospects contacted, or—worst of all, and more about this in Chapter 8—numbers of billable days. These are activities and tasks. You should be focusing on the broadening nature of client work you're able to undertake, the reputation you are building, the longer-term results you're helping clients to attain, and the widening application of your expertise and experience. These are results that build your career, stimulate you as a professional, and, by the way, significantly grow your business. Increased amounts of jobs don't necessarily grow a business, although they can make a business more complex, complicated, and frustrating. But an enhanced career is synonymous with an enhanced business. That's what my friend at Marine Midland was driving at when she wanted to prevent jobs from interfering with careers. And that's what will account for financial growth as well.

Will Growth Cut You Down to Size?

The vast majority of consultants fail to grow their businesses because they refuse to abandon business. A consulting firm is not like an automobile manufacturer who tries to sell as many cars as possible and adjusts production to meet demand. If business continues to grow, more assembly line workers are hired, new plants are opened, more dealerships are established, and additional middle managers are promoted to administer the operations. Conversely, in down times, top management closes plants, furloughs blue-collar workers, fires white-collar workers, and stores unsold cars as inventory.

Consultants are vastly different. Growth is dependent on abandoning some lines and types of business in the pursuit and acquisition of other, more productive lines of business. (Remember, growth is not just financial. It includes broadening experiences, higher-level contacts, more sophisticated work, and an enhanced reputation.) For the consultant whose very lifeblood was originally sustained by $2500 one-shot contracts and $300 speaking engagements, the attitude is usually, "*All* business is good business, and I'll never turn down a paying engagement."

There are just a few things wrong with this attitude, but they are all deadly:

1. *The paint-yourself-in-a-corner syndrome.* Reputation works in all directions. If you are known as an "inexpensive alternative," or a "very reasonable speaker," or "desperate to accept any job," that's the way prospects will approach you. If word-of-mouth stipulates that your fee is $750 on a per-diem basis, a prospect will estimate that your services are required for a week and be confident that you will cost him less than $4000. The fact that the project is worth $75,000 in productivity enhancements to the client won't matter, nor will the fact that it would cost $25,000 for the client to accomplish the job with internal resources, even if that were possible.

2. *Quality, not quantity, is the sole measure of success.* A friend of mine, Mike Robert, has established a worldwide training firm from scratch. In fact, from less than scratch—he resigned from a former employer, struck out on his own, and never looked back. In 1988 we collaborated on a book,[2] during the writing of which he commented

[2]Michel Robert and Alan Weiss, *The Innovation Formula: How Organizations Turn Change Into Opportunity,* Harper & Row, New York, 1988.

that approaches to direct mail were off-base. "People are looking for a response of one and a half to two percent to represent success," he pointed out, "which is simply an arbitrary number. If you mail out ten thousand pieces, all you need is one *very high quality* response." Mike has based his business on that premise—find one client and do a great deal of work there, rather than find 10 clients and do a little work with each. As a consultant, you are far better served doing $50,000 in business with a single client than doing $5000 with 10 clients. Accepting all business as quantitatively equal, no matter the quality, dilutes effort and confuses perceptions.

3. *Effort = task while payoff = results.* While managing a national field force for a training company, I discovered that it requires as much time to sell a $10,000 project as a $100,000 project. The amount of calls, the nature of the proposals, the types of competitive threat, and the overall time required are amazingly consistent. So if each of my salespeople had X hours in a day, and both sales required the same amount of time investment, which kind did I want them pursuing? This was real rocket science, right? The only difference is in the attitude of the salesperson, and a similar attitude is necessary for the consultant. The efforts required to attract, administer, and deliver small assignments are virtually the same as those for larger assignments, so you are not making up in volume what you lose in size. By accepting any business that comes along, the consultant is doomed to poor investments of time, and he or she will find it increasingly difficult to break out of the box.

Every time you raise your fees and/or refuse to make concessions to gain business, you will lose the bottom 15 percent of your market. Million dollar consultants regularly abandon the bottom 15 percent of their market as a growth strategy, because it frees them to expand the upper reaches of their market.

Every two years or so you should be able to look back and identify assignments that you would not bid on or accept today. If you are accepting the same type of assignments at the same fees today as you were two years ago, you have not abandoned the bottom 15 percent of your market and therefore probably haven't expanded the top 15 percent of your market. *You cannot retain all types of business and expect to grow.* Continuing to take on everything means that your growth-in-expertise and repute aren't advancing.

Abandoning Clients Gracefully

I've been speaking rather harshly of abandoning business. But that's because you must not equivocate on this issue. You must stop accepting the business. But there are alternatives to simply dumping the client, and there are ways to attend to clients who, while they may not represent your future, were certainly instrumental in paying the rent in the past.

- Establish alliances with consultants who were where you were two years ago. There is always a wealth of such talent eager to align itself with more established practitioners in order to learn, obtain business, and network. Refer your bottom-end work to talented protégés, who will do an excellent job, bring credit to you for the reference, and provide continuity and support for a valued client.[3] (It's generally *not* a good idea to have such people on your own staff to perform that work, because your firm will still be associated with it, which is no different from *you* being associated with it. Talent agents who handle regional theater actors are not called by major stars.)

- Explain to the client personally that you can't cost-effectively handle such assignments any more, that you *are not* using that fact as an excuse to raise fees, and that you will refer some people to the client for consideration as a replacement. In this case the client knows that you are helping make the transition at no charge, and that the people you are referring may not be well known by you. The responsibility for choosing someone appropriate and compatible is then clearly the client's.

- If it is a regularly scheduled series of assignments or appearances or workshops, let the client know that the next one, or the next month's, or this year's will be the last you can do. Provide the client with that

---

[3]Although it's not the topic of this chapter, a word on *finder's fees*, or commissions: whether you take a percentage of the fee for the referral is a matter of individual strategy. If you do, I feel you have a heightened ethical responsibility for the quality of the results. Moreover, you are exacting a relatively small amount of money for yourself and a relatively large amount of money from your colleague. My preference is to create a "win/win/win" situation by expecting no consideration yourself other than your colleague's inclination to ask you to participate in projects too large for him or her to handle in the future.

kind of leeway and advance notice, and continue to demonstrate that you are doing the exact same high-quality job you've always done.

- Offer to transfer the skills to the client, if appropriate. Suggest some internal alternatives, and work with them to replace your expertise. Demonstrate the value of the catch-fish-for-yourself approach in Chapter 1. It is fair and reasonable to charge a fee for such transition, and it's generally easy to justify it in terms of the cost-savings of having the skills present internally, whenever required. Offer to support the internal person by phone and mail whenever help is needed.

- If the client is a local site of a larger organization, explain that it's time to move up to the parent. You've gone as far as you can go with the excellent support of local management, but you have assessed that the time is right to try to influence changes of policy at corporate level. You are not abandoning your local client, but there is little more you can effectively do without intercession from higher authority. In this manner, you are moving to a higher level in your market by moving to a higher level within your client organization. If you have a good relationship locally, management should be willing to make introductions at higher level. If management refuses, you are in a business relationship that you should abandon anyway.

Business You Should Abandon

Whether you are a one-person, entrepreneurial consulting practice, or lead a growing firm of professional and administrative people, you must consciously and consistently abandon business that is:

1. Beneath your growing fee structure
2. Unchallenging ("I can do this with my eyes closed")
3. Providing a reputation that does not fit your growth strategy ("They train secretaries")
4. Overly specialized ("They know everything about packaging")
5. Unable to attract the kind of talent you want in your firm
6. Unable to attract the kind of references you need
7. In areas and industries which themselves are not growing

Finally, there is a clarion-clear call that demands you carefully examine your markets and clients to make hard, steely decisions about leaving some of them. No matter how easy it is to accept a small assignment that comes over the phone without effort, or how relieving it is to make a concession for a lower fee when business is hurting, these bottom-end pieces of business are simply not that profitable. They bring in revenue, not profit. I've seen consultants spend $4500 of their time, materials, and overhead to deliver a $5000 assignment. "Oh, it's OK," they assure me, "because the business comes in at $5000 like clockwork five or six times a year." Yeah, and they spend $4500 like clockwork each time (or, worse, $5500).

It doesn't matter at all—not at all—what your billings are or how much you make. The only thing that matters is how much you keep.

Ninety percent of all of my billings go to the bottom line. That's right, I lose only 10 percent of revenues to expenses and overhead. If you generate $100,000 in revenues, an overhead of 35 percent will provide $65,000 of pretax income, while an overhead of 10 percent will provide $90,000 in pretax income. The trick, of course, is to increase revenues while decreasing overhead, and that's exactly what million dollar consultants do. One of the most important elements of that strategy is abandoning the bottom 15 percent of your market on a regular basis. Another is in being crystal clear about your business goals.

Establishing the Ideal Goals

Every consulting business—large or small, local or international, specialized or general—has a motive force. This force is its raison d'être, its self-concept. The problem is that while this should be a conscious force, it's often an unconscious one, created by default, by the market, by the clients, or—worst of all—by the competition.

Financial results are only one indication of success. In fact, it's the ability to meet longer-term, predetermined goals that dictates the true measure of ultimate financial success. Without such nonfinancial goals, your ship is rudderless, dependent on the winds and tides of the marketplace. Strategic goals are intended to provide not just the direction, but also the propulsion that enables you to navigate despite the treachery of the currents. In our marketplace, "currents" are better known as fads, "winds" as perceptions, and "tides" as economic conditions.

What goals do you have for your business? When I ask most consultants/principals that question, they say something like:

- "We want to be the biggest firm of our kind."
- "To continually grow our business."
- "To help clients to achieve the best results possible."
- "We will be on the leading edge of developments in our field."
- "To reward the people in the business commensurate with contribution."

This is hardly the stuff on which to plan your future. Oh, they are all noble enough sentiments, but they could apply to dry cleaning, driveway paving, or accounting, not to mention muffler repair and tractor maintenance.

During one stage of my life, I used to travel over an hour to Boston just to have my hair cut by a woman who did a superb job. I don't have great hair, but she had great scissors. She was in constant demand. I asked her one day why she thought she was so successful. (Consultants have a way of always trying to find the common denominator. It ain't poetry, but it's good consulting.) Her response was a revelation: she thought she was in a unique business.

"Hairdressers have the consent to touch the customer," she explained. "This creates a very close bond, although it doesn't seem it. That's why I find out so much about my customers, and why they share things with me that they would never share in any other business relationship."

"Isn't that a rather glorious view?" I pontificated. "After all, most people would simply say you cut and style hair, wouldn't they?"

"Name me another professional in your life who physically touches you and moves your position around like this."

"Ahhhh...a doctor."

"Right! And that's who most people pick. But a doctor is threatening. You see, I'm as close to people as their doctor gets, but I'm non-threatening. People come to me not just because I do their hair well, but because they enjoy the relationship. So do I."

I thought about that conversation long and hard, and came to realize that her success was largely based on her personal, clearly defined image of her business and her place in it. It was irrelevant whether you agreed with her or not. (After all, I finally concluded, manicurists touch you, so do tailors, and people seem very willing to talk to strange bartenders who never touch them.) Her vision of her business and her goals was unique, clear, and tangible enough for her to act on. In other words, she encouraged people to talk (the few who didn't like to would go elsewhere), was an excellent listener, remembered details about customers from month to month, and was acutely aware of her role in the relationship. She often asked about my kids, would tell me stories of her own kids, but didn't offer advice, and was *never* judgmental except about what looked good on top of my head.

Here are some of the best goals I've heard from consultants—best because they are clear, unique to the profession, and tangible enough to base tactics on, day in and day out.

- "We will undertake consulting assignments that result in direct contributions to the client's profitability as measured by quarterly results."
- "We will assist in the outplacement of people in a cost-effective manner while always respecting the dignity and needs of those leaving the organization."
- "We will design and implement workshops that result in demonstrable behavior change on the job as determined by customer feedback."
- "We will enter into collaborative relationships in which responsibility is shared with the client, skills are transferred to the client, and dependence on us is gradually diminished to the point of disengagement."
- "We will assist clients in enhancing the productivity of their people through needs analyses, enhanced communication, and joint decision making."
- "We will accept only short-term, value-added consulting assignments with specific result objectives and measurements, which will be fee-based. We will unconditionally guarantee our work."

You don't need pages of goals. In fact, they should be brief enough for you and your colleagues to keep in mind at all times, particularly when in front of a prospect or during an engagement, since operating decisions should be dictated by those goals. I've found that sound goals are not hooked to any particular financial figure, do assume personal responsibility, are unequivocal (I will or we will), and include some form of outcome. They are often based on the specific kind of expertise or talent you bring to bear (outplacement), philosophy (collaboration), process skills (needs analyses, decision making), and/or timing (quarterly results, short-term assignments).

Specific goals are extraordinarily useful in explaining to prospects why they should hire you. Your goals should appear in your literature (see Chapter 6 for specifics) and should serve to set your firm apart. You should be able to explain them in 60 seconds to anyone who asks. (Any consultant who can't explain precisely and specifically what he or she does in one minute needs to go sit in the corner. How many cocktail parties have you been to in which someone is asked what they do and takes the next 30 minutes rambling on without giving a clue. You can bet 5 to 2 that the person is a consultant, and 10 to 1 that he or she is not good at it. Would it take any of your clients over a minute to tell you what kind of business *they're* in?!)

> *Goals provide a rudder for you to steer with and enable clients and prospects to understand what you can provide. How can a client clearly understand what you provide, and distinguish you from others, if you can't do that yourself?*

Figure 2-2 provides a basis for establishing goals. If you can't articulate what it is you stand for and what you are trying to accomplish in a client engagement, then don't even walk out your door. If you do, you're likely to accept assignments for monetary reasons alone, which means you'll often be over your head in expertise or up to your rear in alligators. Your goals *will* be set, if not by you consciously, then by the marketplace, or the situation, or the client. And those goals will be impossible to live with because they will change each day. Your business won't be growing, it will be circling.

One final thought: Goals can change as your business grows and matures. They should be reexamined regularly (particularly if you are successfully abandoning the bottom 15 percent of your market) for modifications. You don't want to be known to prospects as something

■ Expertise and talent	■ Types of client interaction
■ Contribution to profit	■ Productivity of employees
■ Enhanced communication	■ Employee participation
■ Market share	■ Customer satisfaction
■ Quality and service	■ Innovation and creativity
■ Strategy formulation	■ Problem solving
■ Employee assistance	■ Research and development
■ Motivation and morale	■ Priorities/time management
■ Community service	■ Safety and regulatory matters
■ Design-to-market timing	■ Adult learning

Figure 2-2. A basis for establishing goals. Goals can be based on personal talent, or client need, or both.

you used to be, and you don't want to invest in actions dictated by your own outmoded perception of who you are. A firm whose call was "to provide the best objective and rational decision-making skills" for clients may now see itself as "providing the best thinking skills, combining rational and intuitive approaches" as it has found and adopted additional technologies and disciplines. If your consulting business is to grow, your goals have to grow and expand. The more frequently that occurs, the better you're doing.

As in Show Business, Timing Is Everything

I recall watching Johnny Carson's *Tonight Show* one evening when his guests were Richard Pryor and Milton Berle, the former seated on the couch and the latter holding court in the guest's chair. Berle and Carson had established some nice shtick when Pryor attempted to interject, which had the result of throwing cold water all over the proceedings. In the ensuing awkward silence, Berle leaned over to Pryor and hissed, loud enough for the mike to pick up, "I told ya, kid, pay attention to the timing. Everything is timing."

There is neither a good time nor a bad time to enter the consulting profession or to attempt to enlarge an existing practice. Many people assume that poor market and economic conditions augur well for consulting, since firms are in trouble then and need more help. Fortunately or unfortunately, this axiom has never applied to my firm, since we tend to work with excellent companies that don't use hard times as a trigger for consulting assistance. Similarly, good times don't automatically generate business because, during good times, few firms are enlightened enough to look beyond the short term and focus on fundamental needs and challenges.

The timing I'm most concerned with is that of being in the right place at the right time, and that means in front of the buyer with a back scratcher when the buyer has an itch. You don't have to be physically present, of course, but you must be present in spirit. Now many marketers who are expert at their work will tell you that it's your responsibility to create the need (or at least to help the client to express it in such a way that you are the likely candidate to meet it). But I'm not all that adept at marketing myself. (The overwhelming chances are that most readers aren't either.) Also, I don't like to sell, and I don't associate selling with the consulting business I like to generate—especially if selling means convincing the prospect that he or she has a need and I'm the one to fill it.

You see, such marketing and selling is dependent on what I call the "one person, one situation" approach. That is, you must personally visit, convince, follow up, and attend to the various leaks that occur when you're trying to float a proposal. So you're limited to the number of people in front of whom you can reasonably appear, and you're limited by their lack of initial agreement on the exact need you're trying to convince them exists.

I prefer a timing approach to increasing business. That timing is based on the prospective client (or current client) feeling an itch at any given moment and immediately thinking of you as having the back scratcher. Note that this isn't dependent on your being someplace, nor on your convincing the client of the need, nor on carefully constructed proposals. The client is calling you. This approach is not mutually exclusive with other approaches, but it does make life a whole lot easier.

As you read this paragraph, potential buyers of your services are reaching decisions all over the country (and the world) that they need help. And over the ensuing day, week, month, or quarter, they will go about securing that help. Some will choose consultants they already work with; others will rely on recommendations; still others, probably the majority, will engage in some type of hunt, from the informality of making phone calls to the formality of requesting bids and proposals. In Chapter 1 I talked about the ways in which organizations choose consultants, and in Chapter 9 I'll talk about how to maintain contact with clients and prospects over the long haul. What I want to address here is the combination of those two elements: the merging of the prospect's need (occurring at some unanticipated time) with the awareness of your potential to fill that need (from repeated contacts and visibility). This is the essence of the timing approach.

This is a state of mind that you must buy into philosophically and strategically before you can make it work tactically. That is, you must be convinced that it is far more powerful to have the buyer call you than it is for you to call the buyer. The traditional response to growing personal service businesses has been the atavistic feet-on-the-street approach. Hire more people to make more calls to close more business. But that is a quantitative approach to selling, not a qualitative one, and failed companies' obituaries are filled with overly optimistic sales forecasts based on the numbers of people seen and the likelihood that they would buy simply because someone managed to get into their office. When you're *invited* into someone's office, the equation changes considerably. Instead of justifying your presence and demands on the buyer's time, you are working together to collaborate on a problem the buyer feels comfortable addressing with you.

Thus, your marketing thrust should *not* be the number of people you see, promoting your approaches to likely buyers, or — heaven forfend — making cold sales calls. You should be endeavoring to make your name, firm, and talents known to as wide a variety of prospects as possible. We'll examine specific options in Chapter 9, but it's important to acknowledge and embrace that fundamental position here.

During a typical week, my firm receives two requests for proposals, four inquiries about speaking engagements, ten orders for books, and a dozen or more inquiries for literature about our consulting activities from organizations for which we have never done any work. These are leads exclusive of current client work and extensions of current work. Conservatively, that's about 100 leads per month, or 1000 per year. If 10 percent of those leads results in short-term business (within 12 months), and the average contract is $25,000, that's a quarter of a million dollars generated from prospects developing a need and knowing that they should contact me. In actuality, 10 percent is a fairly low figure and over the longer term — 12–36 months — we (and you) are likely to do business with 20 percent or more of those leads.

Although we are focusing on strategy for now, here's a quick example of how to stimulate this prospect-based timing approach. Let's assume that *no one* is asking you to bid on work for them. Ground zero. Standing start. Do the following:

1. Talk to colleagues and find out which governmental agencies (i.e., Department of Defense, Federal Aviation Authority, Bureau of Prisons) and which private sector organizations (i.e., the local utility, a department store chain, the American Bar Association) have sent out unsolicited requests for proposals. Then write to those agencies and organizations requesting that you be placed on their bid list. You should then receive bid requests in the future, or an application to be placed on the list. Once you've bid on any such work, irrespective of your success, you will almost always be included on future bidding lists and often will find yourself on similar lists from sister agencies. I bid on work for the Housing Authority in New York and found myself receiving requests from the Department of Human Services shortly thereafter.

2. Call the major organizations that have resource centers[4] that keep track of consultant offerings to provide for internal departments. These are typically the very large employers. For example, 3M has

---

[4]A resource center is simply a unit that provides information about outside resources to all other units in the organization, making the process time-efficient and uniform. To find one, simply call a company's main switchboard and ask if there is one. Ask for the center's director or manager, and ask how you can get onto their resource lists. You'll probably be asked to send various materials, brochures, offerings of services, references, and so forth.

an active resource center that frequently updates its listings, as do Chrysler and GM. A half day on the phone with a good business directory should produce those appropriate for your talents and expertise, and you can then put together a package to forward to each.

> *If you are dependent on seeking out prospects and convincing each one to buy your services, you are limited by the amount of time in a day. If prospects are dependent on seeking you out to secure your assistance, you are limited only by the amount of growth you are willing to accept.*

---

3. Network at local association meetings and find out who's acquiring outside consulting services. Ask about new activities and developments and how the organizations have secured the expertise.

4. Contact chambers of commerce in major cities and find out whether they have a referral service for members seeking consulting help. Determine what, if anything, is required for your firm to be listed.

5. Check the want ads in major cities to find out which major organizations are hiring human resources help, specialized help (i.e., market analysts), and/or expanding in certain fields, and approach them with your services. Frequently, organizations seeking to acquire internal help are also experiencing growth that requires external help.

6. Network like a fanatic. Let everyone you ever knew (and everyone *they* ever knew) know that you are consulting and where to reach you. I learned recently of a consultant who obtained a $50,000 contract because the wife of a social club member is the secretary to a marketing vice president in a company searching for customer survey work. She alerted her husband, who alerted the consultant, who was able to bid on a project he would never have known about. It might not be the best way to plan your growth, but a couple of these a year can't hurt.

One of the techniques employed in creativity sessions is called *reversal*. Its intent is to generate new solutions by reversing the way in which we generally view problems. (For example, retailers traditionally sought ways to get shoppers into their stores. Catalogs are a reverse technique, which allow the store to come to the shopper.) There are legions of consultants concerning themselves with how to get in to see prospects. They will be forever limited to the amount of people they can physically see, interpersonally influence, and eventually convince. The reverse position—which I call timing, because it relies on the prospect's own "right time," not your creation of it—is to get prospects to seek you out. This significantly enhances your leverage and allows you to respond in any number of ways: by mail, phone, in person, subcontracting, delay, collaboration, and/or respectful decline. ("We don't handle that type of situation, but we can recommend three firms that do, and we hope you'll continue to call on us for work within our capabilities.")

Up to this point, I've tried to establish what the lay of the land looks like, and why it's important to clarify what's in your head. Your growth—personally, professionally, and financially—is predominantly a function of your view of the marketplace and your role within it. If your mind focuses on making phone calls from the moment you awake, for example, then you will take pains to ensure that you are uninterrupted in making phone calls while you are in the office. Your behaviors and actions will adjust accordingly, and you will tend to view your success in terms of your ability to make phone calls. However, if your philosophy of the business calls for a more strategic focus—let's say, to establish a reputation with a certain type of buyer—then your behaviors and actions are likely to be much broader and more innovative in scope, organized to establish that reputation through a variety of means (within which the telephone will play a proper, minor role). Only *you* determine how you act toward your business; the market doesn't, the prospect doesn't, and the competition shouldn't.

The introduction to this book cites Matsuo Basho, and his philosophy is as applicable now as it was three centuries ago. Don't look around at other consultants and decide how to do what they do, only better. Look at the marketplace, evaluate what you have to offer, and to which buyers, and decide how best to get those buyers to come to you, while continually abandoning the bottom slice of your market to expand the top slice. If you can maintain that state of mind, you're ready to grow.

3

Prerequisites for Growth

Expanding the Envelope

The Success Trap

Success may be responsible for the death of more consulting endeavors than failure is. When a strong person fails, he or she is likely to examine causes of the defeat, determine what must be done to prevail in the future, and take steps to try again. Strong people learn from their setbacks and emerge all the stronger. Success, after all, is never final, and defeat is seldom fatal; it's perseverance that counts. (Woody Allen said once that 80 percent of success is "just showing up.")

When a proposal I've submitted is not accepted or I find that a competitor is chosen for an assignment that wasn't offered to me, I *always* investigate the reasons. I'm relieved on those occasions when I find that I didn't get the business because someone else had an "in" with the client, or because a competitor offered to provide something completely beyond my capabilities or motivation or fee structure. I call this kind of situation an *uncontrollable rejection* because it's unlikely that anything I could have done would have changed the outcome. However, when I find that the competition provided for an intervention I just hadn't thought about, met a client's need in a more innovative way, or brought better resources to bear, then I devote my full attention to understanding how I was outflanked or out-thought, and how I can prevent a recurrence. This is a *controllable rejection,* which is business lost because I failed to do something which I could have done and would have been willing to do, and which might have changed the outcome in my favor. The good thing about studying controllable rejection is that you learn a great deal about how to improve your business.

For example, I can't learn or improve much by determining that I lost a contract because the client preferred someone who happened to be located a mile from the site, while I was an airplane trip away. But I can learn a great deal by determining that the competition attended preliminary discussions using three people who, acting as a team, provided the client with a feeling of depth and competent support that I, acting alone, couldn't provide. I now bring associates to most preliminary prospect meetings. I once lost a survey project for which I was a finalist because the ultimate winner offered in his proposal to train management in how to convey to employees both the survey results and the actions management intended to take as a result of those results. I had never thought to do this because every prior survey project I had obtained involved long-distance data gathering only, with one-on-one meetings with the top executive to discuss results. But I would have been quite willing to do it, I had the capacity to do it, and I could have done it in a cost-effective manner. As a result of this particular controllable rejection, I now provide the option of management education in every survey proposal. Quite a few clients and prospects have complimented me on this follow-through, and have been willing to pay slightly more to utilize it. As an extension of this tactic, I've since added six-month and one-year follow-up days to all my strategy work. The extra days cost me virtually nothing, yet provide the client with a sense of continuation and long-term interest, and enable me to remain visible on a scheduled basis.

Although very disciplined about finding out why I'd been rejected, I found that I seldom asked for the reasons that led to my being *selected* by a client. Success will do that to you. After all, you were trying to get the business, did a fine job in your preparation and proposal, and the client demonstrated superb judgment in selecting you. What else is there to know?! But enough of those successes can lead you into a trap, because you're so busy scheduling implementation and cashing checks that you aren't growing in any other dimensions. Million dollar consultants don't get that way by doing one thing well, over and over. They succeed to the extent that they do because they evolve with the times and grow with increasing challenges. Consequently, you should always try to stretch your applications and abilities until you are rejected, so that you can find out why. I alluded in the introduction to pilots "expanding the envelope." They don't know what a plane can do until they discover what it *can't* do. Then the designers can try to improve on that.

> **The only way to improve upon success is to experience rejection. Successful consultants do not experience uninterrupted success. Instead, they ensure that they stretch their abilities until they are rejected so that they know what additional growth is required. Uninterrupted success leads to inevitable failure—the success trap.**

A couple of years ago I received a request for a bid from the New York City Housing Authority. It was for design and implementation of comprehensive middle management programs, something we don't normally do, particularly on the scale requested. After determining that we could provide (or acquire) the expertise and resources needed, we bid on the project, the bid alone requiring about 25 hours of work. The award day came and went, and we heard nothing, so I followed up, facing that particularly perverse bureaucratic delay that public agencies have such expertise in. But I persevered, and found out three months later that the project was awarded to Booz Allen. I also found that:

- They had provided much more detail than we had.
- They had provided for more participant materials than we had.
- They had attended the preliminary conferences (we did not).
- They had provided more biographical information than we had.
- They had bid, successfully, for over $100,000 more than we had!

My follow-up on this rejection had become quite a learning opportunity. When we are requested to bid on large public projects now, I make careful calculations about such factors, determine first *whether* to bid, then *how*. We now bid on only a third of such requests, and are quite careful about how we do so. But bidding on that project and finding out why we were rejected made a significant contribution to our learning curve. As a result, we have had very productive relationships with dozens of public organizations such as the Federal Bureau of Prisons, the New York Office of Business Permits and Regulatory Affairs, and City University of New York.

When I meet consultants who claim to have experienced unfettered success (and by the way, I *never* meet consultants who are doing poorly; it's as rare as meeting a losing politician who isn't proud that "we got our message across"), I find that such success is usually lateral. They continue to do their thing in a repetitive manner. While they may enjoy modest financial growth, the other measures of growth (reputation, experience, expertise, etc.) remain stagnant. But most important, their financial growth will be arithmetic, and will never lead to geometric increases. These are the consultants to whom conventional wisdom does apply—they are "capped" by the logical extensions of their particular content and personal time.

Richard Foster has developed an S-curve theory that explains why organizations do not become more innovative than they are.[1] I've modified it somewhat in Figure 3-1 to demonstrate how million dollar consultants become innovative through constant expansion of their potential clients and projects.

In Foster's S-curve, a product, process, or performance begins a steep growth pattern (point 2 in the figure) after it is accepted by buyers. That growth continues until it plateaus (point 3)—usually due to competitive offerings, changes in perception, changing conditions, or buyers simply tiring of the offering. Then a new S-curve begins. I've modified this for consulting firms' growth.

The magic number for a new consulting firm is about three years. After that, original contacts have probably been exhausted, contracts from a former employer have expired, and start-up momentum has been spent. In other words, it's time to determine whether you are a going concern or simply a person who had good contacts. *All* firms plateau periodically (point 3 in Figure 3-1). This is due to the factors I've just mentioned for start-up operations. For well-established firms it is due to one's technology and expertise becoming dated (i.e., left brain/right brain thinking has been authoritatively debunked), expanded competition entering the picture (to offer "managing total quality," "total quality management," "total management quality," etc.), and/or client and market conditions undergoing basic change (economic downturns don't favor placement firms, and economic upturns don't favor outplacement firms).

Unexamined, repetitive success in limited fields will lead to a perpetuation of the plateau which, ultimately, results in the success trap. By the time the lack of growth begins to take its toll in the form of a diminished client base, declining visibility, weariness from lack of stimulation, and inability to attract talent, it's often too late to try to expand the envelope. That exploration must come from a position of strength, not desperation. So, beware of the success trap and the false security of lateral growth. *Ironically, to grow you must fail periodically, so that you are continually aware of opportunities for improvement and for expanding your envelope.* This discipline will not only provide for internal stimulation; it will also influence how the external world views you.

[1]Richard N. Foster, *Innovation: The Attacker's Advantage*, Summit Books, New York, 1986.

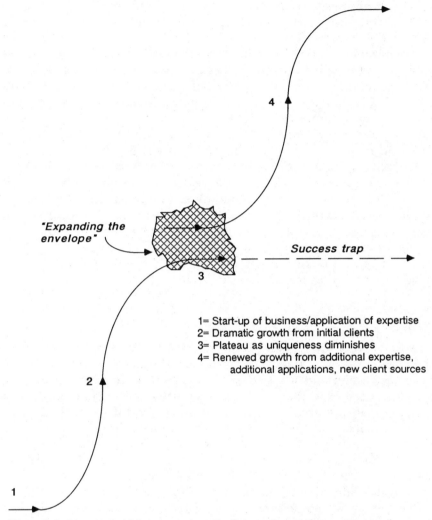

"Expanding the envelope"

Success trap

1= Start-up of business/application of expertise
2= Dramatic growth from initial clients
3= Plateau as uniqueness diminishes
4= Renewed growth from additional expertise,
    additional applications, new client sources

Figure 3-1. How to avoid the success trap: the S-curve theory of geometric growth.

Establishing the Firm's Image

If you think that people *don't* judge books by their covers, just take a gander at the cars around you on the freeway. People buy cars to say something about themselves, whether the object of their affection is a staid Volvo, a rakish Corvette, a middle-American Taurus, or an aloof Mercedes. In fact, an automobile is the most expensive life-style statement that most people ever make. Yet that extension of one's personality into the acquisitions one makes—a sort of anthropomorphism gone wild—embraces ballpoint pens as well as works of art, and jogging suits as well as cultural events.

Organizations make the same type of statements about the vendors with whom they choose to do business. In fact, a number of large organizations that have won one or more of the major quality awards have begun demanding that their *suppliers* show evidence of similar commitment to quality standards. Motorola has been a leading force in this philosophy, and some firms are demanding that their vendors not only meet the award requirements but actually apply for the awards.

My belief is that a consulting firm's image—or lack of one—will play a key role in influencing a buyer one way or another as to whether that firm is right for the buyer's organization. The consulting firm's image will be most dramatically and clearly conveyed when the buyer interacts with the firm's principals. But prior to that interaction, there is opportunity for the buyer to taste the consulting firm's flavor, and it is those *first impressions* that this section will address. While there are no perfect images to convey, there are some to avoid.

Name

The first corporation I ever set up was called AJW Associates. Perhaps the main reason for establishing such names is that they are easy to use in incorporation and are seldom the trademark of anyone else. The trouble, of course, is that to a buyer such names shout "one man band" from a great distance. Don't choose a name—and if you already have such a moniker, change it—that conjures up a lone-wolf image. If you must use a name, then several are better than one, á la a law firm: Stevens, Dworkin, Reisenberg & Company. Generally, single names, such as A. D. Little & Company or Bain & Company, were established around the fame of the founder, not in anticipation of such fame.

The name you choose should also convey something basic about who you are. My firm is Summit Consulting Group, Inc. It simply says that we are consultants, and we are an incorporated business, and that's all I want to convey in our name. The Center for Creative Leadership gives you a good idea of what they're up to, as does The Executive Edge. Names such as Sage, or Quest, or Tracom leave you a bit in the dark, but that's not a cardinal sin. At least they clearly convey "company" and not "individual."[2]

----

[2]See "Picking a Name for Your Firm? Watch Your P's and Q's," *Wall Street Journal*, April 10, 1991, B2.

Logo

This is so obvious that I have to grimace as I write it, but too many people ignore the obvious. Create a logo or look that is used consistently on your stationery, business cards, brochures, labels, and any other document that might appear in public (i.e., course materials, presentation folders, etc.). These simple pieces of paper are the first and primary conveyers of your image, and they are not the place to economize. A good graphic artist can create, design, and execute the work for you for less than $1000, and these days all your print materials can be produced at one of the local storefront printing franchises (with the exception of multicolored, sophisticated brochures, which ought to be done at a conventional printer).

My logo looks like this:

Figure 3-2. The author's business card, showing logo.

This is called a print solution because the name of the company is spelled out within the logo without excess graphics and design. It appears in two colors, one of which has three different screens, and the background paper is always a classic ivory. I went through this exercise once, nine years ago, and I still receive compliments on the look.

You don't need to be fancy, but you do need to be consistent on all your print media, and you want to convey an image of professionalism and responsibility. If you don't care about the look, who's to know if you'll care about the client?

Legal Entity

My overwhelming bias is that you should utilize a conventional C corporation as your legal configuration. This is how major businesses operate, and it helps dispel the sole-practitioner image. S corporations, in which the funds flow through the principal's personal finances, are sound alternatives when the financial people so advise. This alternative allows for the "Inc." to appear after your firm's name.

If you are not incorporated, then your legal affairs will probably appear in print as "Harvey Jones, d/b/a (doing business as) Global Consulting Group." Moreover, you will have to receive 1099s from clients paying you anything over a low threshold of fees, since there is no legal entity to pay taxes except for you personally. And that means that the client will require a social security number (rather than a federal I.D. number), and such matters can come to the attention of your buyer. Would it make a difference? Sometimes it will, so why take the chance?

In the unlikely but horrible possibility of a lawsuit, it's helpful for the company to be a legal entity because, as such, *it* can be sued as a company, instead of *you*, as an individual. A full-fledged corporation can take in partners, provide equity for them, establish credit lines, obtain insurance, maintain bank accounts, and, in general, act in a manner that the accountants like to refer to as "a going concern." On occasion, I've had to write out a check to a client to return an overpayment, provide a discount, or reimburse a client for expenses when my wife has travelled with me to a client affair. I've always felt better seeing a company check—no different from the client's own—going into the envelope. (There will be more about incorporation in Chapter 6.)

Visibility

At a minimum, you should have your business listed in the local Yellow Pages, in trade publications catering to your field, with personal professional organizations you join, and with those trade associations that apply to any specialties you offer.

At a later stage, you should consider a toll-free number for clients (they are remarkably inexpensive), regular mailings or newsletters to clients and prospects, advertisements (for visibility purposes only, i.e., as a supporter of a trade association's convention), and specialty mailings tailored to particular clients (a client you know that is undergoing a reduction in force receives copies of articles on helping displaced workers, whether or not you are being used in a consulting capacity). (We'll discuss the tactics for client contacts of this type more in Chapter 6.)

Office Requirements

I knew I was missing the boat when an auto dealer with whom I was discussing a purchase asked me for my fax number so he could send me the newest financial data as soon as he received it. Then there was the deli that accepted fax orders for their luncheon take-out business...

If auto dealers and deli owners are into that level of technical sophistication, then where should your consulting firm be?

These are the basic requirements for a professional office, irrespective of whether it's in an office complex, a suite that is subleased, or
your home:

- A dedicated business phone with at least a call-waiting feature and,
  preferably, several lines. The phone should have a hold button as well
  as a conference feature. (Estimated cost: $250.[3] There are many ex-
  cellent models.) Also, if you don't have full-time office help, select an
  answering service (never an answering machine) that is as personal as
  possible. Send them some literature and meet with them to describe
  the kinds of calls you'll receive and what to expect. For example,
  never allow the answering service to tell a caller, "There's no one in
  the office right now." Instead, they should say, "Ms. Harley is travel-
  ling. May I take a message and have her call you?" A good answering
  service should cost less than $100 per month in most locales.

- A dedicated fax phone line, with a fax that can be left on automatic at
  all times to receive at the sender's convenience. The fax should have
  the capability of automatically feeding multiple sheets, and have a paper cutter to separate incoming sheets. (Estimated cost: $1000. My
  preference is Sharp.) I actually did run into a consultant who asked
  me to send him his faxes with a specific cover sheet so that it wouldn't
  accidentally be read by the travel agency whose fax he shared.

- A high-speed copier that can enlarge and reduce flexibly, handle various sizes of paper and, ideally, automatically feed multiple sheets.
  (Estimated cost: $2500. I've always used Canon products.)

- A first-rate computer with hard disk drive and laser printer. There is
  simply no other way to create the kind of proposals you must produce. (Estimated cost: $2500 and *declining* steadily. I was totally com-
  puter illiterate and found Apple exceedingly user-friendly.)

- A postage meter and minimum five-pound scale. Your correspon-
  dence needs a meter for professionalism, and this combination will
  also save you a lot of time in the post office having packages weighed.
  The meters can even include your logo or message in the indicia. (Estimated cost: A wide variety of leases and purchase plans are avail-

---

[3]All costs are retail prices. You can do far better at one of the giant discount houses
that handle name brands. However, the advantage of dealing with a local merchant is in
the proximity of service and personal attention. I find that for smaller, less complex items,
such as a fax machine or phone, discount houses are fine. But I deal locally and pay a bit
more for computer hardware and copiers.

able. Pitney Bowes pretty much has a monopoly, although you can acquire other brands, such as Frieden, if you search.)

Other equipment, such as slide projectors and document binders, is a
matter of individual preference and frequency of need. A basic, professional office — discounting rent and utilities — such as the one described
above, will probably require $5000–$10,000 in initial investment, depending on your tastes, computer capability, and so on. It's a small price
to pay in order to be perceived as a professional firm.

I've found that you can't go wrong by erring on the side of *too much*
investment in your firm's image. A corporate brochure that folds three
ways and fits nicely in a #10 envelope is like a neon sign proclaiming, "We
are small-time, because this is what I can afford and what I am happy to
have represent my firm." A multicolored brochure of 15 pages, with testimonials, examples of work performed, summary of corporate philosophy,
and other matters that represent your approaches, might not be read
cover-to-cover by the prospect. But it's there if it's needed, and it certainly
says, "I care about our image and how you perceive me, so a lot of thought
has gone into this representation of our firm. Money was not the object."

I talked earlier about "shooting yourself in both feet." No one is as
knowledgeable about what you've done in the past or what your potential is for the future as you are. Others can only look about them and
receive images. For better or worse, those images are the keys to the
early acceptance of your participation. The good news is that the image
is manageable and can convey exactly what you want it to. That image
should represent what you can do for your clients in the future, not
what you've accomplished in the past.

Abandoning the Past

The moment you decide to become a consultant, you automatically possess a particular approach to client interventions and relationships that
has been formed and honed by your experience. If you've been a member of a large business organization, you have a view influenced by the
internal and external consultants with whom you've dealt, the difficulty
of pushing change through the bureaucracy, the difficulty of implementation versus the ease of relying on others' advice, and the comfort
of comprehensive resources supporting you.

If you've been a member of a consulting firm, you've been influenced
by the difficulties of reaching the key buyer, the discomforts of travel to
undesirable sites, the pressures of meeting business quotas and demands, and the importance of retaining business.

If your background is in academia, the influences have included find-ing the time to pursue private interests, scarcity of resources, lack of pragmatic application to the business world, the credibility that comes with a Ph.D, and so on.

It's tough to break out of the experiential boxes in which we find ourselves. But breaking out is important, because the past is a woefully in-adequate base upon which to build a successful consulting firm. Its major drawback is the limiting model you possess with which to shape client in-terventions. The more flexible that model (or set of models), the better you'll be at developing interventions that can meet the needs of specific buyers at specific points in time. The more you can adjust and still get the job done, the less the client has to adjust.[4] In Chapter 1 I spoke about the pragmatic range of client interventions. Those were the *roles* the consult-ant plays in working with the client: i.e., facilitator, coach, or intervention-ist. When I speak of models, I'm referring to the *processes* that the consult-ant utilizes while operating in any of those roles.

The one thing consultants should be certain about is that there is no one way to help a client. You should know twice as many ways to help a client this year as you did last year, and twice as many next year as you do today.

Models are largely determined by the recent past and the route you've taken to establish your consulting firm. Although they may have worked fine for the firm you used to be with, and they may work well for you at the outset, no firm grows dramatically with just one stock-in-trade. The best example I know of this phenomenon is the "personality assessment."

There are scores of personality tests, or instruments, on the market today, many of which are available to consultants for use in their work. They range from commodities like Performax®, which is a forced-choice, self-scoring word selection that provides astrology-like profiles, to the Meyers-Briggs Type Indicator, a well-respected and fairly well-validated instrument, to the social styles quadrant, utilizing peer input,

---

[4]I'm not referring to massive organizational transformation efforts here, in which near-traumatic change is exactly what the client must endure. I am referring to the vast majority of consulting assignments, in which the consultant intervenes to improve a spe-cific client condition.

popularized by Wilson Learning but appearing under a wide variety of names and applications. These instruments, and others like them, can, and often do, provide useful feedback on behavioral predispositions when interpreted within the context of the environment and interactions people experience.

However, rather than as a means to an end, the instruments often become an end in themselves because they constitute the only technology, or model, the practitioner has available. For example, a consultant hired by Providence Energy to facilitate interpersonal communications came up with the idea of profiling all the managers and having their profiles printed on their coffee cups. This (so the idea went) would enable colleagues to "read" one another's salient characteristics and respond accordingly. (One can only wonder what happened when a manager borrowed a colleague's cup!) Similarly, efforts to improve communication or create a higher level of customer service often wind up in the hands of label-happy, self-limiting consultants as exercises in telling people they're introverts or ISTJs or "driver expressives," without any regard for what the client really needs.

I once observed a consulting team trying to convince top executives to set corporate strategy based solely on a calculation of future shareholder value. Rationally, one might ask why considerations such as values, technology, future markets, and the like were not included, but I realized instantly that the firm's sole model—for doing *anything*—was its formula for calculating shareholder value under the conditions it stipulated. The apotheosis of this self-limiting dilemma occurred during a meeting in which the consultants showed their latest calculation and asked the president if that shareholder value would be acceptable in five years.

"Probably not," he said. "Investors could do better elsewhere."

"Right," replied the team leader. "So what can you do now to change the strategy that is leading you there?"

"That's an impossible question to answer," said the executive. "I'm not comfortable sitting here and speculating on alternatives that might or might not affect value five years from now. It seems as though there must be a more orderly and systematic way to generate alternatives."

He was right, of course, except that the consulting firm didn't have such an orderly and systematic way because it was a one-horse wagon even though it had four people holding the reins. These four had never taken the time to break out of their particular box, although they *had* taken the time to dress up the box and make it as appealing as possible.

"Why was I so uncomfortable in there," the president asked me later, "when their formulas appear to be accurate and there's no question that we'd want to improve on the value they calculate?"

"I think," I replied, "it was because you know, viscerally and intellectually, that your firm is not in business merely to enhance shareholder value. Your acquisitions, personnel policies, product development, and even financial decisions have never been made solely on that criterion. Your own annual report talks about contribution to the environment, respect for employees, customer orientation, and so forth. Investor return is obviously important, but it's never been the sole focus and probably won't account for your future success if you allow it to be the sole focus."

The firm did not pursue that consulting team's help in strategic planning, and I found that the consultants had invested quite a bit of money and time in the work and calculations that led up to those preliminary sessions. They were good people, with significant and valuable expertise—but all within their box.

As a dynamically growing consulting firm, you must continually investigate, evaluate, and decide on the applicability of additional models to use in helping clients. Some may be compatible with others; some may be mutually exclusive. In this business, however, past success is virtually never an indicator of future performance. The issues, situations, personalities, external forces, and legitimate trends change too frequently to depend on past success, no matter how substantial, as the sole basis for future interventions.

In the 1920s, Frederick Winslow Taylor introduced the application of rigorous time and measurement techniques to human performance and demonstrated significant improvements in productivity. "Taylorism" was the beginning of the consultant as "efficiency expert." In the 1950s, the humanists appeared, and the need for more concern for people led to "personnel experts" and personnel departments. Theory X and Theory Y typified the poles of management (centered on task or people), and Blake and Mouton's "management grid" specified an ideal manager who considered tasks and people in beautiful harmony. In the 1960s and 1970s, "participation" became the hot topic, "personnel" gave way to "human resources," and we heard about "T-groups," management retreats, and suggestion boxes, along with individual and corporate est. The 1980s gave us "customer-driven emphasis," "just-in-time manufacturing" (Taylor redux), employee involvement through "quality circles," the search (and passion) for excellence, treading hot coals, and "people issues." And the 1990s? Well, "quality awards" seem important, "empowerment" is big, "benchmarking" has made an appearance, and we'll probably suffer through some variation of still another degree of self-awareness.

In business, the past is seldom an accurate indicator of the future, and those prone to forget history are sometimes the least burdened.

Million dollar consulting is not about embracing the latest (or anticipated) fads, nor about predicting what will happen to a client's business.
It *is* about growing as a consulting firm, so that you can help clients to
grow. If you are using the same technologies, approaches, and models
next year that you are using this year, you aren't growing and you may
well be in the success trap. *You can't help an expanding number of clients in a growing number of ways if you continue to use the same old tools
and knowledge.* The way to grow your business is to grow your approaches, and that requires that you take some risks.

Accepting Prudent Risk

> *If you never accept an assignment that calls for
> your doing something you haven't done before,
> you will never earn significant money.*

There is a piece of conventional wisdom that admonishes the consultant to underpromise and overdeliver. The reasoning here is that the client's expectations should be kept well within your delivery capacity.
Your actual delivery will then exceed those expectations, creating great
joy in the heart of the client. There are only two things wrong with this
approach. First, it presumes that the client is at best too stupid to divine
the manipulation, and at worst an adversary who must be duped: a win/
lose dynamic. Second, my observations of the most successful consultants I've known reveal that they simply don't abide by such bromides.
While they never promise results they can't achieve, they are always willing to expand the envelope.

Underpromising and overdelivering is just another of those empty
phrases that average consultants like to pontificate about. It's easy to remember, sounds great when you're giving advice, and imparts an aura of
lofty notions and uncompromising behavior. But in actuality, if consultants
underpromised on a regular basis, clients would begin to question the degree of value-added assistance being provided. They would also critique
the nature of the fee structure (the corollary for the client would be over-
demand and underpay). And finally, consultants would never grow because they would forever remain within the safe confines created by
underpromising.

In the end, all such pat advice and conventional wisdom—particularly
the kind that comes accompanied by finger-wagging and the phrase,

"When I began in this business…"—should be ignored. In fact, you can afford to ignore any and all advice on how to expand your business except this: there are times when the whole future direction of your career may hinge on your willingness to take a prudent risk. Should you or shouldn't you?

I spoke earlier about two aspects of consulting that are key prerequisites for growth. One was the talents and expertise you gain as you acquire and learn from a wide variety of assignments. Growth is not just a matter of increasing revenues, but equally—for the longer term—a question of expanding expertise, talent, reputation, and experience. I also spoke about the goals for the business, your vision of what you stand for, what you believe in, and what your image should convey to prospects and clients. My own vision and goals are clear to me and to my clients. To accomplish those goals, it is imperative that I continually broaden my talents, expertise, reputation, and experiences. (That is why underpromising is anathema.)

One of the fields my firm is fairly well known in is that of surveys and market analysis. But we only began that type of work about four years ago, and we did not deliberately acquire such expertise, nor did we have experience in the field. A client for whom we had done a variety of projects wanted to discuss a sampling of management opinion on the proliferation of technology within the organization, including its impact on productivity, interpersonal communications, and personal comfort. The client didn't ask about our vast survey experience (we had exactly none), nor did we ourselves focus on the particular instruments to be used. Instead, we discussed the *results* the client wanted to achieve, how the feedback was to be used, and the collaborative responsibility each of us would have in the endeavor. For example, I suggested that we create the instrument and questions, but that the client be responsible for reviewing the entire package for cultural acceptability, clarity, the accuracy of data being requested, and its conformity with corporate legal policies. I committed to revise and refine the package until the client was completely satisfied. We both agreed on what would constitute an acceptable rate of return (50 percent of 2500 managers). We also agreed that the client would distribute the survey internally with a prepaid mailer addressed to our firm. Finally, I recommended that the survey be supported by focus groups and one-on-one interviews (which we did have significant experience in), and the client concurred.

The factors I considered in undertaking survey work that we had never done before were:

- Were the client's expectations reasonable?
- Did we have, or could we develop, the expertise, talent, and capacity to implement the project?

■ Did the client have a significant accountability, so that success would be jointly shared and problems be jointly resolved?

My knowledge of surveys and of the organization supported the 50 percent return as reasonable. Knowing the organization and questioning techniques I frequently employed, I believed that creation of the survey was within our capabilities, *especially* since the client had joint responsibility in several key areas (cultural fit, legal compliance, etc.). We had the capacity to administer the project; I chose two psychology professors who frequently work with us to assist in the computer programming and scoring, and they, in turn, used students on an hourly basis for computer input. Finally, we and the client had entered into still another collaborative venture, in which the results represented a shared effort.

As always when venturing into new territory, I was careful to oversee every step of the process. The result was an 80 percent return rate, which shocked the organization's executives (and me, though I feigned lack of surprise), and a wealth of data. Henceforth, survey work was added to that client's expectations from my firm. It added to my firm's image in the marketplace, since I proceeded to offer surveys as an option in a variety of other projects, wrote some articles about procedures for high response rates, and listed the firm in several guides under "survey: employee and customer."

When assignments are undertaken as collaborative ventures with a client, you are able to expand the nature of your activities with prudent risk. The difference between prudent risk and imprudent risk can be clearly stated. *Imprudent risk* would occur if you represented yourself as a survey (or outplacement or strategy) expert to a prospect who hired you on the grounds that you were responsible for total implementation and results. You might actually have the capability to deliver such a project, but the fact that this was your first, the lack of client involvement and accountability, and the lack of a prior relationship with the client would create a high-risk situation. You might well have overpromised and there would be a significant chance of underdelivering since the client's expectations might be very high. *Prudent risk* would occur if you did not represent yourself as an expert in a field new to you; if there were a collaborative partnership in which you and the client were jointly accountable for design, implementation, and outcome; and if you were working with a client with whom you had a strong history.

Now you may well ask, regarding the situation involving heavy client participation, would there even be enough value-added benefits to the client to merit your outside assistance? The answer provides a fail-safe system for moving into new areas of expertise. If the client does not

	yes	no
■ You now possess or can quickly acquire/develop the expertise required.	☐	☐
■ You are motivated to accept the project for reasons beyond revenue.	☐	☐
■ There is the clear potential to apply these skills in other clients/projects.	☐	☐
■ The client is willing to participate actively and accept accountability.	☐	☐
■ The client's expectations are reasonable and achievable.	☐	☐
■ You possess the capacity to administer and implement the project.	☐	☐
■ You are willing and able to be involved in each step personally.	☐	☐

Figure 3-3. How to determine prudent risks for growth assignments. All these questions must be answered "yes" without qualification.

perceive sufficient value-added benefits ("If I'm doing all of this, why do I need you?"), then you won't be retained for the project, and you shouldn't pursue it further. But if the client agrees to retain you, understanding the joint accountabilities required ("We can only achieve these results by working as a team"), then the client's own decision regarding your contribution validates your approach.

Figure 3-3 provides an evaluation aid that may be useful in determining when you are taking a prudent risk in attempting to grow in new expertise and applications. *All* of the questions must be answered "yes" for you to undertake a new project. If you can answer all seven with a confident "absolutely," you have minimized the risk to yourself and the client, and have established a strong basis for growing your expertise. If you answer "no" or find yourself equivocating about any, then you are embarking on the project for the wrong reasons (money, ego) and/or with insufficient resources, and/or with inadequate growth application for your firm.

You are reading this book, presumably, to help achieve growth. *To grow, you must accept prudent risk by entering new areas of expertise and application.* To enter new areas, you have to disregard the rubrics and bromides. It's time to begin breaking paradigms.

4

Breaking Paradigms

The Worst Piece of Advice
I've Ever Received

A Surefire Strategy for
Growing Your Firm

Let's get down to cases. The first step necessary for most of us to learn how to grow a consulting business is to *unlearn*. We've all been conditioned to automatically believe certain tenets and take on faith certain axioms. I've been calling these deceptive pieces of advice "rubrics" and "bromides" and lumping them all together as "conventional wisdom." You may well feel that I'm simply being *contrarian:* trying to be different by being unconventional.[1]

Well, you're absolutely right. If the conventional wisdom about consulting were accurate, virtually everyone could make it as a consultant, and most of them would be wealthy. That's not what actually happens, and the reason is that the conventional beliefs about our profession are wrong.

A few years ago, a fellow by the name of Joel Barker attracted great interest by debunking paradigms. *Paradigms* are those thought patterns that we take for granted and let limit us. For example, Barker cites the discomfort of most bicycle seats, which have survived for a century in their current form. He invented a radically different seat, consisting of

---

[1] Being contrarian has its wonderful moments. See Chapter 10 for advice on contrarian consulting.

two separate padded supports, which is much more comfortable under one's derriere. Barker maintains that this was hardly a conceptual breakthrough in design, but it *was* a paradigm breakthrough. You see, bicycle seats are still called "saddles" because they take their form and function from horse saddles. He claims that such a genesis restricts innovation in design until someone consciously breaks the paradigm, which in this case means that there's no earthly reason at this stage to pattern bike seats after horse saddles.

I call these self-limiting mental restrictions "thinking blinders." Here's a classic example. Connect the nine dots in Figure 4-1 using only four straight lines without taking your pencil off the paper, without folding the paper in any way, and without retracing any lines:

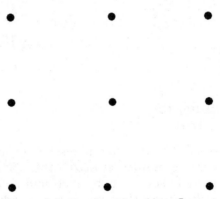

Figure 4-1. The nine-dot problem. Connect the nine dots with four straight lines.

There are two things to be concerned about if you didn't solve this problem immediately. The first is conceptual: you are clearly restricted by paradigms. The second is pragmatic: this is a *very* old exercise that is used in classrooms and workshops all over the world. If you haven't seen it, then you are not up-to-speed on basic group techniques.

The solution to the nine-dot problem appears in Figure 4-2. As you can see, the problem is easily solved *if you go beyond the illusory border formed by the dots.* No one told you that you couldn't extend the lines beyond the dots or through the caption and title. But, seeing this for the first time, most people assume that they must stay within a boundary that they've created in their mind. All of us are prone to do this every day. Here's one final example. What is the reason for the logical sequence of these numbers? Anyone looking at them should be able to

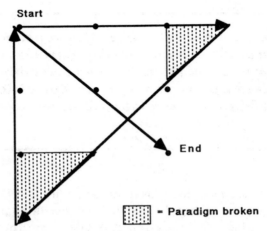

Figure 4-2. The nine-dot problem solved—by breaking the boundary paradigm.

tell. In other words, they do not represent someone's phone number or tax code. The answer is amazingly simple.

8   5   4   9   7   6   3   2   0

I have run this particular exercise with thousands of managers over the past several years, and only *one in twenty identifies the correct reason within five minutes.* Most give up (including my 16 year-old son's math teacher, who surrendered after two days because he couldn't break out of his math paradigm).[2]

Assuming that I now have your attention, I want to attack the most pernicious paradigm of all, which is also, and not coincidentally, the worst piece of advice I've ever received:

> Find your unique niche, then narrowly market within it. Otherwise the competition will eat you for breakfast. Differentiating your services is the key to success for consultants.

I received this advice *before* I started my firm, *while* I was growing it, and *after* I had become a major success. I'm *still* getting it. And it couldn't be more wrong.

---

[2]The numbers are in alphabetical order, i.e., "eight" begins with "e" and "zero" with "z."

> *If you learn nothing else from this book, heed only this. Consulting is a relationship business. A special product might make you competitive. Differentiated services may make you distinct. But only carefully crafted relationships will create a breakthrough firm.*

The strategies available for growth hinge upon the relationships you are able to forge, nurture, and expand. Average consultants attempt to market a repeatable product, which may take the form of a training program, a canned speech or workshop, a survey instrument, etc. Such predefined products seeking their niche are nothing more than commodities, and buyers view commodities almost exclusively from a cost-sensitive position, as well they should. A pound of nails is a pound of nails, and I'll buy them wherever they are cheapest (which includes price, cost of transportation to get there, and so on). The difficulty with such commodity consulting approaches is that the greater the consulting resources, the greater the economies of scale. Seminar factories, using mass marketing and razor-thin margins, are turning out $95-per-person seminars all over the country. Independent consultants may be successful implementing workshops in limited locales or within specific clients, but high costs and low margins prohibit geometric expansion. You don't make a million dollars doing this kind of work.

Better-than-average consultants differentiate their services so that they convey some distinction to the buyer. For example, providing a needs analysis prior to the actual proposal, offering computerized comparisons against national norms with survey work, and providing free follow-ups at periodic intervals are all methods that tend to set one consultant apart from another. These techniques provide for more of a value-added appreciation by the client, but are still self-limiting in terms of the specific nature of the services involved. Many consultants are successful with this approach, but they are probably also the ones who say, "Three hundred thousand is the most you can generate as an individual."

The best consultants strive to establish special relationships with clients, irrespective of their products, services, techniques, and other offerings. Relationships differ from products and services in many ways, but the most fundamental difference lies in the simple matter of payment. Clients perceive *products* (such as manuals, reports, newsletters, art work, and job aids) as commodities for which they pay a fee. Clients also perceive *services* (such as improved presentation skills, better communications, shorter meetings) as commodities for which they pay a fee. But clients perceive *relationships* as intangibles, whose value transcends commodity calculations. Relationships represent an incalculable, intrinsic worth that clients don't even try to put a price on.

My auto dealer is 45 minutes from my home, but I take my business there, rather than to a dealer of the same marque 5 minutes away, because of the relationship I have with him. My dealer's products are comparable to other dealers'; after all, they are the same cars and parts. His services are comparable and standard with his manufacturer: roadside assistance, a hot-line for questions, state inspection on-site, and so on, but my dealer's relationship with his customers is special. He thinks nothing, for instance, of personally picking up and delivering cars to customers' homes, leaving a loaner vehicle for their use in the interim. His staff embraces the same principles of helpfulness. The salesperson who sold me the car keeps in touch periodically, provides the names of new restaurants she's discovered which she thinks we'd enjoy, and occasionally sends my wife a flower with a note about local cultural events in her town. The dealer has taken me to lunch, and makes a point to come over and say hello when he knows I'm at the dealership.

When it's time to buy another car, guess whom I'll call? I'd feel disloyal doing anything else. And now for the kicker: even when such intangibles are actually built into the cost structure, the client still perceives them as free. And if the relationship is sufficiently developed, clients will pay more for products and services that accompany the relationship. How much more? Would I remain with the dealer if he were $1000 more expensive than the competition? How about $3000? Surely I'd leave for $5000, right?[3] In the final analysis, it largely comes down to the relationship.

The strategies available for growth are legion, *as long as they focus on developing unique relationships with clients*. Let's examine a method for selecting them.

Fine-Tuning the Strategy

We've established that there are three basic interactions you engage in with clients. You may sell them a product, which is a paid-for tangible. You may provide them with a service, which is a paid-for intangible. And you establish a relationship with them, which is a free intangible. In any of these areas you may be competitive, distinct, or perceived as

---

[3] These were actual questions I addressed with the North American management team of Mercedes-Benz. We worked together to try to convince dealers of the need for an emphasis on customer service and customer relationships. These dealer-profitability seminars turned out to be wildly successful.

special—which I like to call "breakthrough" positioning. The combination of these interactions and dimensions is expressed in Figure 4-3.

You may not sell any products at all, or they may be peripheral to your major business. For example, we provide books and cassettes on a request basis, and we often design interactive and self-paced learning programs for clients, but these tangible products are not our leading edge; they are the results of our relationships and services, and not the primary factor for our selection by a client. As a rule, products are viewed as commodities and are very price-sensitive. You can be competitive by providing professional, high-quality materials when requested, but to be unique or "breakthrough" in this dimension requires a substantial investment to compete in a margin-thin business. My advice: if you must provide products as a component of your consulting work, keep them to a minimum, keep them high-quality, but *do not* use them as the distinguishing feature of your work.

All of us in this profession provide services—the paid-for intangibles—to the client. The service may be formal and contractually specified, such as a needs analysis or series of focus groups, or it may be informal and ad hoc, such as a review of the client's sudden personnel problems or recommendations for a meeting agenda. This advice and counsel needs to be better than competitive, or else the client will see no differentiation and will select consulting help based on logistical and objective factors. ("All the consultants ask me for my watch and tell me the time, so I might as well carry the cheapest watch and ask the nearest consultant.") However, it is difficult to be in the breakthrough category

	Competitive	Unique	*Breakthrough*
Product			
Service			
Relation			

Figure 4-3. A systematic way to establish strategy. (*Adapted from a model first published in Alan Weiss,* Making It Work: Turning Strategy Into Action Throughout Your Organization, *Harper & Row, New York, 1990.*)

in service, because there is a limit to what you can do in terms of resources and availability, especially when compared with larger firms. A high-quality personal report to the executive board with handouts, graphics, and relevant data from the competition is enough to be special. Flashing lights and dancing animals probably aren't required, because consistently special service is very powerful in the eyes of the client. Breakthrough service can be seen as cloying, self-aggrandizing, and "overkill."

Thus—if you haven't already guessed—my contention is that the breakthrough category for you should be your relationship with the client. Ideally, your strategic mix should look like the one shown in Figure 4-4. The reason for this is that your competition is probably either trying to emphasize breakthrough characteristics across the board (virtually impossible and extremely expensive), or is sidetracked by a particular strength or weakness in any one of the areas on the grid. There is no need to be more than competitive in products, and you are positioned ideally—and cost-effectively—if you are deemed distinctive in service. If you can then achieve breakthrough *relationships*, you are on the way to a long-lived, growth-oriented, highly lucrative clientele.

Products and services tend to be based on *objective* assessment of *what* you are providing and *how* you are providing it. You are being compared to others, to past experience, to expectations. There is an attempt to quantify. You might call this the *science* of consultant selection and acceptance. But relationships represent the *why* of your involvement; you are assessed in terms of the client's *comfort* in dealing with you, and these are *subjective* determinations. While it can be much harder to establish these connections, and is always time-consuming to do so, they

	Competitive	Unique	*Breakthrough*
Product	High-quality Minimum amounts Support, not leading edge		
Service		Polished, professional Anticipate need Client-centered, not consultant-centered	
Relation			Anticipatory Helps "unrelated" areas Personal bonds Visceral and trusting Based on judgment

Figure 4-4. The ideal strategic mix, emphasizing relationships for dynamic growth.

are the most important connections, because they are qualitative instead of quantitative. And herein lies the *art* of consultant selection and acceptance.

The ideal client relationship is one in which the client trusts the consultant to make determinations about capabilities, meaning that the client approaches the consultant with a fundamental assumption that the consultant will act responsibly to improve the client's condition.

The ideal relationships with clients are based on total trust and candor. As opposed to the traditional client-consultant dynamic, in which the client asks the consultant to prove that the latter can meet the former's needs ("Perform for me, so I can evaluate you"), the breakthrough relationship is one in which the client asks the consultant to collaborate to meet a need ("Work with me, so we can be successful"). The client trusts that *the consultant will make the assessment as to whether the goals can be achieved within the consultant's capabilities.* In this act of trust, the critical judgment passes from client to consultant, because the client knows that the consultant is the far better judge of his or her own capabilities, and has no reason to believe that the consultant will do anything other than act in the client's best interests. This, indeed, is breakthrough stuff.

Over the past decade, we've seen virtually all the major accounting firms launch consulting divisions. This is because there is an unyielding cap on growth in the accounting business; after all, how many times can you audit the books? These firms realized that they had established, by the very nature of their confidential work, a special, trusting relationship with clients. By laterally transferring that trusting relationship to related areas (most of these firms began their consulting work by heavily basing it on financial and MIS issues), these organizations have dramatically expanded their business base within existing clients even though their products and services were not known in any area other than financial work. There is simply no growth mechanism as dramatic in our profession as a trusting client who wants to use your services, believing that you will provide a reason not to if you can't accommodate the request. *In effect, the selection responsibility moves from the client to the consultant.* That's not a responsibility to be abused or taken lightly, of course. Taking on a project you can't handle can, in two weeks, sour a relationship it took you two years to establish.

Ten Ways to Develop Breakthrough Relationships

How do you create powerful, breakthrough relationships? With patience, insight, legwork, and specific techniques like these:

1. Provide Valuable Information

You cannot overcommunicate with clients if you are providing information that enhances performance and improves the working environment. Keep a set of files on all important issues facing your clients and key prospects, irrespective of whether you are personally working on those topics or even being considered for them. Our files have titles that include Ethics, Customer Satisfaction Measures, Interviewing Techniques, CEO Development, and the like. We clip articles, note ideas we've heard, and collect competitive product and service literature, and file it all away under appropriate headings. Once a quarter we review the files, eliminate duplication, create a unifying theme or sequence within each topic area, and send the contents to every client and prospect listed for that category. We have never had recipients request that they be removed from the mailing list. We scrupulously avoid any self-promotion other than the inclusion of articles we've published in the field and reviews of our relevant books.

2. Provide Essential Phone Numbers

Make the following numbers available to every client (and "client" means every key individual within the client organization): regular office number, toll-free number (if you don't have one, get one), fax number (ditto), and home number.[4] About three times a year a client will call me at home in the evening or during a weekend with a critical request or question that simply can't wait. Three at-home calls a year is a small price to pay to cement relationships. This privilege is never abused, is a sign of great trust, and goes beyond mere service. One sign that I've established the relationships I seek occurs when clients offer me *their* home numbers.

3. Raise Crucial Issues

In as responsible and professional a way as possible, raise issues that demand the client's attention even if they are not part of the project on

---

[4]A personal bias: don't offer car phone numbers and *never* put them on your business cards or letterhead. Advertising the fact that you have a car phone can insult the client who doesn't have one or believe in them.

which you are working. Make it clear—and live by the pledge—that you are not raising the issues because you want to expand your project to include them. (If the client insists you take them on, request that the client consider other alternatives before making a decision. This sounds crazy to short-term thinkers, but nine times out of ten, the client asks you to help anyway, and fee is no issue at all. See the fee/commitment equation later in this chapter.)

While undertaking a survey of customer satisfaction for a client, I found a severe morale problem among field employees centered on two middle managers. I informed my client in a private meeting on the principle that he ought to know and that I would not be acting professionally and in his best interests if I didn't inform him. He took independent action after consulting with his staff members, and told me that the situation could have gotten out of hand if I hadn't raised it with him.

4. Recommend Other Resources

Don't hesitate to suggest other service- or product-suppliers. I keep lists of resources I can call on to fulfill assignments that I cannot handle because I lack the competency or time. Some possess highly specialized skills, such as outplacement counseling, and some are adept at routine needs, such as workshop facilitation. When a client asks me to take on a project that I cannot handle (the client is trusting me to make that decision), I call upon these resources as alternatives. The client is pleased that I can offer this help (because my recommendations carry my credibility), the person selected is appreciative of the business, and my long-term standing is enhanced. Although I request periodic summaries of the work in progress, I seldom accept a finder's fee or commission on such referral business for two reasons. First, I don't want to convey the impression that I profit from such referrals. Second, I am then able to influence the person chosen to my best advantage (i.e., "If you learn anything about my former sales project results, let me know"; "Please provide your best rates"; "Keep me informed of anything I should convey to the buyer").

5. Go the Extra Mile

Fulfill even tangential requests with grace and timeliness. As I wrote this chapter I received a call from an excellent client with a friend who needs a job. The client felt that his friend could profit greatly from an hour spent with me discussing opportunities in my field and in my experience with clients. I could simply have agreed to speak with the friend by phone when I had the chance, and the client would have been happy with such service. But I don't want to provide service, I want to build relationships, so I immediately called the client's friend and invited him to my office and to lunch as my guest at a mutually convenient time. I dropped a line to the client to close the loop, and gave him a summary of our discussion when I saw him again.

6. Facilitate Client Publicity

Recommend clients for publicity opportunities that may have nothing to do with your work for the organization. Since I'm very active in the media, I am often asked for interview subjects, examples of excellent performance for profiles, people to serve as judges and on panels, and so on. I not only recommend certain clients, but provide a synopsis of why they would be appropriate or qualified, and some background on their organization. I tell the interviewer or selector to be sure to mention my name so that the client gives them priority in his or her busy schedule.

7. Send Appropriate Gifts

Now before you race for the ethics books, let me explain. I send two types of gifts. One is sent at year's end (sometimes it's to welcome the New Year, sometimes for Thanksgiving, but it's never sectarian) to all core clients as an unabashed way of saying "thanks for your business." If their organizations permit (and I *always* find out what the rules are first), I send something like a reference book, a paperweight, a traveling-office kit, or business magazine subscription. If that is not permitted, I might send a contribution to a cause I know they support in their name. If nothing is permitted, I'll send a card.[5] Of course, I can always send an autographed copy of one of the business books I've written, which never prompts a problem.[6] The second type of gift is a "situational" gift. I found out that one client's son saved beer cans (which happens to

---

[5]Interesting dynamic: I've found that the higher level the client and better the relationship, the less there is any problem in sending a gift. Lower-level managers tend to have the most trouble accepting them, as do clients who are ambiguous about the relationship. In nine years, I've had one gift returned, from a client with whom I still conduct business but who felt awkward accepting a book.

[6]When I sent my book on strategy to Roy Vagelos, CEO of Merck, I commented that he had been proud of telling me that he had read only one business book (not mine, unfortunately), in his entire life, and he had never seen the need to read another. I told him I realized the challenge I was facing. I got back a one-line note, which I keep in my office. He said, "Who knows? I just might make an exception."

be a wider pursuit than I ever imagined), so I found a local Rhode Island brew that he wouldn't come across in his Midwest locale, and sent it along. These efforts cost virtually nothing, are never seen as inappropriate, and contribute to solid relationships.

8. Help Subordinates Unstintingly

Go out of your way to help lower-level people whether or not they are directly involved in your project and irrespective of whether they have any direct influence on future business. They *always* have an indirect influence.

While conducting focus groups with field managers, a manager asked if I would be willing to do something similar for his representatives, even though it wasn't part of my charter and was "only" for his personal assistance in managing his people. I told him that if his boss agreed, I'd gladly do it for expenses only. We had a wonderful time, he was able to provide something special for his people, and his feedback to senior management on my help was something that only my mother could write. On another occasion, I agreed to see a staff person after hours who couldn't be scheduled into a focus group, but who wanted to make her views known. I received information from her that I hadn't heard before and that I was able to raise with future groups, enabling me to provide additional insight in my evaluation for the client.

9. Don't Be Afraid to Take a Stand

Never back away from controversy, and don't hesitate to tell the client he or she is wrong. Being a sycophant is not being a consultant, and the chances are that the client has more "yes" people than any organization needs. Your worth, your integrity, your value-added to the organization will be illuminated by your stand on important matters. Jefferson said, "In matters of taste, swim with the current; in matters of principle, stand like a rock."

A year ago I delivered the results of a survey on ethics to a division vice president and his top reports. Three minutes into the presentation the subordinates — obviously feeling threatened — raised every conceivable objection, from the nature of the questions in the survey to the legitimacy of the responses. I told them that they could agree or disagree with the data, but that in my opinion it was rock solid. After the meeting, I took the vice president aside so as not to embarrass anyone, and told him that I thought the kind of resistance and defensiveness we had just witnessed was no doubt responsible for a great deal of the survey results from subordinates. I also offered to cancel the remainder of the project, which called for workshops to disseminate the results, if he were the least uncomfortable, even though I had a noncancellable contract. The result was that he chose to confide in me about sensitive people-issues, asked for advice in his presenting of the results to subordinates, and has enlarged the earlier scope of our work together.

10. Treat Clients as Partners

Always view the client as an equal partner. The client is not just a buyer whose decision puts bread on your table, and you are by no means the expert-all-mighty, without whom the client cannot open the mail. The two (or three or seven) of you are a team, each reliant on the other to provide talent and resources to meet mutually agreed upon goals. I do nothing for you, you do nothing for me; we do things *jointly* for a common purpose. We don't seek blame, we seek cause. We don't relish activities, we rejoice in outcomes.

After a highly successful year with a client, during which his organization beat its plan for the first time in six years, I met with his boss, the group president, to review the past year and prepare for the next. The president said, "You must be ecstatic about the results we had. You were an essential part of the process." I can think of no greater accolade. Every year for the past six, Merck & Co. has been named America's Most Admired Company in *Fortune* magazine's annual poll of executives. Every year, Merck sends all employees a gift, thanking them for their contribution. And every year *I* get a gift, from the vice president of worldwide personnel, personally thanking me for *my* contribution to Merck's success. That is the ne plus ultra of client relationships. Chapter 14 will discuss how a succession of such relationships turns into a million dollar business.

The Core Value of Your Firm's Success

I've labored to explain that the core of your firm's success is the relationships you form with clients. The yardstick of the success of those relationships will be the growth you enjoy, and I've stipulated that such growth must go beyond short-term economics and embrace your learning, reputation, expertise, and experience. The sum total of this broadening is multidimensional growth. Such comprehensive, across-the-board growth establishes a clear, targeted position for the firm. You should not let your-

self be lulled by growth in one area. For example, an increase in your expertise alone is insufficient if your reputation in the market does not reflect it, if you are unable to apply it to new projects, and if you make no
money from it. Yet many consultants continually add expertise—in the
form of new people, the licensed approaches of others and personal research—without regard for the total growth picture.

Similarly, consultants often evaluate growth in terms of numbers of
new clients—a single *quantitative* measure which can ignore the *qualitative* consideration that all the new clients require the exact same treatment, providing no growth in expertise or diverse experience. Figure
4-5 illustrates the power of striving for multidimensional growth. Financial growth must accompany the other growth factors; it is not independent of them.

Obviously, that financial growth is essential for our businesses and
our lives. My intent is not to downplay it—far from it, as the name of
this book should make clear—but to dramatize that real wealth in this
business is a function of longer-term thinking and avoidance of compla-
cency in shorter-term revenues. Here's a very simple equation to try to
prove the point.

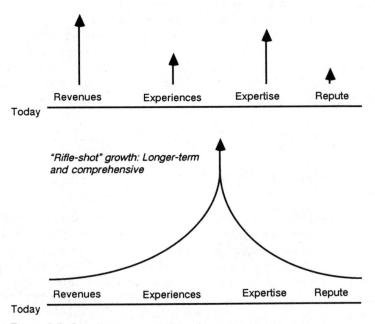

Figure 4-5. Singular versus multidimensional growth.

Establishing high-level, high-quality relationships takes more time than does a quick sale to a lower-level buyer based on such single factors as fee, deliverables, timing, etc. In fact, it often means passing up some short-term business. But the patience this requires is always worth it in the long run because of the fee dynamic shown in Figure 4-6. The higher the commitment of the buyer, the less resistance there is to fees. And the higher the level of the buyer, the less resistance there is to fees. (Low-level buyers are notoriously budget-bound, and consulting services are usually *not* in the budget. Higher-level buyers are results-oriented, and can approve budget exceptions or change existing ones.) Quite simply, the time it takes to develop solid, high-level relationships will always be rewarded with higher fees. Of course, you still have to *ask* for them, and there will be tactics for doing that in Chapter 8.

> ***Financial growth is not the beginning of strategic planning for your business. It is the result of planning for growth in all dimensions through high-level, high-quality client relationships.***

When I help other consultants to evaluate their fee structure, I never do so without evaluating the dynamic of their relationships with clients and prospects. This chapter *began* with a discussion of strategies for growth and *ends* with a discussion of fees based on relationships that are

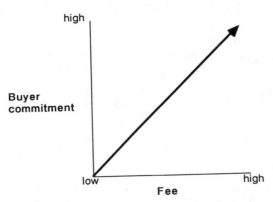

Figure 4-6. The fee-commitment dynamic. The two are directly proportional.

intrinsic to such growth. Your approach to your business must do the same. If you care to evaluate your existing sales potential, you can do so with the chart in Figure 4-7.

Low buyer commitment faced with a high fee is no sale, period. But when buyer commitment is low, a low fee isn't the answer to create the sale you need because the result is indifference. On the one hand, the buyer feels that the outcome isn't very important, because not too much has been invested; on the other, you don't feel the outcome is very important, because you aren't earning the type of fee you think you deserve. *Fees should never be established at a level designed merely to acquire the business to compensate for low buyer commitment. No one will be pleased with the outcome.*

When buyer commitment is high and the fee is low, you have placed yourself in a self-defeating position. No matter how pleased the buyer is or will be, you are working "cheap" (and, perhaps, losing money). Your alternative is forced: you feel you must use this sale to springboard to a larger, more lucrative one. This can be dangerous because once you have placed yourself in the position of using a current project to justify another, you are likely to skew results to justify further work; begin thinking of the next project at the expense of the current one; work uphill, since the client now has a mindset of your fee structure; and view the client relationship as one dimensional, based on finances.

These are the very reasons why I advocate *never* undertaking a job at a reduced fee (or, run for the exits, as a "loss leader!") just to get in the door. But that door can lead you straight into a relationship you'll soon

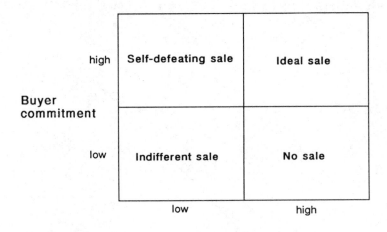

Figure 4-7. Evaluating the outcome of fee/commitment relationships.

need a window to escape from. The whole point of establishing relationships which result in high buyer commitment is to be able to establish a high fee structure.

The only desirable, win/win dynamic on the board is high commitment *and* high fees from the client. This sounds mercenary when stated boldly, but it's the logical outcome of forging the relationships I've been expounding. It's amazing how frequently these very simple dynamics are ignored by the consultant through ignorance of the process, undue focus on short-term goals, lack of appreciation for the relationship aspects of our business, and/or the success trap.

I've explained in this chapter the need to escape traditional thought patterns and eschew traditional wisdom: how to break the paradigms. If you can embrace the notion of relationship-building as the core value of your consulting success, you've gone a long way toward getting ahead of the pack. Before we turn to the specific tactics of million dollar consulting, we need to take a look at the strategies required to transform a firm into the type of consulting business I've described. It's time to turn the corner.

5
Turning the Corner

The Light at the End of the Tunnel

Surviving Transition Periods

I'm going to make some assumptions in this chapter about the readers who have ventured this far, viz.:

- It is in your self-interest to dramatically increase your business.
- You will be more valuable to clients if you accomplish such growth.
- You are already engaged in consulting work of some type.

This chapter will deal with making the transition from what you are doing to what you should be doing if you are to engage in million dollar consulting. If the assumptions above do not reflect your position and you've read this far anyway, you might want to proceed to Part 2: Tactics, because for now we are going to discuss how to sustain yourself while you modify the manner in which you operate. There are two essential considerations.

Step 1: Create a Plan

You'll need a personal plan to keep you focused as you modify your business techniques. This needn't be lengthy or convoluted, but should serve as a daily reminder of what must be accomplished. Figure 5-1 represents a sample of such a plan which might cover your next fiscal year.

Category	Result Desired	Deadline
Marketing	New brochure reflecting generalist image Book idea accepted by agent or publisher Deliver average of two keynote speeches per month	
Relationships	90 percent of business is based on project fees 90 percent of seminar/workshop business is subcontracted 75 percent of total business is "repeat" business	
Finances	One year of operating/personal expenses in the bank Credit line of at least $100,000 established No receivables of over 60 days' duration	
Resources	All legwork handled by colleagues or subcontractors No project turned down due to lack of resources Capabilities gained in Field X or Topic Y	
Personal	Net worth has increased by 25 percent or to a total of $X Family time and quality of life continually improving Nonbusiness, personal goals being pursued and met	

Figure 5-1. An example of a transition plan.

The categories will change, based on where you are and where you want to be, and the results desired will probably be much more specific, with deadlines coordinated to allow for proper priorities.

At the beginning of each year I write down my plan for the next 12 months. One year I decided that it was time to raise my speaking fees. These are 25 percent of my total revenues, and speeches are one of my prime marketing vehicles; predictably, a higher fee gets me in front of higher-quality buyers. Since my speaking is often booked six months or more in advance, I realized that I had to begin to raise the fee *immediately* when responding to inquiries and submitting proposals, and that the effects of the increase probably wouldn't be felt for nine months. At another point, when I decided to abandon personal, multiday seminar work as too labor-intensive and restricting, I found that longtime clients felt unfairly treated. As a result, I modified the plan to refuse any new work in that area, and negotiated with existing clients for an increased fee and more latitude in the content of the courses (more "live" work, fewer case studies).

Without having the plan in writing and constantly before you on your desk and in your daily calendar or planner, you will be unlikely to make the transition. We all tend to follow the path of least resistance, and that path inevitably keeps us doing exactly what we've been comfortable doing all along—and headed straight for the success trap. If, at the end of six months, you see that your plan was to accept 80 percent of your consulting assignments in the $35,000 to $150,000 range, and you've bid *solely* on assignments below $30,000, you know that you haven't applied the discipline necessary to make the transition. Neither the marketplace nor the competition controls such change. Only you do.

2. Set Up a Triage System

There are three kinds of existing or repeat business you will be faced with during your transition period:

- Category 1: business that is not consistent with the new strategy, but that you want to retain because it can be developed into the kind you're after
- Category 2: business that already represents your new, growth-oriented strategy and that you want to retain
- Category 3: business that is strictly the "old" image and that should be abandoned

Triage, of course, is generally applied to the medical system employed during a catastrophe, when casualties are high and resources scarce. Victims are separated into those who will survive if given immediate attention, those who will survive even without immediate attention, and those who probably won't survive in any case. Resources are generally allocated in that priority order.

Now let's apply the triage system to your repeat business:

Category 1 deserves priority treatment. This is sound, historically valuable business. *You want to retain it and further develop the relationship, but you don't want to retain the current format of the business.* Over a prolonged period you want to educate your buyer about the mutual benefits to be had by evolving the nature of your relationship. The basis for accomplishing this transition—the relationship—is in place.

Category 2 is business that is already where you want it to be. It requires nurturing and the relationship-building we've discussed elsewhere, but it's not as sensitive as the preceding business, which must be changed in form. Category 2 business will survive without extra intervention.

Category 3 business is not salvageable. It may be work that you simply don't want to do anymore, or business that creates an image or association that is undesirable. This is excellent business to refer to others, a technique we've discussed in prior chapters. *Retaining this business can be more damaging than not obtaining new business, because it will glue you to wherever you are today.*

Here are examples of each condition:

Category 1.   I increased average project fees by a multiple of 5 over a two-year period by forsaking a policy of "getting the business through the lowest proposal" to one of "I only want business that results in a minimum profit margin of X." I did this by formally specifying services I had to perform anyway (i.e., needs analyses, on-site observations, comparisons with industry norms) and developing relationships with buyers that helped me determine what other needs could legitimately be built into the project (even if those needs were unstated by the client). Then I substantially increased my project fees (this was not especially noticeable, so long as I didn't charge on a per diem basis, and continued to demonstrate high value-added outcomes) from what I would have charged had I not had a tangible transition plan for growth. I can still remember the very first $55,000 proposal I submitted, with my heart racing madly as the client reviewed it in front of me. When he accepted it with a simple, "OK, it reflects everything we've agreed on, so let's do it," I knew that I had turned a corner in my career and my life.

Category 2.   I had accidentally developed a high profile as a keynote speaker in the newspaper industry. I maintained that profile through mailings and ongoing appearances at the American Press Institute and utilized it as a model for the types of speaking I wanted to do cross-industrially. This was a business approach that didn't require modification, and I invested the majority of my time and energy elsewhere.

Category 3.   I had done individual behavioral assessments for clients by providing a written or cassette description of predispositions based on an instrument we utilize. I didn't want to be known as a testing firm, however, and the clients using this service tended to be small, one-site operations, a market I did not see as important to our future or reputation. Consequently, I offered this business to a woman who frequently worked on projects for us, and provided free rights to use our instrumentation. I also provided those clients (and future inquiries) with alternative sources of such testing. Finally, I recorded the entire test and its interpretation in a book,[1] so that the approach could be easily accessed and attributed to us.

These categories will be discussed at more length in the following two sections of this chapter. Before we get there, however, I want to summarize the keys to successfully making the transition to million dollar consulting:

---

[1] Alan Weiss, *Managing for Peak Performance: The Power (and Pitfalls) of Personal Style,* Harper & Row, New York, 1989.

1. Set up a specific plan for the major categories of your business, and use the plan as a daily management tool to influence your decisions in running the business.
2. Establish a triage system to protect attractive business, nurture evolving business, and abandon inappropriate business.
3. Assess your progress monthly, cognizant that some changes will be short-term and other changes longer-term, and determine whether you are performing in an accountable manner as your own client.
4. Do not waver.

A fundamental confidence builder during times of transition is the sound client base you already have and which you will be retaining in the future.

There is no external force that will compel you to change the way in which you secure and deliver business. You must have a clear, tangible plan for turning the corner, hold yourself accountable to it, just as if you were your own client.

Eight Secrets for Retaining Key Personal Business

To make a successful transition from lone wolf to thundering herd, you will want to safeguard key personal business and relationships. These are represented by categories 1 and 2 above. No matter which category the business relationship falls into, there are some techniques available to protect it while your business changes its image and the manner in which it operates. I've found that the following eight methods apply, irrespective of size, location, type of client, or your consulting role.

1. Involve the Client in the Change and Seek Feedback

The worst thing you can do with an established client who has a clear image and understanding of what you've represented to the organization, is to present an abrupt change in that image and understanding. Rather than present the client with a fait accompli and hope for the best, invite key people within the organization to comment on your proposed changes. Share your reasons with them—i.e., you are moving away from conducting three-day seminars and toward on-site observations and one-on-one coaching because your experience indicates that such changes produce higher quality, longer-term client results. Ask the client personnel for feedback and suggestions. Keep them apprised of progress. Ask them directly if there are aspects of your relationship with them that might be endangered or enhanced in light of your new strategy.

2. Present the Changes as Opportunities, Not Threats

Determine how your new positioning will help your client, and prepare a cogent explanation of the advantages. *The client will tend to view change as threat; you must provide the counterpoints.* Demonstrate that it's been the very nature of your relationship with this client and others that has inspired your evolving view of your work and its emphasis. Be upbeat and positive about the anticipated changes and place them in perspective. They are natural evolutions of your growing business that you want to explain personally to the client because of your unique and ongoing relationship; they are not watershed events that will permanently alter the relationship.

3. Don't Explain the Changes and Raise Your Fees Simultaneously

Remember, these are clients in categories either already suited to your new strategy or capable of developing into that role. Even if you've embarked upon a survey technique the client is now obtaining elsewhere, or you are providing customer surveys at a lower fee here than you've begun charging elsewhere, don't propose or implement such changes too early. First allow the client to understand, react to, and acclimate to the changes in your business approach. Then you can introduce new services or fee structures. This could take six months to a year, depending on the original nature of your business and the client's identification with it.

4. Request Ongoing Feedback

Especially when there is a new company name, logo, materials, letterhead, and other print material, be sure to send advance copies or rough concepts to the client and request feedback. Whether or not you agree with and utilize the feedback, by soliciting it and listening to it you will create ownership of your changes with the client. This will lessen the perceived sense of change and make the client a party to it rather than a perceived victim of it. Most importantly, since your image is dependent, not on how you see it, but on how others see it, client feedback is very useful in alerting you and your designers to whether the proposed look is effective in conveying your image in the marketplace.

5. Introduce Changes to Clients as a Group

Convene one or more small, informal meetings in a hotel conference room convenient to a group of clients, offer a continental breakfast or lunch, provide your intent, and elicit their feedback as a group. This is an excellent investment, because

1. Groups are self-sanctioning, and generally adopt a middle-of-the-road attitude about change
2. The clients will see themselves as advisers to you, which will enhance the two-way nature of the relationship
3. The clients will have the opportunity to speak *to each other,* which can only enhance your perceived value in helping diverse organizations
4. Better ideas emerge from a group setting, leading to valuable feedback

I've concluded such sessions by presenting everyone with a best selling business book or reference work as a token of appreciation for their participation.

6. Offer to "Grandfather" or Otherwise Safeguard the Services Being Phased Out

For example, if you are no longer marketing the three-day effective listening workshops that a particular client has requested once a quarter for three years, offer to continue them for one final year. During that time, introduce a colleague or another consultant who will provide the overlap and continuity beyond the year. These offers are effective only if you

1. Establish a definitive cutoff point beyond which you will cease offering the product or service

2. There is an offer (whether or not it's accepted) of a qualified replacement who can smoothly continue as you bow out

Offer a sufficiently long phaseout so that the client has time to consider options and the change does not seem imminent. (Do *not* offer these phaseouts unless you are certain the client will consider them integral to a continued, effective relationship. They are time-consuming and deflect you from your future emphases, and are too frequently offered because the *consultant,* not the client, doesn't want to end the service.)

7. Time Your Explanation to Coincide with Successful Assignments

After verbally reviewing a consulting project that the client is pleased about, survey results that the client has found enlightening, or workshop feedback that praises your techniques, use the moment to explain the changes that will occur within your firm. *Tie the changes in with the ongoing development and evolution that has already been employed in the highly successful assignment just completed.* Demonstrate that you are merely formalizing the effective techniques which you've been informally applying to the client's benefit for some time. Hence this isn't an abrupt change, but an acknowledgment of the changes already incorporated into your work and approaches. (Conversely, do not introduce a proposed change in the way you will conduct business in the middle of a client project or after one that has produced ambiguous or unacceptable results.)

8. Be Prepared to Switch Intractable Clients to Category 3

This is easy for me to say, and no one easily forsakes today's certain income for tomorrow's uncertain prospects, no matter how attractive they may be. But here's the reality. First, very few clients, if any, will be this intractable if the relationship was solid to begin with. After all, you've had to accommodate client changes, and most clients do not find it unreasonable to accommodate yours, especially if they are presented and articulated in terms of the client's best interests. Second, if several of your clients react negatively, your proposed changes may well be too radical for a great deal of your existing business. This means that you are either making necessary large-scale changes to achieve dramatic growth, or that your changes are too ambitious given your relationship with those clients. In either case, the feedback is essential for you to re-evaluate your course of action. Third, as we've stated above and will stress again below, *you must abandon certain no-growth business relationships if you are to establish high-growth business relationships.* You just can't have it both ways. If you make your best effort to retain key personal business relationships during a transition period and those efforts fail anyway, then those relationships would not have contributed to the high-growth business you are seeking to create.

Deliberately forsaking current business and current prospects seems alien to everything we're taught about marketing. Why should you lose business at all? Can't a smart marketer retain the past *and* develop the future? In my experience, this attempt only results in your being a captive of the past and a passive viewer of the future.

Raising Capital

Chapter 11 will deal with managing and exploiting capital once you've earned it. But while we're on the subject of strategy, I want to talk about the lifeblood of your growth plans: how to raise capital. In my experience, the overwhelming reason for most small business failures in this country is undercapitalization. Excellent products, wonderful ideas, and beautiful relationships are undermined and sabotaged by inadequate funding.

If you truly intend to change your business into the type of dynamic and growth-oriented enterprise this book addresses, you will need, at a minimum, access to the following:

- The type of office equipment described in Chapter 3
- Excellent legal help (for incorporation, contracts, subcontracting, litigation, and amendments to bylaws)
- Excellent financial planning help (for credit lines, retirement plans, tax work, and references)
- Bookkeeping services (for trial balances, general ledgers, and balance sheets)
- Insurance professionals (for liability, equipment, accident, and especially disability—the most overlooked insurance need in our business)
- A personal travel agent (for maximizing and coordinating all travel savings and rewards, and for saving you time in scheduling)
- Desktop publishing and traditional printing professionals (for products, stationery, and "deliverables")
- Graphics resources (for slides, video, and textual graphics)

Do not scrimp on legal and financial help. The attorney who closed on your house and the accountant who does your personal taxes are unlikely to have the expertise your business requires. Seek out specialists, using references from colleagues in the business or other personal service business acquaintances. (Did you know, for example, that there is a national insurance company that offers special group products, including dental insurance, for consulting operations, *including even one-person operations?*)

My attorney recommended items to include in my bylaws that cover all family medical expenses not covered by insurance, provision for attractive auto reimbursement, and the demand for scheduled and planned directors' meetings at company expense. My financial adviser has provided contacts for bank credit lines, structure for retirement plans, counsel on cashflow and investments, and has served as a key reference for large new clients who require evidence of financial stability before sending along a deposit of $100,000 or so.

If you are undercapitalized, you will most likely fail in your growth plans, no matter how excellent your consulting expertise. If you are adequately capitalized, you will have the latitude to refine and modify your approaches until they can generate the growth you desire.

As a rule, my guidelines for financial resource needs are:

- Money required to establish the office and services mentioned thus far

- One year of personal, pretax expenses, including recurring (utilities bills) and one-time liabilities (tuition, annual insurance premiums), plus a 10 percent contingency based on current lifestyle

- Six months of nonreimbursable daily business expenses, such as postage meter costs, telephone bills, and office supplies

At any given time, the sum of these three areas should be exceeded by cash-on-hand, accounts receivable, signed but unbilled business, company securities on deposit, and/or access to credit lines. My belief is that access to credit lines should represent no more than 35 percent of the total need. Thus, if your office start-up requires $10,000, a year's living plus contingency requires $125,000, and office needs represent $25,000, you'll need at least $100,000 in the bank, in contractual business, or in securities, and about $60,000 available on a credit line. Your working capital — the excess of current assets over current liabilities — is the key to funding your continuing growth. (See Figure 5-2.)

There are two basic ways to raise the capital you require: debt and equity. If you're serious about building your business, I strongly advise against using equity for the following reasons:

1. Equity investment means that you are surrendering partial control of your business in return for funding. The most extreme form is represented by venture capitalists. These are high-risk investors who will lend money under conditions that conservative investors wouldn't consider, but who demand high payback in return. In addition, they demand that the principal (you) make a demonstrable and heavy investment, so that your motivation is clearly to make the business successful. That heavy investment is often in the form of all liquid assets, a mortgage on the house, and a low personal salary during start-up and initial growth.

Understandably, venture capitalists want to own a piece of your business *and* a piece of your soul. Under such conditions, you can hardly serve your clients well and you can't reward yourself very easily. This is not the route to pursue.

2. You can also attract equity financing through personal investors. These may be family members and friends. The disadvantage of this route is two-fold. First, there is considerable pressure to make repayments, given the personal nature of the relationship. Second, the money

One year of living expenses plus 10% contingency plus Six months of office expenses plus Start-up office expenses (if any)	*Equals basic capital requirements*

Cash and securities on hand plus Accounts receivable plus Contractual, unbilled business plus Credit line access	*Equals sources of capital*

Figure 5-2. The working-capital equation: do you have sufficient working capital— assets over liabilities?

raised through such a route is seldom a large enough amount except for the purposes of short-term working capital.

3. Another avenue in equity financing is that of providing colleagues with a piece of the action in return for their investment. Once you're a going concern with strong cashflow and attractive prospects, you can use equity as a method of attracting good people (or even of establishing partners), which we'll discuss in Chapter 7. But at the outset, such equity value is more problematic, as is setting a definition of its worth. (For a $25,000 investment, does a colleague receive 5 percent participation, or 15 percent?) These early investment/worth decisions can return to haunt you if you've been too generous, or cause dysfunctional ill-will if you've been too miserly.

The advantage of colleague equity investment is that it can create highly motivated stakeholders who identify personally with the enterprise's success. However, such participation severely limits your freedom to abandon business and raise fees, as prescribed earlier. I've found equity participation a much more useful tool for long-term commitment and reward than for short-term capital needs.

4. Finally, some consultants achieve equity financing by providing their products and services for use by other consultants on a fee or license arrangement. I don't consider these to be client relationships, since the purchaser has unrestricted use of the proprietary material and represents it as his or her own. While this can raise short-term cash, the disadvantages of losing control over such approaches and receiving only a percentage instead of the whole, make this approach a shortsighted one. In summary, selling a piece of your ownership and/or a part of your technology is at best a short-term solution and at worst a long-term drain for anyone serious about dramatic growth.

In contrast, debt financing (however forbidding the term sounds) leaves you in complete control of your destiny.[2] The best method I know of involves a credit line with a local bank that demands only that *you make monthly interest payments, with principal payments at your discretion.* This allows you the leeway to repay when cashflow is strong and to minimize payments when cashflow is weak. Yet all payments are legitimate company expenses.

When I first organized for dramatic growth I had a solid client base producing $200,000 to $300,000 a year in revenues. But the contracts

---

[2]I'm using alternatives and likelihoods that apply to a typical economy. In the mid 1980s, for example, debt financing was as easy as having lunch with a banker. By the late 1980s, many sources had completely dried up. Normally, debt financing is available if you prepare carefully and use a strong financial adviser.

were never multiyear, the cashflow varied tremendously (one January I made $55,000, followed by a $250 February), and my track record was of only two years' duration. At times I had to scramble for working capital, while at others I had to use certificates of deposit to absorb the excess funds. Should I have invested in higher-interest instruments that carried penalties for early withdrawal, or have kept funds liquid in the event clients did not pay promptly and sacrificed the interest? That question taught me the value of a heavy investment in financial advice.

My financial adviser used his contacts to arrange meetings with three different banks. I chose a personal banking relationship with the bank that offered a credit line (secured by a second mortgage on my home) of $150,000 for personal use and $100,000 for business use. The bank required only monthly interest payments on each. Remember, if I didn't use the lines I owed nothing, and I could pay back any balances at my convenience. I've since raised the limit by another $100,000, on the dramatic showing of the growth I've achieved.

Is there a danger in using your home for collateral for potential use of investment money in your business? Well, there's less danger in using *it* than in using the money of others, in my opinion, *provided you're serious about growing your business.* If you're going to use such investment capital for skiing vacations or fancier offices, then you're in big trouble. But you don't need this book to tell you that. *The reason that we've tackled strategy in the first part of this book is that your focus and beliefs must be crystal clear concerning the wisdom and advantages of multidimensional growth. If they're not, then don't pursue financing, because you've nothing definitive in which to invest.*

If you cannot use your home for such credit purposes, there are other options to explore. You are best advised to consult with your financial adviser about what they are, but here are some areas to discuss:

- Receivables can be used as collateral, which may be attractive if you have long-term contracts that pay at specified intervals and you want to accelerate the use of the cash. Banks will typically lend up to 80 percent of the amount of such receivables, although you should be advised that they frequently inform the client that the receivable is the basis for collateral. Some financing institutions may also demand a percentage of the collateral from you. There is a derivation of this financing called "factoring," in which the lender assumes the risk and collection of the receivable. It is generally more expensive and I don't recommend it, particularly since it is often (though wrongly) inferred to be the resort of a company in financial trouble.

- Inventory can often be used to generate up to 50 percent of its worth for financing purposes. If your business involves a large product inventory, then this is an option. Be careful about the bank you choose, since many do not understand the nature of the worth of proprietary products and technology in our profession. John Humphrey, when CEO of the Forum Company in Boston, told me once that he actually took his bankers into the vault, showed them the master copies of the company's training materials, explained the copyrights and the revenue they represented each year, and helped them make the conceptual breakthrough that monies could be lent against such inventory.

- Other personal or corporate assets can be used as collateral—from vehicles to copyrighted computer programs and from office space to securities. Your financial adviser should create the most attractive combination of debt possibilities once you've collaborated on the growth needs and current assets.

Obviously, the less indebtedness the better. But don't be afraid of it. The only way to make money is to invest money. We tap into our credit lines frequently with the intent of exploiting business growth opportunities. Our clients, our banker, and our business are all the better for it.

The Ten Basic Principles of Million Dollar Consulting

Million dollar consulting is based on these ten premises:

1. The consultant will *improve* the client's condition.
2. The interactions with key clients will, strategically, be based on competitive products (if products are required at all), distinctive services, and breakthrough *relationships*.
3. Those relationships will be developed as *collaborative*, long-term, mutually reinforcing, and mutually rewarding.
4. As a result of these relationships, the consultant can achieve total conceptual agreement on project *outcomes*, as opposed to tasks, after which fee is a relatively minor issue.
5. Fees are based on *value*[3] as perceived by the client.
6. The client trusts the *consultant* to make the decisions as to whether the latter can accomplish the former's objectives.

[3]More about this in Chapter 8.

7. The consultant must achieve *multidimensional* growth in repute, expertise, experiences, and income if high earnings are to be a long-term, ongoing phenomenon.

8. To grow the high end of the business, the consultant must *abandon* the low end of the business.

9. The consultant must invest money to make money, and adequate capital is *fundamental* for growth.

10. No one becomes wealthy as a function of the revenues they generate. It's not what you make, it's what you *keep*.

Most of these precepts have been examined or at least raised in the previous four chapters. At times, we've even crossed the line into tactics, i.e., techniques to develop breakthrough relationships, secrets to retaining key personal business, and the range of interventions available to use with a client. However, my overarching goal so far has been to set the stage and allow you to view the entire scene. The tactics that follow in Part 2, while effective and important no matter what your business looks like strategically, *will only create the dynamic growth we've discussed if they are embraced within a framework that exploits their potential.*

The reason I've dedicated the first third of the book to understanding and selecting your strategic options, is that your philosophy and basic beliefs about your business will—unequivocally—determine how you actually act and perform with clients and prospects. And my experience is that most consultants are too busy trying simultaneously to deliver current business, send out proposals, service key clients, market their services and, occasionally, spend an evening at home, to afford themselves the luxury of thinking about strategy, because it's "long-term." But that's another piece of conventional wisdom run amok. Strategy is intrinsically neither long-term nor short-term. It has to do with *what you are* and *what you want to be,* so that the tactics you employ—*how you get there*—are consistent with the intended destination. If there is no intended destination because there's no time to think about it, much less consciously formulate it, then at worst you will spin your gears in frustration and at best you will find yourself ensnared in the success trap. In any case, you will never reach the top of this profession.

And make no mistake about it, the top of this profession is worth reaching, and the million dollar tag I've hung on it means a great deal more than simply money in the bank. At the top there are client opportunities, collaborative offers from other consultants, publishing alternatives, speaking invitations, and travel options. Taken together, these opportunities can enhance your personal and professional growth in a way few other professions in the world can match. But this isn't merely about getting rich, although that's not an altogether unpleasant aspect. It is about excellence.

> **Strategy is the framework within which you make the decisions that determine the nature and direction of your business.**[4]

When consultants tell me that they are happy with their current size and capacity, or that they really don't want to grow because they couldn't handle the business, or make some other excuse justifying the plateau they're on, I don't feel sorry for them; after all, it's their life. But I do feel sorry for their clients. Because *ultimately, consultants who refuse to grow are shortchanging the clients who hire them,* no less than an auto company that refuses to include new technology in its cars or a bookkeeper who charges by the hour and refuses to use a computer. Client organizations cannot survive, much less dominate in their markets, if they are content to be sitting on a plateau. The consultants they want are just as committed to the dynamics of strategy, tactics, growth, and achievement.

Million dollar consulting utilizes *a belief system and strategy* that prevents mere jobs from getting in the way of careers. It's not easy, because it requires highly focused self-discipline. But that's nothing less than you'd require of your clients. It is this long-term and strategic approach that ensures that the light at the end of the tunnel is new territory, not an onrushing train. Let's turn now to how you thrive in that new territory.

[1]From Benjamin B. Tregoe and John W. Zimmerman, *Top Management Strategy: What It Is and How it Works,* Simon and Schuster, New York, 1980.

PART 2

Tactics: Implementing Your Vision of Your Firm

6
The Look of the Business

Prospects Believe What They See and Hear

Memberships, Networks, and Affiliations

Whether you are a lone wolf, a wolf pack, or a thundering herd, you'll need outside stimulus to help in your growth. For those who have left a larger organization, don't assume that one of the "luxuries" you can no longer afford is membership in professional organizations. This should be a priority, since it is a way of learning about others' techniques and experiences and maintaining a necessary visibility level of your own.

I once belonged to the Instructional Systems Association (I don't anymore because you have to produce instructional systems — training materials — to belong). While a member, I became friendly with the president of a $3 million consulting firm that specialized in organizational change. Over the past 10 years he has provided very valuable advice for my growth, and he has called upon me to return the favor. He has also provided a dozen or so referrals that I never would have received otherwise, and these have resulted in over $125,000 in business so far. If you think that sum isn't anything to get too excited about over 10 years, multiply that friendship times two dozen others of similar reciprocity and you can begin to appreciate the power of such indirect marketing.

Because that's what memberships, networking, and affiliations do for you. They are indirect, painless, cost-effective marketing avenues.

Several years ago, I joined the National Speakers Association. I attend meetings irregularly and am not interested in their various awards and honors. But I read the publications and listen to the tapes faithfully. Three or four times a year I learn something that is immediately helpful to me. Is that too little a return on too great an investment? You be the judge.

At one meeting, I heard one of the organization's "name" speakers, whom I thought was dreadful and who would quickly sour a relationship if I ever introduced him to a client as a resource. However, halfway through a condescending presentation he mentioned that he always provided a client with the option of paying the full speaking fee in advance in return for a discount. I immediately came to life. In this business, control of receivables and management of cashflow is essential. I'd gladly provide a discount if I received payment at booking rather than after delivery of a speech. (I require a deposit to hold the date anyway, so the client has to send a check in some amount.)

I began offering a 10 percent savings to clients for speaking dates, and to my amazement, *80 percent of all such clients took advantage of it.* So I went a step further. I offered the 10 percent reduction only if the client paid the speaking fee *and* travel expenses in advance (the reduction applied only to the fee). I calculated the expenses and guaranteed that I would be responsible for any increases in airline fares in the interim. This did not affect the acceptance rate, so now I was receiving full fee and expenses months in advance of my appearance; this not only solidified cashflow but also made it extremely unlikely that the client would cancel or change dates at the last minute without careful conversations with me.

Then I came upon the really big idea. If this option was so attractive to speaking clients who were investing $5000 to $6000 for an appearance, wouldn't it also be attractive to consulting clients investing 10 or 20 times as much? Absolutely! As a result, 50 percent of my consulting proposals are now accepted on the basis of full fee in advance for a discount of 10 to 15 percent, depending on the nature of the business. In fact, as the economy gets shaky, clients prefer this option. (Several of my best clients, making excellent profits and at the top of their industries, operate internally as if they're *losing* money. When a buyer sends an invoice to purchasing that stipulates a dramatic savings if payment is made immediately, the check arrives in my office with the ink barely dry.)[1] And what do you think the

---

[1] No, I do not inflate fees so that the discount is a phantom reduction. My discounts are legitimate and come out of my margin. The worth to me of money in hand, no receivables or periodic billing, and the client's full attention to someone already paid is monumental.

impact is on my bankers when they see I collect a high proportion of my fees in advance and the money is on deposit? They can't do enough for me. I'll expound of how to use such techniques to manage your bankers in Chapter 11.

Thus, from an otherwise horrible meeting and an unpleasant speaker, I learned of a technique to dramatically improve my cashflow and financial options. In all candor, I don't think that I would have come up with this myself because I thought that asking for 50 percent on commencement was state of the art. In any case, I wouldn't have implemented the technique as soon as I did, even if I eventually had the brainstorm.

I always seek to identify what I call "keepers." These are single-sentence, easy-to-remember ideas that can have exponential impact on your business. Here are some examples.

- Send all proposals and key confirmations by courier express, not regular mail.
- Contact every client and prospect once a quarter with *something*.
- Base fees on value, not time or tasks.
- Provide your own written introduction when making a speech.
- Create a blue-chip reference list to automatically include for prospects.
- Don't provide written reports unless there's a client need for them.
- Create and continually update a standard press kit.

These and similar techniques are discussed throughout this book. All of them were generated by networking and through memberships and, at least in my case, have been applied immediately and continually to improve business.

This is not the place to attempt to provide a comprehensive listing of organizations, periodicals, and networking activities. You must be selective because there are so many options that you can invest all of your time in pursuing the full range. Some will apply more than others, based on your specialties, preferences, stage of growth, and so forth. Instead, I'll prime the pump by suggesting specific activities of varying types for your consideration. If you were to adhere to this list, I suspect you'd be in excellent company, and your list of keepers would be growing considerably.[2]

---

[2]Annotations and locations of various resources are in the Appendix.

1. *Join at least three organizations that offer regular meetings and the opportunity to interact with your peers in the industry.*[3] The American Management Association is excellent because it provides seminars and workshops, breakfast meetings with influential authorities, books, videos, cassettes, a fine reference library that you can access by phone, and a "presidents' club," which you qualify for by dint of being president of your consulting firm. The dues are reasonable (less than $200 a year for regular membership at this writing), and the benefits considerable. Finally, it produces several high-quality publications, including *Management Review,* an attractive option for publishing and book reviews, aside from its useful content.

Other organizations for consideration include the National Speakers Association, if speaking is a large part of your practice; the American Society for Training and Development, which is oriented toward workplace issues of a broad variety and has heavy human resource representation; the various consultants associations, such as ACME or IMC,[4] and trade associations that represent your present or targeted client base, such as the American Bankers Association. Three of these may be all you can handle, and you may choose to change memberships until you find a combination that provides the best networking and the most keepers. As a rule, if you're contributing but not learning, then you're engaged in pro bono work, which is laudable, but don't get it confused with networking. If you're not taking notes that you later use and you're not making contacts whom you later call, you're not benefiting. If you find membership is a chore that falls to the bottom of your priority list, you haven't understood the marketing value of this investment or you've joined the wrong organizations.

Joining organizations and taking the time to network is an investment no different from buying office equipment or creating a marketing piece. You are negligent if you don't focus on achieving the maximum return from that investment.

---

[3]Run like crazy from outfits that grant you initials representing such things as "Certified Management Consulting Professional" for a $250 membership fee. These are bogus, and everyone knows it. Similarly, don't pay for services that will "provide 50 leads a month" or "provide all the materials you need to set up a consulting operation." You're better off investing your money at the tables in Vegas.

[4]ACME is the Academy for Consulting Management Engineers, which offers membership by company, and IMC is the Institute of Management Consultants, which offers membership for individuals. Both now operate under the single banner of the Council of Consulting Organizations. Kennedy Publications, which publishes the single most authoritative newsletter on consulting, recommends joining CCO in some capacity if you do nothing else.

2. *Create a reference library.*   It should include marketing resources such as *National Trade and Professional Associations of the United States,*[5] *Marketplace Directory,*[6] *Consultants News,*[7] *The National Directory of* [business] *Addresses and Telephone Numbers,*[8] and other publications that will assist your marketing, implementation, and travel. I subscribe to the *Official Airline Guide*[9] pocket edition, since I'm often forced to make changes in my schedule en route. I also keep a wide variety of atlases and travel planners near the phone.

3. *Establish a circle of informal advisers and contact them monthly.*   Put them on your mailing list, and treat them as you would a prospect. That is, send them items that may be of help in their pursuits, offer assistance whenever needed, and keep them abreast of your plans. Then seek their feedback and counsel. Are the mailings effective? What image are you conveying? Does your firm stand out from the crowd? How can you improve your approaches?

Your inner circle should include other consultants, clients, vendors (i.e., your printer or graphics artist), professionals (your attorney or financial adviser), and others whose judgment you respect, including friends, business associates, and community leaders. You can't get too much feedback, since you can always ignore irrelevancies, but you can be in a position to get too little, which is an occupational hazard of our profession (and a shadow of lone wolves). Networking doesn't mean "selling"; it means establishing quid pro quo relationships with others that result in improved conditions for both of you. That's right, you're serving as consultants to each other.

4. *Establish collaborations with other consultants.*   I have often been asked to subcontract on a project by another firm, and I've often asked others to perform in that role for me. This is a high-margin approach to business because no direct marketing is required—only a relationship with a kindred firm that contacts you at the right moment. Some firms might call me every two years, but they do call, at no more cost to me than a quarterly contact or offer of help.

I invited the principal of another consulting firm to bid on a project at Merck a few years ago. A division of Merck required a training program that I didn't provide, and designing one was inappropriate for the client, since there were existing, excellent packages on the market. I asked for no

---

[5]Published by Columbia Books, 1350 New York Ave., N.W., Suite 207, Washington, D.C. 20005.

[6]Published by *Training Magazine,* 50 S. Ninth St., Minneapolis, Minn. 55402.

[7]Published by Kennedy Publications, Templeton Rd., Fitzwilliam, N.H. 03447.

[8]Published by General Information, Inc., Bothell, Wash. 98011.

[9]Published by Official Airline Guides, Inc., 2000 Clearwater Dr., Oak Brook, Ill. 60521.

fee or commission, and the client evaluated my recommendation along
with several others. When the firm I recommended was chosen, the client
decided that the program was to be placed in a configuration (competency-
based, self-paced learning) in which it had never existed. As a consequence, the buyer and the consulting firm both approached me with the
request to adapt the material, since my firm was ideal for that type of design work and no such configuration currently existed. Merck got exactly
what it needed, my counterpart obtained a key business relationship with a
superb organization, and I profited with another project. This "win-win"
affiliation is an enduring and highly profitable way in which to conduct
business.

Memberships, networking, and affiliations are *aggressive, proactive marketing tools* if you use them in that capacity. Assuming a leadership position
in an association not only enhances your ability to market yourself but also
creates excellent visibility for your firm and enhances your reputation, a
key growth element. Prospects believe what they see and hear, and the
more there are others talking about you and representing you, formally
and informally, the more your phone will ring.

Promotion and Publicity

Figure 6-1 provides a checklist for publicizing your firm and its work.[10]
How do you rate at the moment as your chief publicist?

There's no need to pursue all 16 areas. In fact, it would be dysfunc-
tional to do so. At any given moment, you should be actively involved in
at least a third of them, however, and those six might change as your
firm and its clients evolve. Here is a brief rundown on each of the options and my assessment of their value.

Mailings to Clients with
Items of Interest

This one is a must.[11] Some of my colleagues in direct mail and
marketing tell me that you can't contact clients too often.[12] My own bias

[10]I'm working on the assumption that the admonitions from Chapter 3 about brochures
and letterhead have been heeded and that your mailings include these standard items.

[11]Periodic client-prospect communications, publishing, speaking and pro bono work
will all be discussed in detail in Chapter 9, since they are, in my opinion, the most dramatic marketing vehicles available for growth, and since some readers may desire step-
by-step techniques.

[12]By *current client* I mean an organization for which you have conducted assignments
within the past 12 months. The term *client* without that qualification refers to any organization for which you've done work, irrespective of the time frame.

	Pursued		
Option	Always	Sometimes	Never
Mailings to clients with items of interest	☐	☐	☐
Mailings to prospects with items of interest	☐	☐	☐
Published articles in relevant periodicals	☐	☐	☐
Pro bono work for community, government, nonprofit organizations	☐	☐	☐
Speeches at trade associations and conferences	☐	☐	☐
Exhibits at trade shows	☐	☐	☐
Requests from satisfied clients for referrals	☐	☐	☐
Interviews in newspapers and magazines	☐	☐	☐
Book publishing	☐	☐	☐
Listings in directories and trade publications	☐	☐	☐
Advertising for visibility and/or leads	☐	☐	☐
Business listing in the Yellow Pages	☐	☐	☐
Audiocassette series or recordings of speeches	☐	☐	☐
Networking with other consulting firms	☐	☐	☐
Membership in client industry trade associations	☐	☐	☐
Professional publicists and agents	☐	☐	☐

Figure 6-1. Sixteen options for publicity and promotion.

is that once per quarter is sufficient for current clients, since you're interacting with them on an assignment anyway, but inactive clients could probably be communicated with monthly via a newsletter, "briefings," or some other kind of consistent device. We've already discussed the clippings files and similar techniques to gather relevant or provocative information, distill it, and send it to appropriate clients.

Mailings to Prospects with Items of Interest

This, too, is mandatory, because it is a cost-effective way to keep your name in front of potential clients. If your resources and time permit, a quarterly or monthly mailing is appropriate. You will also learn from these mailings when key people leave their position as a result of promotion, reassignment, or departure for a new firm. This allows you to update your mailing list. My firm is now mailing twice a year to all clients and prospects and mailing situationally during the year based on the information we've distilled and its application to those on our lists.

Published Articles in Relevant Periodicals

It is easier to be published than you may believe, and once you're published the first time it gets easier and easier thereafter. I once submitted an article to a training industry monthly publication for no fee. Once it was printed, I suggested a column, again for no fee. Once the column was running, I used it to (1) send to my mailing list and (2) gain credibility with larger publications to write for them. Eventually, the publication began paying for my columns and, more importantly, I generated over 30 articles, with reprint rights, on topics most productive for my business before I moved on to other marketing pursuits. If you have no writing experience, begin modestly by offering free submissions to publications that need pieces—local newspapers, industry newsletters, trade magazines. Use these to gain credibility at the next level. Be patient. My first article was for no fee to *Supervisory Management* in 1969. By 1975, I was in *Management Review,* and by 1979, *The New York Times.* Publishing of virtually any type provides tremendous credibility, and this effort should be an ongoing one.

Pro Bono Work for Community, Government, and Nonprofit Organizations

Is the town establishing a search committee to choose a new police chief? Does the school board need help with its human resource planning? Are the Girl Scouts looking for local board members? Does the chamber of commerce need consultants to work with small businesses? This work provides the opportunity to gain visibility, meet potential contacts, and demonstrate how you can successfully apply your craft. Chapter 14 will address pro bono work as a professional ethic, but for now we'll simply recommend it as a pragmatic method to gain publicity and contacts. You will be interacting with other community leaders, many of whom are executives in local and national businesses. There are usually minimal expenses attendant to this work, and your time is well-invested. I've just offered my services to the governor of Rhode Island to advise his ethics commission, which is suffering from budget constraints. I don't know yet whether he'll accept the offer, but I do know he couldn't accept it if I hadn't extended it!

Speeches at Trade Associations and Conferences

Even if speaking is not an income source for your firm, it should be a publicity technique. There are local, state, regional, and national conventions of bewildering assortments for nearly every industry you can think of. I've spoken in front of the Eastern Region Nurserymen's Association, the Pharmaceutical Manufacturers Association of Canada, the Inland Press Association, the Executive Round Table of Jacksonville, the Central Illinois Employer's Association, the International Association of Professional Women, and over 300 other groups. As in publishing, you can begin for no-fee, local groups (Rotary and Kiwanis chapters are always seeking business speakers for weekly meetings) and move on to larger groups. My fee is $5000 to $6000 for a keynote speech, during which I have the opportunity to address several hundred to a thousand people, and after which I'm besieged with requests for more information. Usually, you receive bookings for more speeches from people in the audience. (This is when it pays to have reprints of articles and a first-class brochure available for distribution.) Every time I think of the opportunity to address hundreds of potential clients at one time, with the credibility provided by being a featured speaker, I wonder if I've died and gone to heaven. (By the way, forget about speakers' bureaus and agents at the outset. They do not help the neophyte, and once you're of interest to them, you've reached a level at which you don't need them unless you prefer to give part of your fees away as an act of charity.)[13]

Exhibits at Trade Shows

This is an option that many of my colleagues pursue, although I don't. Virtually all trade shows have exhibitors' areas where participants can learn about your services, pick up free literature, and ask questions. For my money, it's too much of a commodity undertaking: most firms that are successful at it sell products of some type, be they course materials, books, or equipment. Exhibiting costs are fairly high: the space rental, display creation or rental, and local drayage costs can easily reach $5000 or more. It is difficult to interest people in abstract services in such an environment, and the leads you do get are apt to be from all over the country, making it very expensive to engage in any type of personal follow-up. The one exception I've found is this: if you're a featured speaker at the conference, you may do well in attracting people to your booth. Of course, you're still faced with the problem of qualification and follow-up.

Requests for Referrals
from Satisfied Clients

I once had an insurance agent who saw me twice a year, every year, whether I needed additional insurance or not. And he ended *every*

---

[13]OK, there are exceptions. Once you're an established draw, a bureau can be helpful in booking new clients for higher fees. But good bureaus are few and far between.

meeting the same way: "Alan, give me two acquaintances you think might be able to use my help with their insurance needs." He was relentless, and I know he did this every day, with every client he saw. If you don't request such information, you might never receive it. And if you've established the types of client relationships we've been discussing, it's easy to ask the question. "John, you know a great many people in this industry, and in the business community in general. Given the kinds of results we've achieved together here, do you know of anyone in need of similar assistance whom I should call on?" When you get those names, whether or not they will see you immediately, they should go directly on your prospect mailing list. In this manner, with discipline, you should be able to increase that list by at least 100 names a year. With a quarterly mailing, this represents 400 contacts a year.

Interviews in Newspapers and Magazines

Human interest stories are often written about a local consultant who assists major organizations, or who has written a book, or who has designed a technique to aid in performance improvement. Keep local and national editors on your mailing list. I've been interviewed by a local newspaper twice for my consulting and writing, then by national media such as *USA Today* for my views on behavior in light of Wall Street venality. On three occasions I've been cited and quoted in *Boardroom Reports,* which I discovered while reading the issues and seeing my name under a particularly brilliant quote! Editors are always looking for a new slant or a sidebar on an existing debate. They will never know you're a source if you don't keep your material and ideas in front of them. This is particularly true of in-house organs. Client publications are always looking for articles and interviews. You can reprint these with impact equal to an article appearing in the trade press. Although I have written four books and had numerous mentions in the national media, one of my most influential reprints is a full-color, four-page interview run in an internal Merck magazine on the subject of ethics and values. In return for the interview, the client provided me with 500 copies and the right to reprint. Consumers Power, a utility client, provided a splendid layout—with illustrations—for an article on risk assessment that has turned out to be one of my most popular publicity pieces.

Book Publishing

This is simply an extension of article publishing, with one or two distinctions. First, an agent helps, and you can get one if you put together a professional presentation of your articles, your consulting clients and results, your credentials, and a couple of sample book chapters. Video- and audiocassettes of any speeches you've done will help, since they will indicate that you're a professional with marketing potential. My first three books, however, were published without an agent, working directly with major publishers. Second, don't publish a book "merely" for publicity. You must have something worthwhile to say to your audience or you will waste your time and money. This is where literary agents earn their keep. The agent will tell you whether you have a marketable book, and if not, why not. The chances are that if you can sell an agent on representing you, the agent can sell a publisher on publishing you. *Do not self-publish or vanity-publish,* at least not to help your promotion as a consultant. These efforts are completely transparent, and executives (just as reviewers) are not impressed. But a book from a major publisher is worth tens of thousands of dollars in promotional punch.[14]

Listings in Directories and Trade Publications

You can be listed for free in many publications, or for a fee in others. An example of the former is the annual listing of consultants published by *Consultants News*; an example of the latter is the *Buyer's Guide and Consultant Directory,*[15] which requires about $150 for a synopsis of your services and firm. We receive frequent inquiries from the listings, but even more valuable is their use by firms sending out bids in certain subject areas. With a minimum of legwork and modest investment, you can easily be listed in a dozen directories each year. (Eschew the Who's Who listings of various types, which require people to pay to receive the book. These are nothing more than vanity listings, and everyone knows that they carry no significance other than the fact that the checks of the firms included cleared the bank.)

---

[14]I'm advocating here the effectiveness of using book publishing as a promotional alternative. The how-to technique for writing a book is a subject for a book in itself. The interested reader is referred to the monthly magazine *Writer's Digest* and the annual reference book *Writer's Market*, both published by Writer's Digest Books, 9933 Alliance Rd, Cincinnati, Ohio 45242, for specific ideas, sources, and publishers. In addition, there is an ocean of tapes, seminars, and guidebooks extant on book publishing offered through the auspices of organizations such as the American Management Association, which is why membership in such groups is advocated in the prior section of this chapter. See Chapter 9 for more on publishing options.

[15]Published by the American Society for Training and Development, 1640 King St., Alexandria, Va. 22313.

Advertising for Visibility and/or Leads

These are really two separate objectives. I rarely advertise for visibility and never for leads. My experience is that people are not influenced by ads when choosing consultants. However, they may be somewhat more sympathetic to a consultant whose name or firm is familiar. Consequently, I do run a full-page ad in a national speaker's directory because buyers often do peruse speakers by topic area to generate alternatives and an ad might create the extra incentive for someone to contact us. However, I've found that placing ads for the purposes of generating leads is not a fruitful pursuit, and my colleagues in the industry bear that out. *Exception:* A highly targeted ad in a special issue or theme publication when you also have an article appearing in that issue can attract responses. If you do advertise, be as specific as possible. Cite client names, specific types of projects, and any results that you have permission to publicize.

Business Listing in the Yellow Pages

You get one for free if you have a business line. For a modest amount you can use bold print and some descriptive lines, and for a bit more you can run a display ad. This is money well-spent *if your prospects and business expansion are local.* It is not money well-spent if you simply live near an airport and your business is primarily out of state. But make sure you always have a business listing. Many organizations have called directory assistance to locate us after reading an article or hearing about us, knowing only the city in which we're located.

Audiocassette Series or Recordings of Speeches

Whenever I make a speech, I provide in the contract that the client may record the session on audio- or videocassette with no additional fee due me and may distribute those tapes to participants. *However, the client must provide me with two master copies of any such recordings for my own use.* These are "free" marketing tools, which I've used to great advantage. Many speakers charge for such recordings, insist on royalties, or want to sell their own tapes. I simply want to make copies that I send to prospects. It costs about $1 to duplicate an audiotape in volume, including a label and a box. (Videotapes are more effective as audition tapes to acquire more speaking assignments, but audiotapes are wonderful for prospects to listen to in their cars to understand what your approaches are about. And they are far more credible when recorded in front of a live audience, even if there are flubs or minor problems.) I've taken several such tapes and had them packaged as a series on various topics, which lends the same kind of credibility that publishing does, since the production company name, not ours, is on the material.

Networking with Other Consulting Firms

This was mentioned in the previous section. It is an effective marketing tool in that it is free and unlimited. Put other consultants on your mailing list, keep them apprised of what you're doing, and develop those relationships. If you look at other consultants solely as competitors and "threats," you will never benefit from them. But if you see them as colleagues and the sources of opportunities, sooner or later one of them will pass your name along for a project that they cannot handle. This is long-term marketing, but it's a niche that shouldn't be ignored.

Memberships in Client Industry Trade Associations

If permitted, join the trade associations that the preponderance of your clients and prospects belong to. You probably couldn't get into the American Dental Association but I'm not sure there are prohibitions about becoming a member of the National Retail Merchants Association, or the International Association of Tourism. Sometimes associate memberships are available. These affiliations will keep you abreast of what's happening in industries important to your business, afford the opportunity to meet key people in the industry regularly, and provide the inside track on speaking at conferences or publishing in industry newsletters and house organs.

Professional Publicists and Agents

There is a plethora of agencies that will publicize you. I pursued several to see if they would undertake a pay-for-performance option. That is, they would get a commission on business generated through their efforts. As you might expect, there were no takers. Most such firms will charge a monthly retainer to "guarantee" that you will get articles in print, be interviewed by print and broadcast media, and, generally, receive a heightened image. With the exception of a good literary agent, I'm skeptical. But the option exists, and you might just find the right

108

chemistry with someone. But be aware that this is probably the most expensive option on the list.[16]

Personal Conduct

I've just retrieved a business card from my Rolodex that was given to me by a fellow consultant whom I will call Marty Scott. The card is illustrated in Figure 6-2. If you think the information looks crowded on this page, you can imagine how it looks on a business card. And when was the last time you saw *both* "Dr." and "Ph.D." surrounding one person's name like a pair of bookends? Then we must have the professor title and the university, of course...

I see this kind of ego trip as poor form, not just in terms of professionalism but also in terms of endangering any chemistry that one seeks to build with the prospect. A card should state your name, position, and firm. It's a reference piece for the client, not an advertisement. Even sillier than Marty's card are those that say, "Mary Jones, M.A." I'm not familiar with a protocol that shows graduate degrees listed after one's name. What's next—Alan Weiss, licensed driver, registered voter?

I happen to have a Ph.D., but as one of my college professors explained, I choose to use my "maiden name" in most instances, particularly in business documents. I will use the honorific when such credibility is needed or requested by clients or prospects, but not simply as window dressing. Using any other initials at all, whether graduate degrees, certification of courses completed, or professional recognitions,

---

Dr. Martin Scott, Ph.D.
Professor of Management and
Human Resources

Global Human Resources	School of Management
Strategies, Inc. (GHRS)	Famous University
100 East West Drive	Big City, SS 01010
Arrogance, RM 10101	(010) 765-4321
(555) 123-4567	

Figure 6-2. A business card "billboard."

---

[16]An exception is Media Relations, 7850 Metro Parkway, Minneapolis, Minn. 55425 (800/999-4859). They guarantee radio and TV interview time and have delivered consistently for me.

are unnecessary at best and amateurish at worst. The National Speakers Association, for example, loves its alphabet soup, bestowing CSP (Certified Speaking Professional) and CPAE (Colleagues' Professional Award of Excellence—they also have a Latin translation, for goodness' sake) on deserving members. The point, of course, is that such designations help to establish a pecking order within the association, *but mean next to nothing outside it.* I've never met a buyer who made decisions based on such insider recognition.[17]

Your personal conduct is your primary marketing device. It's the fundamental "look" of the business, and what prospects put most credence in. Consequently, the way in which you comport yourself will determine not just *whether* you obtain the client but also *on what grounds* you obtain the client. This is often the essential element in the type of relationship that ensues. The key relationship aspect of our business is often established prior to the actual "sale," as influenced by the buyer's comfort in dealing with you. "Personal conduct" is not "dress for success," whatever that means. It is, rather, about the integrity of your positions and the candor with which you express them.

> *Whether you have an ongoing relationship with the CEO or are delegated to lower-level managers is often determined before the eventual sale is even made. First impressions will influence whether an executive feels the relationship should exist at his or her level or at a lower one.*

I once fired a salesperson who simultaneously sold two pieces of business in the casino industry. His sales were based on using each organization as a reference for the other, even though, at the time, he was simply meeting with each and had made *no* sales. Although he got lucky and neither buyer contacted the "reference" prior to signing a contract, I knew we would be compromised if they eventually compared notes. Such practices are a recipe for long-term disaster. Before I could even approach the clients, they *did* find out about the subterfuge, and al-

---

[17] I recently called the president of the local speakers' association chapter. Her answering machine produced this unbelievable message: "You have reached Sarah Smith, author, speaker, consultant, and president of Global Beliefs." I assume she consults, writes, and speaks on modesty. The larger your operation, the less you have to hype it.

though they honored the existing contracts, they never sought or accepted any additional proposals from us.

Facing Up to the Challenge

You will often be in a position in which the prospect requests an industry reference, examples of work performed, résumés of other professionals in your firm, and similar information which you literally do not have. The answer is neither to dazzle the prospect with footwork nor to scramble for the exits.

The answer is to treat the request as an opportunity, not a threat.

You see, you are the best possible person to anticipate requests that you will have difficulty fulfilling. For example, if you are a lone wolf and your firm says "Multitudes of Pros, Inc.," you know that you might be asked for background on the multitudes. If you're meeting with a prospect in the airline industry and you've never done business in the transportation field before, you probably know that industry references might be a sticking point. Or, if you're being considered for an employee survey and you've never conducted one (you're "testing the envelope"), then you can reasonably expect to be asked about it.

By anticipating such awkward questions and requests, you can prepare for them. And by preparing for them, you can steer the discussion in the direction of how you can improve the client's condition without being flustered by the question, without trying to come up with lame examples, and without having to sit there like a lump dropped from the skies. The keys are candor, clear preparation for the question, and crisp examples of what you can do for the client. Let's examine some common dilemmas that anyone trying to develop a business might face.

You've Never Worked in the Industry

This is one of the most common challenges for consultants seeking to expand. There has to be a first time in every industry. My advice is to develop examples from similar industries, and demonstrate the relationship. If you are facing an airline executive, explain your work with rental car firms, highlighting the similarities in scheduling, catering to business as well as recreational travelers, administering frequent flyer-driver awards, and the like. If you're approaching health care organizations for the first time, emphasize your work with pharmaceutical companies and their interactions with doctors, pharmacists, regulatory agencies, consumer action groups, etc. You can also describe work done for vendors and peripheral suppliers. Perhaps you've never worked for an auto company, but you have worked with GE sites that provide electrical components to auto makers. Your work with a chemical firm might help you with Kodak film processing. Finally, demonstrate that you've studied the industry, regardless of all else. If you can provide the prospect with key issues facing the industry, how your work relates to them, and what the outcome of their resolution might be for the organization, you will help to overcome the "never worked in the industry" dilemma.[18]

The Client Wants
a Cast of Thousands

Early in the process of embarking on growth, identify at least six people whom you would be proud to use in implementing projects. (For many of you, this may be old hat, or you might have full-time staffs. But bear with me for a moment.) These people often come from the ranks of:

- Free-lance consultants
- Retired professionals
- School faculty with available time
- Self-employed professionals who can invest the time
- Graduate students with specialized skills
- Full-time professional people with situational time available
- Unemployed professionals seeking temporary assignments

As you can see, this is a diverse group. You can best locate good people by networking in the manner described above. My financial adviser is a key source of people seeking to enter the consulting field or abruptly terminated from their positions. A colleague who serves on a bank board with me has helped with professors. Several other consultants provide me with free-lancers whom they use. The beauty of such references is that the people involved tend to be highly qualified.

The next step is to have the individuals provide a detailed résumé of work experiences, in return for being considered for future assign-

---

[18]These tactics are remarkably effective if you do your homework. For example, while trying to convince a computer manufacturer to do business with me, I found that General Motors was the country's leading manufacturer of computers, because so many of them went into every car produced. Since I had worked with GM, I used this as support for my familiarity with computer manufacturing.

ments with you. These résumés, printed on your letterhead, are the documents you will provide prospects — along with other salient company information and brochures — when you are asked for a description of your staff and their qualifications.[19] Tell prospects the truth, if they ask: these aren't all full-time staffers, but are people used situationally, allowing you to cover a wide range of assignments with the least overhead, at tremendous savings *to your clients*.

Finally, have a business card created for every such person who may actually be employed by you. You can get a couple of hundred cards for less than $25 at any local storefront printer. Put your logo, business address, and telephone number on the cards (and alert your answering service to take messages for those individuals). Provide each contract person with your letterhead and literature as required, but try to have all communication go through your office.

Using these techniques, my staff over the years has included college professors who specialize in psychometric testing and surveys, a woman who specializes in testing and assessment, a man who is expert in telemarketing and sales techniques, a woman who is an excellent researcher, a woman who does the legwork for strategy data gathering, and a dozen others who have provided value-added services to me and my clients while receiving significant fees and *their own multidimensional growth* in return.

You've Never Worked on This Particular Type of Assignment

This is a fairly easy one as long as you don't get drawn into a ridiculous exercise in trying to "force-fit" projects you have worked on into the prospect's category. ("No, I've never worked on succession planning, but we did design a retirement program that is remarkably similar.") Once again, stress the opportunity.

Provide the prospect with a clear plan and proposal for improving his or her condition. You might mention that the very fact that you haven't worked on an identical project motivated you to study it carefully, research the background, and create the existing options. Provide several options for undertaking the project, with the pros and cons of each and your preference. The focus on the various alternatives available to tackle the project, coupled with the evidence of the careful thought that went into them, will deflect and subordinate the issue of whether you've done the exact same work before. You also want to emphasize that you

---

[19]See Chapter 9 for what should appear in your press kit.

are adept at the process of improving the client *condition,* not merely the content of the client's organization or of this particular issue.[20]

> *Always, always,* **always** *provide the prospect with a choice of "yes"es, not the single choice of "do it or don't do it." Once the prospect is trying to select which option seems best, the eventual contract is just a formality.*

The Prospect Has Never Heard of You

This will mean more to some prospects than to others, but it's the easiest dilemma to deal with. Have a list of references in your briefcase at all times. Make sure that they are current, and specify exact titles, addresses, and phone numbers. Explain that your firm is in the category of best-kept secret (I refer to mine as a "boutique consulting firm," with such strong word-of-mouth references that we do not need to advertise). Provide your blue-chip client list, provide the publications you've written for or been interviewed by (see the preceding section on promotion), and explain that your strategy is to succeed through dramatic client results, not competitive advertising.

The key here, too, is *being prepared for the question or challenge.* Acknowledging that you've heard the issue raised before, and that you're accustomed to the question, helps relax the atmosphere and adds to your stature. I've often turned the tables and asked, "How do you succeed, when your competitors have better-known profiles?" I'm almost always told, "Because we work harder," or "Our service is better," or "We establish excellent client relationships."

"Really?" I respond. "Then it looks like we have a great deal in common."

The Japanese have a word that I love: *sogomi.* It's tough to translate, but it means roughly "presence" or "stature." I once asked a Japanese colleague how he identified it. "Oh, you don't identify it," he explained. "You simply *know* whether it's there or not. You *feel* it."

---

[20]This is why the role of content expert, as described in Chapter 1, is not the most lucrative or promising in terms of growing your business.

I'm not going to insult you by telling you to shine your shoes, comb your hair, and dress well. But I am going to tell you that *sogomi* is more than just physical appearance. It is the manner in which you handle yourself, which I believe must always be with confidence, honesty, and integrity. You needn't compromise these traits, because you have no reason to. You are trying to help the prospect understand how you can help improve his or her condition in a client relationship. If you anticipate these dilemmas and prepare to deal with them, they are not dilemmas at all, but opportunities to show the prospect how well you conduct yourself and how able you are to meet client needs.

The look of the business is your look. Clients will believe only what they see in you and hear from you. But the people working for you also represent you, and it's important that they embrace your ideals and convey your image as effectively as you do.

7

Acquiring People

Practicing What You Preach
Could Save Your Life

Options for Participation

If your firm is to grow dramatically, you will need people. Those people may be in the form of employees, partners, subcontractors, alliances with other firms, and/or other innovative arrangements. None of these relationships is mutually exclusive. There is one consistent thread, however. No matter what the relationship, you want people who

- Are highly competent and represent your firm well
- Bring their own "value-added" to your needs
- Adhere, strategically and tactically, to your objectives
- Are ethical, honest, and law-abiding
- Understand and accept their role
- Ideally, can be used on a long-term basis

Hiring Employees

Hold on to your chairs, but the *worst* option to attract and utilize people who meet these criteria is to hire them as full-time employees. There are four basic reasons for this:

1. Full-time people are full-time overhead. They must be fed and housed irrespective of business conditions; the government expects certain tax and record-keeping protocols; and the employees expect certain benefit and perquisite arrangements. This detracts directly from the bottom line—your *personal* bottom line.

2. Managing employees is a tremendous drain on time. You will have to conduct and sit through meetings, deal with personnel problems, complete performance evaluations, and attend to the various and sundry needs of others. There is a growth-inhibiting tendency to focus more on internal matters than on client matters.

3. Your personal actions will be subject to the dynamic of an employee-employer relationship. For example, it is difficult to purchase that new Mercedes in a year in which you have frozen salaries or reduced bonuses. Despite what others do or do not contribute, *your* personal decisions will be judged in light of *their* conditions.

4. A relatively small number of employees (under two dozen) will never afford you the scope of talents that may be required as you embark on growth and continue to "test the envelope." Consequently, you will still need outside resources, the acquisition of which may be hampered by the costs and social dynamic of current, full-time employees.

Hiring people is too often a matter of ego rather than business. I've acknowledged that it is important to provide prospects with a feeling of depth and to provide clients with an assortment of talents, but these objectives can be met in a variety of innovative ways. In any business, *people are the most expensive asset*. Consequently, we need to use some imagination in obtaining and utilizing such assets. The only people I recommend hiring as full-time employees are those who provide secretarial or administrative support or highly specialized skills that are required daily (for example, a researcher or programmer who can be kept busy full-time through the bulk of your contractual work, when outside contracting is cost-ineffective). Part-time hires can include:

- Specialists needed for a particular long-term project that will utilize them on a constant basis for the duration of the assignment

- Office support staff to handle exceptionally busy periods of a known duration

- College interns and temporary help who are doing legwork while learning the business for a summer or project

There are three options far superior to any others for obtaining the talents necessary to help develop your business:

1. Acquiring Partners

It's generally better to own 50 percent of a million dollar business (or one-fifth of a $3-million business, for that matter) than it is to own 100 percent of a $100,000 business. If you can find people who share your vision and your growth plans and who bring complementary talents to the table, you have a strong basis for considering a partnership.[1] I have never liked partnerships in which the investment or stake of the partners has been unequal, as in "I'll put up the talent, you put up the money." Partners should be just that, sharing risk and reward equally. (It's fine to allow a person to buy into the partnership over time, as long as the time is specified and full equality is the result.)

Partner candidates should possess the characteristics shown in Figure 7-1. These characteristics may seem self-evident, but they must *all* be met *fully* for *every* partner. Simply bringing in a needed talent, or providing access to a new client base, or being "a helluva person," is insufficient. In fact, it's deadly.

- They bring in complementary new talents, not a duplication of your talents.
- They provide business base or financial investment to equal your own.
- They share your ideals, goals, and vision about the business.
- They have a track record of success.
- They are genuinely likable; the chemistry is positive and rewarding.
- They make the whole greater than the sum of its parts.

Figure 7-1. Essential qualifications for prospective partners.

For example, there's no criterion about being geographically proximate. It may make sense for partners to be geographically dispersed or to live next door. In either event, the partnership equation demands great trust, and trust is based on common goals and beliefs, not on revenue bases. Diverse talents are required, because you don't want to get better at things you're already quite good at. Instead you want to stretch. You'll have to like each other because you're going to make some errors that will affect the other. At times you may be bringing in

---

[1] I mean this in the figurative sense of an equal partner, not the legal sense of the form of the business. The firm can remain a corporation and needn't be a legal partnership. Doctors, attorneys, and accountants have increasingly abandoned partnerships for incorporation.

disproportional amounts of business. Also, you'll disagree on some approaches. These are legitimate business conflicts. They shouldn't be aggravated by personal conflicts. *Partnership is not about equal opportunity employment. It is about a soul mate.*

The result of joining forces must create a whole that is larger than the parts creating it. If you and the partner each have a $250,000 business and, two years after joining, you are 50 percent owners of a $500,000 business, you've wasted your efforts. The nonfinancial gains you might have derived (exchange of ideas, mutual critique, companionship) could have been accomplished through networking and alliances. Partnerships should geometrically increase business, or they're not worth it. As the equation below illustrates, a partnership should create a combined business base at least 25 percent larger than the sum of the two firms. The collaboration of two $300,000 firms should result in combined annual billings of $750,000.

Firm 1 + Firm 2 × 1.25 = minimum for justifying partnership

One final caveat on partners. I have seen partnerships that were made in heaven descend into hell in the blink of an eye. Partnerships are extraordinarily difficult to escape from and frequently result in the demise of the firm. A good friend of mine finds himself in the position of being controlling partner of his firm and being the predominant business generator. His "minor" partners will be seeking to retire by selling their equity to him, which means that he will have to work harder than ever to provide funds for people who haven't been pulling their weight for quite some time. How does he raise the money to buy them out—by remaining on airplanes for the next five years, or selling a portion of his ownership to investors, or some other odious solution?

Make sure of two things before embarking on a partnership. First, diligently ensure that the partnership will provide payback far in excess of the sum of the parts; second, create a "prenuptial" agreement so that you can disengage with a minimum of chaos if the arrangement deteriorates.

2. Forming Alliances

"Alliance" is the hot new phrase in consulting (at least, as of this morning) but it's really an old method with continual practical application.[2] Through networking, memberships, and other contacts, you can estab-

---

[2]Many sources include subcontractors as a form of alliance. I've separated them here, since I believe they fundamentally differ in aspects of control, leverage, and access.

lish strategic alliances with allied firms. It is a reciprocally beneficial relationship in which the smaller firm obtains access to larger markets and organizations and the larger firm obtains specialized expertise and/or situational help in a cost-effective manner.

The membership organizations cited in Chapter 6 are excellent sources for meeting principals of other firms, often on a social and informal basis. I've noted that a major source of business for us comprises the referrals and requests of other consulting firms. These alliances may result in occasional or frequent collaboration. If effective, they are highly lucrative, since the marketing has been done for you. Moreover, your visibility in delivery becomes an important marketing tool. And, generally, since your fee structure is known to your allied partner, your inclusion is not fee-sensitive.

I encourage all consultants to pursue alliances at every opportunity. This is an excellent technique to leverage your marketing impact and visibility and to engage in multidimensional growth as you observe your allied partners applying their techniques and talents. Alliances involve no confining contractual obligations, can be initiated and ended with relative ease, and often lead to still more alliances. But they don't simply happen—they must be pursued through networking and memberships. Remember, placing other consulting principals on your mailing list is not giving away the family jewels—it's inviting in the appraisers.

Alliances and the related subcontracting that follows are superior to partnerships in most cases, because these options retain absolute control while providing leverage for multidimensional growth.

3. Subcontracting

Many of my colleagues hate this phrase. I guess it sounds too much like the builder calling in a plumber. If it pleases you, you may think of these relationships as "short-term contractual," or "situationally dictated," or "nonemployee subordinates." But to me it's subcontracting, and your pipes won't hold water if you don't believe in calling in good plumbers.

In subcontracting, you obtain the services of other consultants for a specified fee arrangement or other participation under your direction. (If the other consultant is on an equal basis with you in terms of decision making and initiative during the engagement, then you haven't subcontracted for specific help; you're in an alliance with an equal partner.) Subcontract work entails specialized skills and/or specific tasks as directed by you. These may include interviews, workshop facilitation, creation of a questionnaire, establishing customer focus groups, researching an industry, and so on. The client may or may not know that the extra help is not actually a part of your firm. However, the client does know that the tasks are to be performed under your auspices, and that you, personally, will not perform them.

I mentioned earlier that I maintain a regular cadre of subcontract consultants whom I tend to call on repeatedly. Their participation is *never* based on the fee that the client pays me. It is *always* based on their fee structure. Some charge me by the day, others by the half-day, and others by the type of project they are responsible for completing (i.e., $2500 per workshop). When I obtain a project that requires subcontract help, I estimate the amount of assistance I'll need and build those fees into the project fee. Subcontractors are paid based on their contribution and work performed, *not based on the size of the project I've obtained.* I will also pay different fees to different subcontractors if they bring a specialized expertise or are simply better at what they do. Each is a separate negotiation, and I am free to pay based on value, just as they are free to refuse work. I never hire based on the lowest fee; I always hire based on most value—the degree to which my condition is improved by utilizing their help.

Subcontractors are relatively easy to find in the networking and membership process. We receive a résumé a week from someone wanting this type of work. We also ask our colleagues in the business to recommend people, as we will for them, thus creating a win-win situation for all concerned. If I am ever uncertain whether I need subcontracting help, I err on the side of using it. This creates more interaction and a stronger relationship with the subcontractor and ensures that extra talent is available for the work. This is another instance of investing money to make money. (For those of you who have identified subcontractors as having established a strategic alliance with you, I have no quibble, just as you might consider yourself a subcontractor to your larger, strategic partner. The categories are worth separating, however, since you may often be in one and virtually never in the other, depending upon the nature of your business and contacts.)

It is always better to grow and retain control than to grow and surrender even partial control, unless the latter provides extraordinary growth.

Of all the options for growth involving other people, I've found partnerships, alliances, and subcontracting to be the most effective in developing the business while protecting your interests. The latter two are the safest. I recommend partnerships only when the synergy of the partners creates a substantially larger business than the mere addition of those being partnered.

No matter what options you choose, there is a need to recognize good people when you trip over them. After all, you are no doubt preaching this to clients. But how do you practice it yourself?

Where to Find Good People and How to Recognize Them

Invariably, the least expensive people you can find to assist on a project are not the best qualified. However, the most expensive are seldom the best qualified, either.

The first step in finding excellent people (whether for subcontracting, alliances, partners, referrals, etc.) is to understand what kind of people you're seeking. Are you in need of people with specific talents, for example, people to run workshops, create learning materials, conduct interviews, design test instruments, counsel employees, etc.? Or are you in need of conceptual and strategic thinkers, who can work in ambiguous situations with a client and identify patterns or suggest procedures? Do you require experts, exemplars, or collaborators?[3] Are you searching for a subcontractor, a sounding board, or a potential alliance?

One critical mistake that consultants commit, one which makes the cobbler's children seem well-shod by comparison, is choosing people on the basis of "chemistry" alone. Interpersonal relationships are certainly essential. After all, you must trust those with whom you are working. However, warm and cuddly feelings are, in themselves, insufficient. The individual must be suited for the *type* of work or relationship you have in mind. I've seen people hire researchers who couldn't understand computer data bases. All too frequently I see content experts used in workshop situations, although they don't know a thing about adult learning and have no facilitation skills. No matter how well you like and respect a person, if he or she is ill-suited for interviewing because of poor listening skills, then that person is a square peg in that particular round hole.

Ergo, rule number 1: Identify the traits, performance objectives, and skills required.

Next, utilize your networking, memberships, and affiliations to meet people. Don't simply try to find people when you discover you have the

---

[3]See Chapter 1 for the pragmatic range of interventions.

need. This will inevitably create undue pressure to turn up a "warm body" and diminish the quality of your selection decision. You should have an established pipeline of people that you can tap into whenever necessary.

We cherish those résumés we receive every month from people interested in entering the field, free-lancers who have heard of us, and people who are themselves networking. (This is just one example of the benefits of growth in repute in the market. Good people come to you.) We evaluate all such inquiries and find about one in twenty of potential use for our various needs. We establish communication with these people and meet them during our normal travels, further paring down the numbers as a result of those interviews. The candidates also go on our mailing list. By establishing this network, we can call upon a variety of resources when the need arises, instead of desperately seeking someone with particular skills. I've often found that certain bid requests will demand a profile of the consultants who might work on the project. If experience in the health care industry is an evaluation criterion, we will include people from our pool with requisite skills who have that background. If experienced sales trainers are considered important, we'll select several of those.

I met an independent consultant at an industry conference who was a specialist in sales training. We became friendly, and decided to share an occasional working breakfast to compare notes. I discovered that he had skills that were applicable far beyond his chosen niche and soon invited him to participate as a field interviewer on several projects. As he has learned my system, he has become even more valuable in a wider range of projects and is now one of my prime subcontractors.

Selecting people who can provide value-added to your business is as important as identifying potential clients.

We maintain a special file for our pool of resources that is constantly being modified and expanded. It's as important as our prospect list, in that these are the people who enable us to leverage our business.

Thus, rule number 2: Aggressively identify and establish relationships with good people as a continuing pursuit.

Finally, once you've recognized your needs and identified potential candidates, how do you know which ones are the right ones for a particular assignment? The client shouldn't be the guinea pig. The answer here is that you must spend time with the people you've identified, no matter what potential role you envision. Here are my recommendations:

- *Alliance relationships.*   Visit their offices, and get to know their staff. Sit in on an internal meeting if possible. Learn how they interact with clients and ask about other alliances they maintain so that you can talk to *those* firms. Offer them the same courtesies. Determine whether there is a philosophical fit and a true complementary connection, rather than a duplicative one.

- *Task subcontracting.*   Ask for samples of their work. Sit in on a workshop they are conducting. Ask for references from their clients.[4] Give them a sample situation, and ask for their resolution (that is, provide some questions they would ask in interviewing under these conditions).

- *Conceptual subcontracting.*   Ask for client references. Give them a situation and ask them how they would react (for example, a client employee approaches the consultant and discloses confidential financial information). Describe the model you intend to use, and ask them to support it *and* attack it. Ask what their favored models are to see if there are conflicts (for example, the candidate believes that "right-brain thinkers" can't be organized in their work habits, a position that you find abhorrent).

- *Potential partners.*   Spend extended time together, professionally and socially. Collaborate on several projects. (I believe this is as important as a test drive prior to purchasing an expensive car.) Share detailed financial statements with each other and with appropriate financial advisers. Check client and professional references extensively. *Bring in a third party to play devil's advocate to the venture.* Convince yourself that the combined business will grow by at least 25 percent in the first year. Clearly delineate responsibilities and duties. Meet the other staffs and subcontractors.

Note that these are detailed, time-consuming activities. A lunch is not good enough for selecting a once-a-year survey designer, much less a future partner in the business. If you're not willing to invest this kind of time and energy, then you will never develop your business effectively. You're leaving your own future to the trial-and-error method of ran-

---

[4]Here is an interesting and important dynamic: as useless as references are in standard hiring conditions, they are almost always highly useful in client references on consulting work. There are no legal problems attendant, and clients will be quite candid if you ask the right questions, for example, "Why is Joan better than other people you've hired for the same type of work?" If a candidate can't give you client references, he or she either has no experience or has not performed well.

dom people selection. Incredibly, most consultants I meet spend more time choosing their electrician or dentist than they do the people who can have such a profound effect on their future. (And they "preach" quite a different sermon to their clients.)

By the way, this type of careful scrutiny allows for candidate *self-*selection. The candidate is often the one who says, "You know, I'm beginning to realize that I'm not quite right for what you have in mind. But I think I know someone who is."

So, rule number 3: Invest all the time it takes for you to be absolutely comfortable that the person is right for the job.

A final word about fees, before moving on to the next section about rewarding people. I *never* offer a fee or per diem rate to subcontractors. In the first place, I want to wait until I'm convinced that the individual is appropriate for my needs. (This is the "conceptual sale" I talked about earlier, as pertaining to clients.) In the second place, I want the subcontractor to cite a fee for *me*. I often find that such fees are extremely reasonable, because the other consultant has not pursued a comprehensive fee strategy (as detailed in Chapter 8), and I might have begun at too high a level. In the infrequent occasions in which their fee is too high in my opinion, but the candidate is excellent, I am in a position to negotiate. In any case, if I've made the investment cited above to determine what my needs are, established a candidate pool, and gotten to know each potential candidate, I'm on extremely solid ground about relative value-added and commensurately appropriate fees. *Remember, never pay subcontractors based on the size of your project or provide them with a "piece of the action."* Only partners get a piece of your action—because they are bringing you a piece of *their* action.

How to Reward Collaboration: The Revenue-Sharing Formula

Your business will grow substantially once your presence is no longer necessary to establish contact with a prospect. There are two conditions that create this salutary situation: (1) prospective clients call you, and (2) others bring prospective clients to you. In the first instance, there is no reward or remuneration due anyone. But in the second instance, there are these possibilities:

- You've received a referral from a client or other consultant, with no reward due.
- You've received a referral from another consultant with whom you have a finder's fee arrangement.

- You've received an assignment within an alliance relationship, and no reward is due since the other consultant has included your fee within the overall fee structure.

- You're contacted by another consultant who needs your collaborative help in securing, designing, or delivering the business.

Let's discuss the two situations in which you'll need clear guidelines for rewarding those situations that deserve reward and are not otherwise covered: finder's fees and collaboration.

Finder's Fees

I said earlier that I don't usually demand finder's fees when I refer work to others, being content with being able to influence the implementation and gain information from my colleague. However, there will be others who may request finder's fees of you when referring business (and you may wish to request such fees of others at times, which is quite proper and ethical).

I'm going to define a finder's fee situation in this manner. *Finder's fees* are paid on business that is referred and that would not have otherwise reasonably been obtained. Thus, it is appropriate to pay a finder's fee for business that would not otherwise have come your way.

My position on the amount of the fee is:

1. Twenty percent for business that the other party has closed and that requires only your introduction to, and acceptance by, the client

2. Ten percent for business for which your introduction has been arranged but your skills are required to close the sale

3. A thank you and small gift for cold leads that require your skills to obtain entry and close the sale, and that eventually result in business

I don't pay, nor do I expect to be paid for, cold leads, which are names and background information that may constitute a marketing opportunity. These are simply professional courtesies that result from active networking and similar favors done for others. If a meeting is arranged for you with the buyer through the auspices of the referring consultant, then financial consideration is due if business results, since the marketing process has been considerably shortened ("velocity" has been accelerated—see below). Because your skills, repute, and decisions are instrumental in obtaining the business, 10 percent is adequate recompense. However, if the business is conceptually closed by the referring consultant, and that consultant's repute, skills, and decisions have

also been responsible for convincing the client to consider your participation, the marketing process has been virtually completed. It's up to
you not to spill coffee on the carpet or insult the buyer's spouse.[5] In
such cases a finder's fee of 20 percent is appropriate.

In both cases, I'm assuming that the referring consultant is not involved in the actual design or delivery of the project. Naturally, these
fees are always negotiable, but I find these percentages to be equitable
and commonly accepted. *You must also stipulate the duration of the finder's fee arrangement.* My position is that they are for the current assignment only unless it is a pilot, in which case there is justification for including the subsequent project if the pilot is successful. In some cases,
when introduced to a key executive in a large organization, I will include a time period of up to a year for *any* business that results. While
nothing is cast in stone, my rule-of-thumb is to ensure that the referring
party feels fairly treated so that they will refer additional business. One
referral is merely a business event. Continuing referrals are a consulting
career. Providing 10 percent of a $100,000 contract may be a short-
term device to maximize cashflow, but granting 20 percent or more for
$1 million is a long-term investment that will dramatically develop your
business.

Collaborations

I've been in some sticky situations about revenue splitting when two or
more consultants collaborate. Otherwise amicable cooperation can be
undermined when a colleague feels shabbily treated, or when you feel
taken advantage of. So I've devised a formula, reflected in Figure 7-2,
for rewarding collaborations, which I communicate to anyone even approaching me with an idea. I want it clear from the outset. I've found
my colleagues are grateful for the concept, and I've never had difficulty
with a collaborator who has accepted it.

In this system, an assignment is separated into three component
elements: closing the sale, providing the technology, and implementing the
project. Closing the sale means getting the buyer's name on the contract,
which may include on-site presentations, personal meetings, providing materials and references, convincing the recommenders, and so on. The technology involved may be formal and tangible, such as test instruments,

---

[5]Do not take this lightly. I was once concluding such a "done deal" when the buyer
asked me if I'd like a cold drink. After cavalierly asking for a diet soda—which required a
search—I took a gulp that went down my windpipe, and I spewed soda all over his desk.
My last recollection of him is wiping soda off his leather-covered calendar and the graduation picture of his daughter. I no longer accept refreshments from anyone whose check
has not yet cleared my bank.

	Sale (⅓)	Technology (⅓)	Delivery (⅓)	
Consultant A:	X%	+ X%	+ X%	= share
Consultant B:	Y%	+ Y%	+ Y%	= share
Combined:	⅓ project	+ ⅓ project	+ ⅓ project	= full project

Figure 7-2. A formula for sharing revenue equitably.

	Sale (⅓ = $42,000)	Technology (⅓ = $42,000)	Delivery (⅓ = $42,000)	
Her:	(100%) 42,000 +	(0%) 0	+ (75%) 31,500	= $73,500
Me:	(0%) 0	+ (100%) 42,000	+ (25%) 10,500	= $52,500
Us:	$42,000	+ $42,000	+ $42,000	= $126,000

Figure 7-3. Equitable revenue sharing: Example 1.

classroom materials, computer programs, and proprietary intellectual material. But technology can also be informal and intangible, such as skills in running focus groups, observations of operations, assessment of communication techniques, backstage counseling, and so forth. Technology encompasses the wherewithal—the talents, materials, approaches, skills, and judgments—that is necessary to improve the client's condition. Finally, delivery is the actual implementation[6] of the technology. Tangible technology may be implemented by persons other than the owner or creator. Intangible technology is usually reliant on the personal skills of the possessor. I can equip someone else to use my model for establishing strategy, but I can't equip someone else with the skills and traits I use to develop the relationship that allows me to "shadow" and provide candid feedback to CEOs. Each consultant provides a portion of each of these three components, from 0 to 100 percent. Here's an example.

A colleague approaches me with a request to use my technology in establishing succession planning systems within a client of hers. She is about to submit a proposal for $126,000.[7] She wants me to help her with the model I use and spend some time overseeing her initial on-site implementation. Using the model, we arrive at the formula shown in Figure 7-3.

I've reflected 100 percent credit to her for closing the business, 100 percent credit to me for providing the technology, and shared credit for implementation reflecting her preponderance of the work but my pres-

[6]Implementation, in my system, includes follow-up activities.

[7]Where did this number come from? See fee structures in Chapter 8.

ence for oversight. She receives 58 percent of the total fee, and I receive 42 percent. I would not have had the business without her, and my implementation responsibilities are important but limited. She could not close the project without my approaches, and she has the main implementation responsibility. I found this fair. So did she.

Let's look at another case. I approach you with a request for help in convincing a prospect to proceed on a strategy formulation project. He requires a "show of force," and your name is recognizable in the field. Your presence could be the deciding factor in the client's choosing our collaboration over the competition. We will both need to be present for implementation, since the client will expect to see both of us regularly. However, the technology is all mine, and you've used it in the past and are comfortable with it. The ultimate proposal is worth $240,000.

In Figure 7-4, we see that I'm receiving 70 percent of the total fee, and you are receiving 30 percent. The sale was primarily set up by me, but your presence was required to help close the business. The technology is mine, and we share equal implementation responsibilities. Is $72,000 fair compensation for you to lend your name to the proceedings and share equally in the implementation, using my technology? Is your involvement worth $72,000 to me?

As you have probably observed, the serious discussions occur around the contribution of the collaborators in each of the three areas. Should you have received more than 40 percent credit for participating in the close of the business? Can we shift the implementation responsibility one way or the other, creating leeway in that area? These questions should be answered prior to the agreement on collaboration; they can also be used to reconcile inequities if conditions change during the collaboration. (I've been involved in projects in which a colleague's technology was required more than anticipated, or the client requested one of us to play a more substantial role in implementation than the other.)

As opposed to finder's fees, this system *is* based on a "piece of the action," because the relative contributions of the collaborators are responsible for the action occurring. And what if one party feels that $72,000 doesn't represent the time investment required for his or her

	Sale (⅓ = $80,000)	Technology (⅓ = $80,000)	Delivery (⅓ = $80,000)	
You:	(40%) 32,000 +	(0%) 0	+ (50%) 40,000 =	$ 72,000
Me:	(60%) 48,000 +	(100%) 80,000	+ (50%) 40,000 =	$168,000
Us:	$80,000	+ $80,000	+ $80,000	= $240,000

Figure 7-4. Equitable revenue sharing: Example 2.

half of the implementation? The answer is, either increase the project fee or don't enter into the collaboration. But don't be lulled into sacrificing the other party's share to make the colleague happy. This creates resentment, inequity, and, ultimately, unsuccessful collaborations. You cannot base collaborative fees on anything other than the total project fee and the appropriate contributions of each party. Individual fee structures or rates are beside the point.

> *Maximizing short-term cashflow is the act of a lone wolf. Creating enduring relationships that provide referral business and collaborations is the mark of an established professional firm.*

My credo is, "Always help the other person get rich." This applies no matter what relationship or fee system you prefer. I don't just want the project to be successful, I want the *relationship with my colleague to be enduring*, whether small referral business, situational alliances, reliable subcontracting, or large-scale collaborations. This is why you can use a reward system for others to dramatically help your business grow.

But the accent must be on using others to develop your business, not using others to abandon your business.

The First Rule of Leverage: Don't Give Up the Ship

As you leverage your growth by working with and through other people, you will find yourself in various stages of disengagement from project details. This is difficult for those who feel that "I'm the only one who can do this correctly" and easy for those who feel that "I'm the deal-maker. Someone else can do the legwork."

The truth of the matter is that you are the key link in the relationship with your clients. While that relationship should evolve to include others who work for you and your firm's image in general, it is nonetheless ultimately dependent on you. If your relationship remains sound, the client will always bestow the benefit of the doubt. A poorly conducted briefing session by one of your people or a misdirected document from your office will not be the match that lights the fuse that blows apart the relationship. Instead, the client will call you with the attitude that the two of you have a mutual problem, or have both been the victim of a performance error.

No matter how many people you employ or subcontract with, focus on sustaining and evolving the personal relationship you've established with key buyers in each client. In some cases, this may mean that a significant portion of the project is delivered by you. For example, you may make the executive presentations and personally counsel the top officers. In other instances, you may simply have to visit the key people once a month or once a quarter to discuss the results that your team is producing. There will often be ongoing clients that require only a monthly phone call and yearly visit.

The balance and perspective that you must constantly adjust apply to what I call the velocity of the sales process. The *velocity* is the rate of change in motion or position relative to time. The elapsed time of a sale in the consulting business is usually lengthy. In obtaining a new client of any magnitude, it's not unusual for six months to a year to elapse from first meeting to signing of the contract. Anything that can be done to increase the velocity—the movement toward agreement on a project in as short a time as possible—is highly advantageous, while impediments to velocity can be deadly.

However, the elapsed time to secure *repeat* business is often quite brief. In many cases the client will ask you to undertake a project as a follow-up to one you are completing or to investigate issues raised that were tangential to the current assignment. Or the client will call you because an "itch" has developed, and your prospect-based timing approach (see Chapter 2) makes you the right person at the right time, meaning you make a sale instantaneously. So where is your investment better made, out on the street spending all of your time trying to sell new business, or working with existing clients trying to maximize repeat business? Where is the greatest potential to accelerate the velocity of the sale? Figure 7-5 shows the forces that influence velocity for both repeat and new business.

> **Employing others is not a tactic to "free" you from a client account. It is a strategy that allows you to further develop your relationship with that client.**

As you can see in Figure 7-5, there are many more forces aligned against sales velocity within prospects than there are within clients. In

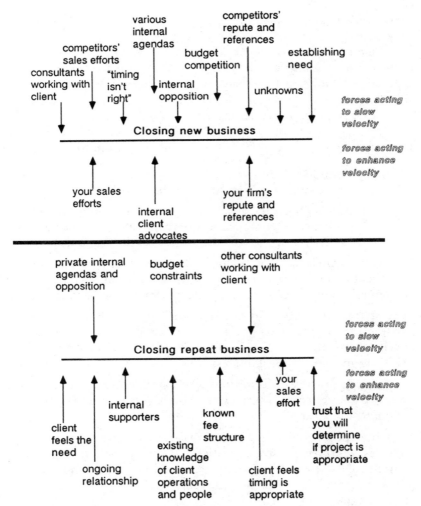

Figure 7-5. Sales velocity comparisons. Velocity is always greater within existing clients.

fact, many of the forces working in opposition to velocity within prospective clients—for example, various internal agendas—can be turned into forces enhancing velocity in client accounts (when you're familiar with the internal agendas you can strive to help meet them). Million dollar consulting means obtaining 80 percent of your business from existing clients, which both increases revenue and decreases marketing expenses. Not only is it more cost-effective to sell to existing clients, and not only is it easier to make that sale, but it's also a *higher velocity sale.*

Consequently, don't make the error of utilizing other people (whether alliances, subcontractors, or employees) to free you up to pursue new business. While new business should always receive attention, *your top priority should always be to nurture and evolve existing client relationships.* This is the pursuit that other people free you up to accomplish.

The fact that you bring a crew on board doesn't mean that you give up the ship. It means that you have the leverage and the time to understand the workings of the ship that much better. When you utilize additional resources, you have the opportunity to do the following:

1. Arrange periodic meetings with the key buyer(s) to review the team's progress and discuss ongoing modifications to the project.

2. Use the team's observations and insight to develop a list of critical issues that should be presented to top management, separating those within the purview of the existing project and those outside it.

3. While the team is fulfilling assignments, spend nonstructured time with the client to observe and understand the essential aspects of the client's communications, operations, and interpersonal relationships.[8]

4. Invest time in getting to better know, and establish relationships with, other key members of management who were not a party to the decision to hire you. (This is one of the few occasions when a lunch meeting may be an ideal alternative.)

5. Investigate practices within the client's competitors, and/or industry practices in general, to provide more insight into the client's condition and the kind of improvement possible.

6. As opportunities emerge, begin to formulate plans for addressing other issues through further projects. (Don't present these in a transparent sales effort. Simply have them ready so that when the client feels the "itch" you are ready to respond, thereby enhancing the velocity of the sale.)

7. Try to establish your team members as members of internal client task forces and committees. This is one of the most effective techniques I've ever observed in creating synergistic relationships, and one that can't be effective if you are a lone wolf trying to do everything. This is a prime example of using others to build your relationship.

[8]Only a fee structure that is not based on per diem rates will afford you this opportunity, which is why I find fees based on time so restrictive, and why fee structure influences so much more than merely the amount of money you are paid. See the next chapter for a detailed discussion of fee structures.

Utilizing other people within a client relationship is a technique to help you gain, not relinquish, control. Once you're on board the vessel, you want to get to the bridge. And once on the bridge, you never want to give up the ship.

We're about to enter the middle of this section on tactics, and it's appropriate that we do so by discussing a central part of your business: fee structure. Thus far, we've covered your personal conduct and promotion, the affiliations possible with others, and the leveraging effect of using additional resources within clients. Let's move now to how that adds up to a million dollars.

8

Establishing Fees

If You're Charging a Per Diem, You're Still Just Practicing

Formulaic Methods to Establish Per Diem Fees

For those of you who have turned directly to this chapter, let me apprise you that there is some material in Chapter 7 that has a bearing on fee structure. By way of review, here are some instances and conditions that might justifiably cause you to cite fees at levels *below* your usual level.

- To gain access to an industry or client with large long-term potential
- As a subcontractor, who is experiencing no marketing expense
- As a referral, who is experiencing no marketing expense
- For a long-term client asking you for special consideration
- For pro bono work, or work for nonprofits and public agencies

Note that none of these reasons includes "tough times" or "business is slow." Whatever your fee structure is—and we'll examine several alternatives in a moment—you must adhere to it. If you do, you'll find your business steadily growing over the long haul. If you don't, then your approach is "whatever the market will bear," and your short-term income will be at the expense of long-term wealth.

Fees are part and parcel of your overall strategic approach to your market. They should never constitute your single driving force, nor should they be dictated by the client or competition.[1] Moreover, there is nothing unprofessional about saying, "I can answer that when I learn some more and have time to consider how we might help you," in response to, "How much?" But once you say, "We charge $1500 a day, plus expenses," you've had it. From that point your fee can only decline and your margins erode.

What I'm calling the formulaic method to establish fees is one I don't favor but that requires explanation, since it is so often advocated for individual consultants and principals of small firms. It's actually a strictly arithmetic approach that begins with your determining what level of income you require to support your desired lifestyle. (Note how delimiting this is from the outset. By establishing what you'll "need" you're already capping your potential.) For our purposes, let's say that Charles Consultant determines that $200,000 in after-tax money will support his lifestyle, pay tuition, provide for a vacation, and afford some savings, after the pretax (company) money pays for medical and retirement plans and assorted fringe benefits. So Charley calculates that a gross income from consulting of $280,000 will provide for company expense, personal expense, and personal taxes.[2]

Now, sharpen your pencils. Charles calculates that there are 220 working days available to him during the year, once he subtracts weekends, holidays, and vacation time. Of these, he estimates that he will be booked 70 percent of the time, meaning he will allocate the remaining 30 percent to marketing, promotion, and other nonrevenue-generating activities. (If you have employees, these nonrevenue days multiply like libidinous rabbits, which is why the previous chapter discourages full-time employees.) That leaves 154 days available to generate revenue. If we divide Charley's $280,000 revenue needs by 154 billable days, we arrive at $1818 per day.

---

[1] In my strategic consulting work with a wide array of organizations, I've found that very few are driven by profit. Almost all businesses are driven by their products, services, markets, technology, or related strategic areas, with profit a derivative of success in that pursuit. Consulting firms are no different. For an excellent discussion of these driving forces, see Benjamin B. Tregoe and John W. Zimmerman, *Top Management Strategy: What It Is and How To Make It Work,* Simon and Schuster, New York, 1980. See also Michel Robert, *The Strategist CEO: How Visionary Executives Build Organizations,* Quorum, Westport, Conn., 1988.

[2] Your firm should always break even at year's end or show a *small* profit or loss. The preponderance of profit should be taken out as salary; otherwise you will pay a corporate tax on earnings, then an individual tax when you ultimately take these earnings out. Any large loans to you will be interpreted as dividends, which will also subject you to double taxation. Incorporated personal service firms should not show large profits. Your banker will be sufficiently happy to see the sales figure that translates into personal income.

So, using this formula, Charley should establish a per diem fee of $1800 per day. Therefore, when he formulates a proposal for a project, he knows that his time must be accounted for at the rate of $1800 per day. Or, if a client asks, "What will it cost for you to spend two days with us?", Charley knows that $3600 will cover it.

Candidly, this backward calculation of a daily rate is amateurish and, worse, severely self-limiting. But so many consultants inappropriately cite daily rates that I want to take the time to explain why they are such a bad idea before moving on to more fertile ground.

What happens if your lifestyle needs are $450,000 a year? Is that so ridiculous? A couple of kids going to good schools, a decent vacation or two, the luxury of a wonderful house to return to after all that time on the road, intelligent retirement planning, elderly parents who need support—these are not uncommon events or desires. Moreover, if you are undertaking the major risks of being on your own, you should at least be in a position to enjoy commensurate rewards. How silly it is to take major risks when your return is less than it would have been staying in traditional organizational life.[3] At $450,000, Charley's per diem would have to be about $3000 a day. That's not all that uncommon for big names in the business, but it's stretching it for most people, no matter how talented and how endorsed. And what of a desire for $1 million? Well, that comes to $6500 a day, or $4500 if you worked *every one* of those 220 days and did nothing else. Daily rates are limited because they are based on a finite resource: time.

There are substantial risks in this profession, and substantial rewards. It is ridiculous to assume the former without capitalizing on the latter.

Why on earth would you want to work every potentially billable day? Wouldn't it make sense to spend increasing time on the other elements of growth we've discussed, including personal expertise and repute? And why not take four vacations a year or spend time to watch your kids play

---

[3]Ben Tregoe, an early mentor and member of *Training Magazine*'s Hall of Fame, once told his staff during a heated discussion of company benefits, "We're all refugees from large organizations—that's why we love this profession." I'm continually astounded by people who seem willing to take significant risk but who are reticent about seizing proper reward. We once advised a strategy client that if his goal was only a 5 percent return on the business he owned, he ought to liquidate the business, invest the equity in CDs, and sleep better at night.

soccer to make up for the nights you weren't there to help with the home-work? "Billable days" place emphasis on activity, not result. The measure of your success at year-end isn't the amount of days you've worked, but the amount of money you're able to keep. Period. Banks won't give you credit lines based on billable days worked, and no one will be impressed by the amount of time you spend on airplanes. A focus on per diem rates, estab-lished by determining financial needs, will focus you on the wrong activi-ties and waste your precious time and energy.

You want to encourage a collaborative relationship with the client, within which the client feels free to call you at any time. This includes people *other than the buyer who signs the checks,* so that a multitude of people can call you without incurring an expense, thereby making you more valuable to more people. When clients are on a daily rate system they hesitate to call for help when they may really need you because they are forced to constantly evaluate their request in terms of real-time, current expense. Consciously or unconsciously, they are calculat-ing, "Is this problem worth $2500 for Charley to come over? What if we find he'll need three days—it's not worth $7500, is it? Even if it is, we're better able to afford it next quarter." These conversations occur all the time in these circumstances.

Let's face it, if days of your time are your fundamental device to make money, you are going to try to maximize the days of your time used. This is human nature and is often, more basically, survival. Conse-quently, when you create a proposal or respond to a request for help on a particular problem, your tendency will be to maximize your involve-ment, *when the consultant's real value-added is to improve the client's condition with minimum involvement.* It is extremely difficult to estab-lish the types of relationships we've been discussing when you are citing a daily rate to a client and then describing the number of days you will be "needed." It's that much more difficult for the client to commit to the keystone of the relationship—allowing the consultant to determine whether he or she can improve the client's condition—when the quali-tative benefit is viewed within the context of the quantitative measure of days required and costs per day.

If you are perceived as selling days, you will not be perceived as an equal partner in the relationship. And the converse of the client's hesi-tancy to call you is your hesitancy to suggest legitimate, additional in-vestigations because such pursuits, no matter how justified by the project, mean you're suggesting more "days."

Finally, your scheduling and energies will be hampered by the need to minimize time use. It's grueling, for example, to conduct employee interviews or customer focus groups. I limit myself to a half-day of in-terviewing or two focus groups a day, for example. But if the client sees two half-days of interviewing, there will be a normal question about why the interviewing couldn't have been combined into one day, saving the client one day's per diem.[4]

Sometimes, you can best schedule client work, or combinations of client work and your own marketing activities, in portions of days. As long as the client results are met within the deadlines agreed, the particular activities and timing you use shouldn't be the focus. But they inevitably will be if the client perceives that the way you spend your time is directly proportional to your fees.

If you want to make a million dollars or more in this profession, charging by time units isn't the route to get there. Not only are the amounts self-limiting, but the opportunity for multidimensional growth can't be exploited if maximizing days at the client is the driving force of your business.

When prospects request a day of my time for which they'll pay a fee if our discussions *don't* lead to a project, I usually request only that my expenses be paid. This pleases the prospect, gives me an opening edge in building the relationship, and makes me very objective about the discussions that day. Personally, it's an essential component in my strategy to "think of the fourth sale" and not the immediate one. You have to invest money to make money. Have prospects "demanded" that I cite a per diem rate? Of course. And I've always declined, stating that I work on a project basis only, and that our collaborative responsibility for results dictates that the client's people should never be hesitant to call me, and I don't ever want to be hesitant about spending additional time on site whenever I feel it's necessary to achieve our goals. If the prospect can't work that way, then I'm never going to establish the relationship I need, and I'm not interested in short-term income.

A final word on formulas that result in daily rates. Yes, I know that attorneys and kindred professionals scrupulously assess hourly fees. But most attorneys don't do as well as Charley Consultant's $280,000, much less $1 million. And attorneys don't establish relationships; as a rule, they provide a technical commodity—legal advice and representation. How many individuals or corporations view attorneys as collaborative partners, and how many as necessary evils? The attorneys who make the most money are those who take contingency fees. If you win, they win. If you lose, they lose. That's as close to collaboration as the legal profession gets.

---

[4]Don't even think about charging by the half-day or by the hour. Assuming you're traveling, you can't use the other half-day for anything else, and your financial calculations for the year are based on a full per diem rate for a day with a client. Besides, can you picture a top executive saying, "We need consulting help. Get me someone who has a reasonable hourly rate!"?

Dick Butcher, a character in *Henry VI*, says, "The first thing we do, let's kill all the lawyers." I'm not certain, but I believe he was reacting to their billing system. Besides, doesn't it bother you that attorneys only "practice" law?

Market Demand Methods
for Establishing Fees

One of the easiest methods to use in establishing fees is simply to emulate the competition. If you are networking effectively and talking to clients regularly, it's relatively easy to discover what the average rates are. Then you can make a determination as to where you want to position yourself within that range. For example, Figure 8-1 shows the average ranges I've found for the activities listed.[5] These vary with experience, geography, and even the client's urgency, but the ranges encompass the predominant fees assessed at this writing.

If you determine that your client and prospect base is accustomed to paying $750 to $2500 for a day's consulting help, and you have embarked upon a strategy of assessing per diem rates, then you must decide where in that range you wish to be positioned. Do you want to be seen as the most economical alternative? Will such a position help you to get in the door and enable you to obtain more lucrative contracts as a result of the quality of your work? Or do you prefer to establish at the outset that the client gets what the client pays for, and your value-added help more than justifies your position at the higher end of the fee range? Do you intend to use the entire range as a negotiating technique and attempt to get whatever the market will bear?

If you are going to use a market demand system for establishing fees, I think it should follow the sequence displayed in Figure 8-2 so that the underlying, consistent basis for your fee decisions also reflects your longer-term strategy.

In the graphic, the sequence calls for isolating the various activities you will be undertaking for which you are assessing fees. You then evaluate the prevailing market ranges for each activity. Now comes a step that most consultants completely ignore: *You should apply your strategy to those individual ranges.* For example, if your strategy is to enter new clients as an economical alternative with the intention of building long-term relationships and increasing revenues as a result of a multitude of

---

[5]Since I've already discussed the weaknesses of being activity-oriented, it should come as no surprise to the reader that I don't favor the market demand approach to fee structure. However, these comparisons should prove to be of help in comparing your current billing practices.

Activity	Range
Consulting day, on-site	$750 to 2500*
Consulting day, off-site (in office, research, etc.)	$500 to 2500
Keynote or other brief speech	$500 to 5000†
Half-day workshop	$1000 to 3500‡
Full-day seminar	$2500 to 5000
Executive retreat, per day	$2500 to 7500
Systems (i.e., succession planning) implementation	$10,000 to 50,000
Employee or customer surveys	$15,000 to 100,000+
Strategy formulation	$50,000 to 150,000
Organization or department diagnosis	$50,000 to 200,000
Organization redesign and restructuring	$100,000 to $500,000

*Many consultants will assess fees by the half-day or even by the hour. I've found hourly fees from as low as $35!
†"More than half [of all associations] employ professional speakers...at convention general sessions and spend an average of $10,000 to hire four speakers per convention." *Source:* American Society of Association Executives, promotional letter, April 9, 1991.
‡These are sometimes billed "per participant," ranging from $100 to $500 per person, especially when the consultant is providing formal, proprietary participant materials. Hence, a class of 25 people might result in a total fee of $2500 to $12,500, depending on the perceived value of the take-away materials.

Figure 8-1. Fee ranges for various activities. Market demand requires that a consultant take a position within a range.

assignments, you will tend to position yourself toward the lower end of the ranges. The exception will occur in those activities for which you may need outside expertise, licensed approaches, subcontracting help, etc. (This is why the activities should be evaluated separately: some will be more cost-effective than others.) Having applied that strategy and

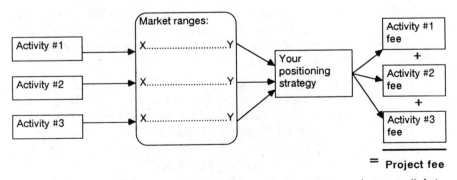

Figure 8-2. Establishing market demand fees. Strategic planning takes precedence over "what the market will bear."

considered your resources, you can assess a fee for each activity, the sum of which adds up to your overall project fee.

> ***The lack of a systematic method to arrive at fees in the market demand approach can result in one bad situation and one catastrophic one. The bad situation occurs when you lose business because your fees are too high when compared to perceived value-added. The catastrophe occurs when you obtain business for which you've cited much too low a fee when compared to perceived value-added.***

That fee may reflect one activity or 20 activities. The total fee may be substantially different from someone else's fee because of the strategic positioning factor. Using this method, however, at least you are able to arrive at market demand fees that *also* reflect your image to the client and your longer-term market plans. It is the absence of this systematic determination which creates a trial-and-error method for the consultant and tremendous confusion for the client. Despite the improvement in using a system to arrive at market demand fees, the entire approach suffers from some severe shortcomings that must be carefully considered when establishing a fee structure:

1. There is a tendency to be constrained by the ranges, never approaching the higher end and settling comfortably in the middle as a safe, noncontroversial position. This will never lead to dramatic growth.

2. You are helping the prospect to make comparisons based on the activity and opening the door to comparative shopping based on fee rather than focusing on conceptual agreement on objectives and consideration of value-added.

3. There is a tendency to charge whatever the market will bear irrespective of value-added and longer-term strategy. When fees are solely based on the client's ability and willingness to pay, the basic collaborative relationship (we will work together to improve your condition) cannot be established since a win-lose relationship (the more you can pay, the more I can make) preempts it.

4. It is very easy to be "positioned" by the market. That is, clients and prospects frequently compare notes (particularly if you are intelli-

gently building referral and repute business). It is difficult to assess one client a higher rate than another for what the client perceives is an identical assignment, regardless of legitimate differences in preparation, tailoring, resource use, and other elements that may apply to one and not the other. "She implements a performance evaluation program for $25,000" is a far inferior statement to "She is the best at implementing performance evaluation programs tailored to your particular needs and situation."

5. A key long-term growth strategy calls for providing current clients (who should be constituting about 80 percent of yearly business) *more favorable* fee arrangements than new clients. After all, current customers shouldn't be subsidizing new ones. A market demand fee system inhibits that strategy, since it's difficult to decrease your position in the range continually without creating excess pressure on your own margins. Also, those current clients will be citing your current—not original—fees when they refer you to prospects. This is a difficult box from which to escape.[6]

Market demand approaches to fee structuring are somewhat superior to formulaic methods based on income needs. But I hope you'll appreciate that they are rather short-term in their strategic orientation and can be highly superficial and transparent to clients and prospects alike.

I've been advocating the improvement of the client condition and the consultant's value-added contribution to that improvement as the litmus test for effectiveness in this business. Let's see how that ethical starting point can also form the basis for establishing fees based on perceived value. This, I've come to realize, is one of the core elements of growth in our profession.

Perceived Value as a Basis on Which to Establish Fees

The quickest way to become wealthy in this profession is to do superb work and to be paid high fees. I've tried to establish a foundation for the position that fees will always be artificially depressed as long as they are correlated with arbitrary, objective measures, such as days, hours, projects, numbers of people, and the like. The secrets of receiving high fees are:

---

[6]One of the surest signs of a consultant simply charging what the market will bear is that of new clients actually paying lower fees than existing ones. When existing clients learn of these inequities, relationships that took years to build can be destroyed in an instant. This is another reason why market demand fees can be antithetical to long-term relationships.

- Base fees on the client's perceived value of your assistance.
- Ask for them.

Here are two examples of the role that value plays in establishing fees. In the first instance, one of my clients approached me with the request to design a training program which his company would market through his offices around the world. However, he wanted me to accept a smaller fee in return for a percentage of the sales. I usually turn down contingency fees and was ready for a healthy negotiation, but he hit me from behind. He opened with, "Alan, this has nothing to do, and everything to do, with your *value*. I couldn't begin to pay you fairly with a fee based on value. It's strictly a matter of my ability to pay. Oh, I could pay you $40,000 or $50,000, but your work here would be worth well into six figures. That's why I want to offer a royalty with no time limit."

Well, he had me. I wasn't prepared for that attack, with him conceding the value issue and turning it into *his* argument! It was one of the few instances in which I've done work for "a piece of the action."

I used that same reasoning with my financial advisers not long ago. I felt their bill was too high because of incorrect billing allocations. (They bill by the hour and fraction, which is cumbersome and, I'm convinced, severely limiting.) Their hours should be declining, even though their value to me is increasing. However, they bill on the former, not the latter!

"David," I explained to one of the partners, "don't misunderstand, your value to me is substantial, and I have no complaints about the quality of the work. But over the past several years, as I've adhered to your reporting and detail requirements, the hours needed to plow through my books should be steadily *decreasing*. I think your people are applying incorrect measures."

My financial advisers are limited. They can only audit my books and calculate my taxes so many times, and they can't raise their hourly rates beyond certain competitive points. Further, my mundane work—the bulk of my financial reporting—increasingly requires junior, lower-billed partners. You see, it wasn't a matter of *value*, just one of numbers of hours. Their loss, my gain.

Establishing fees based on values requires adherence to these conditions:

1. You never cite a fee before you're prepared to do so, no matter how much pressure the client exerts. "Just give me a ball-park estimate," is a request that will always land you in the bleachers, not the box seats. Ball parks are surrounded by concrete walls and iron fences.

2. You must be willing to live with ambiguity. You have no responsibility to provide the client with numbers of hours worked, numbers of reports prepared, your payments to subcontractors, or any expense other than travel documentation. In fact, if a client focuses on these

issues, you haven't made a conceptual sale. You must be willing to cite project fees that fairly represent your value to the client plus your expenses in fulfilling the assignment.

3. You must spend time building the relationship to the point that the sale is conceptually made and *all* important decision makers are on board. At that point, even if your value-based fee isn't automatically accepted, it will meet much less resistance, and any negotiations can be handled much more easily.

4. If the client does want to negotiate the fee downward, do so by explaining *the kinds of value that will be lost with each decrement of the fee*. Never take a position in which you lower the fee but do not remove services and value. The client has the choice as to how much value justifies what investment, but should never have the choice of benefiting through your sacrificing your margins. That is not collaborative. That is a transfer of wealth from you to the client (value provided for no investment).

5. Be prepared to walk away from business. Once you are perceived as someone who will negotiate fees downward, you will always have pressure on you to do so. I once worked for a training firm that was so poorly managed that it *always* lowered fees in the fourth quarter in order to meet its plan. New, fourth-quarter clients benefited, often at the expense of long-time clients who ordered earlier in the year. Consequently, everyone began to wait for what our clients called "the fire sale," and *65 percent of the company's business occurred during December!* You must be perceived as someone who does superb work, requires a high investment, and will not lower fees without the client commensurately sacrificing value.

One of the most fundamental distinctions of million dollar consultants compared to the rest of the field is their willingness to turn down business. The vast majority of consultants accept any assignment on the grounds that something is better than nothing. They ultimately relegate their professional lives to such trade-offs.

Not long ago, I had to find a subcontractor to produce a video to accompany a project I designed for a client. I knew that more such collaborations would be necessary, so I needed a firm that I'd be comfortable with for the long term. I searched in Providence, Boston, New York, and Chicago. Video production firms provide estimates based on black-and-white commodities: editing time, number of crew, number of actors, background music, visual effects, and so on. The estimates for my video work—the exact same specifications were provided for all of the 12 firms I'd selected—ranged from $10,500 to $47,000! All of the bells and whistles were the same. However, the firm which established the best relationship with me (collaboration in choosing actors, invited me to lunch, showed an interest in longer-term work, actively listened to my editing ideas) cited a fee of $11,400.

There are several lessons here, not all of them obvious. First, there is that terrible box constructed by citing fees based on activities and tangible deliverables. The comparisons were odious at the high end. Second, it helps to shop around with such firms, and *your* prospects will shop around just as I did if they can make such clear comparisons. Third, if you are at the high end in such commodity offerings, you'd better be able to differentiate your services. ("Why are you charging $40,000?" I asked a New York firm's account representative. "Because that's what we all charge," he replied vaguely.)

Fourth, however, is the fact that the company I chose could easily have charged me three or four times as much and I would have accepted the fee in light of their excellent relationship building, had I not been placed in a limiting fee structure of their own making! They could easily have cited a fee of $30,000 without breaking it down by number of crew or actors' pay, and by emphasizing the way in which they would work with me, their willingness to hold unlimited meetings and involve me in the editing.[7] Those are valuable opportunities that I can't easily put an individual price tag on. In fact, I ultimately invited my client to the shooting, with the blessing of the production company, and he was very impressed at the effort on his behalf. That was worth a lot to me, and my value was enhanced in his eyes.

Believe it or not, a great deal of my advice to other consultants—as well as to contractors who work on my house, local business people, and entrepreneurs—is that they are charging *too little*. But, guess what? Except for a tiny fraction, all are afraid to raise their fees because they are unable to embrace the five conditions above.

---

[7]"Unlimited meetings," like "an open-door policy," are offers that are virtually never abused. I've never experienced a client requesting unnecessary meetings, because the client's time is as valuable as mine. Hence, this is always a good offer to make, and I always make it in writing.

Establishing the Value of a Client's Investment

When you boil it all down, how do you know how much to charge? Figure 8-3 contains the questions I ask. Now, remember, these are asked in view of the five conditions cited above being met. Many of them I ask the client, and some of them I ask of myself. Note that none refers to the client's budget. If that turns out to be a constraint in terms of the fee you arrive at, you can then negotiate down by sacrificing value.

Also, the client must view the fee as an investment, no different from an investment in education or new equipment or better security. The focus then turns to the *return* on that investment, and the return is a far superior point of negotiation than is your "fee."

Case Study 1

Let's say that you've been asked to design and implement a new performance appraisal system for a client. You've done these before and have a

---

1. What is the outcome of this project worth to the client?
   a. If quantitative, what is the amount?
   b. If qualitative, what are the effects?
   c. How does the client describe a successful outcome?
   d. To what degree is the client's condition improved?
2. What is your direct contribution to that outcome?
   a. Are you accelerating what would have occurred anyway?
   b. Is the outcome dependent on your unique talents?
   c. Are you facilitating or also delivering?
   d. Are you observing, diagnosing, or prescribing?
3. What is your current relationship with the client?
   a. Is this a longtime client?
   b. Does this assignment provide for professional growth?
   c. Does the assignment present stressful conditions?
   d. Are there difficult deadlines?
4. What are your costs to complete the assignment?
   a. Was there marketing cost or other costs of acquisition?
   b. To what degree are subcontractors required?
   c. Are there extensive travel requirements?
   d. Are there materials or other deliverables required?

Figure 8-3. Establishing the value of the client's investment. These questions help to determine value-based fees.

model that has been very effective. You've done a succession of projects for this client, and you know the operation well. You estimate that you'll need about 20 days of your time and two subcontractors for 10 days each. There will be some administrative work and a few reports, plus the new forms you'll design. You estimate the following project fee:

Personal time	
15 days on-site @ $1500	$22,500
5 days off-site @ $1000	5,000
Subcontract time	
20 days @ $750	15,000
Administrative time	
40 hours @ $25	1,000
Materials and deliverables	
Printing, collating, art work	1,000
Total project fee	$44,500

Assuming the client pays all expenses, your gross margin is 62 percent, out of which you're paying for lights, rent, phone, and so on.

Case Study 2

Let's apply the questions in Figure 8-3 to this scenario.

1. The client estimates that the performance appraisal process requires about $400,000 a year in management time, and feedback indicates that about a quarter of all time spent is redundant—correcting errors on feedback sheets caused by poor directions; misunderstandings of the process, necessitating retraining; and ratings overruled by superiors who don't agree with subordinate assessments because of earlier inability to reach agreed-upon performance goals. A successful outcome would also vastly improve morale, since the current evaluation system is widely viewed as a paper-pushing exercise and not as a legitimate assessment of contribution.

2. The client knows the system must be changed, but was particularly impressed by your approach, which utilizes employee focus groups to create ownership of the new system, and by the fact that you've implemented it successfully in organizations that provide glowing references. You are prescribing the solution and designing the system, working with the client's human resource group to implement and assume responsibility.

3. This is a long-standing client who has been a pleasure to work with. It will be a relatively easy project, since you know the client and pos-

sess the model. It should allow you to be considered for increasingly sophisticated organization-wide assignments.

4. There was no marketing whatsoever on your part. Time demands on you personally are reasonable. Other costs equal $17,000. The client will pay all travel expenses.

Based on these considerations, the value to the client, and your contribution, the client's investment will be $86,000. That's a gross margin of 80 percent.

The worth to this client is a minimum of $100,000 in salary annually, plus the morale factor. The conceptual sale is tight. On the other hand, this is a long-term client with significant potential, and the model is already in existence.[8] You know you have fixed costs of about $17,000, and you should allow for inevitable contingencies bringing that to $20,000. So the range for this project is probably from about $50,000 to $100,000. Given your positioning strategy, you decide that $86,000 represents an equitable investment given the return. (The client agreed, in real life.)

Could you have charged a fee of $79,500 or $91,750? Probably. Just as you could have charged the $44,500. Now, don't go screaming down the hall. I said there would be ambiguity. You have to determine a comfortable fee — an acceptable client investment, in light of the value which is the client's return on that investment. *That's your responsibility.* Excellent restaurants charge not merely by the cost of the meal ingredients, but also by the ambiance and service: the entire dining experience. First-class air fare is not based on the size of the seats, and certainly not on the caliber of the food alone.

The ultimate test of a value-based fee system is the client's acceptance of the investment in terms of the value perceived.

How much is a kidney transplant worth? How about a cast for a broken leg? Almost any doctor can do a good job with a cast, but very few can transplant the kidney. And do most people choose doctors by fee or by bedside (well, office) manner?

---

[8]This is strictly a pragmatic consideration. You have every right to charge for proprietary intellectual material and approaches every time you apply them, just as a royalty is paid on a song every time it is played commercially or a book every time it is sold.

Value-based fees are not a technique for the faint-hearted, in the sense that you have to make some bold decisions (albeit with input and cooperation from the client) about the improvement in the client's condition and the justifiable investment in achieving it. That's why the conceptual "sale" is so important and why value-based fees are utterly dependent on it. Once the client agrees on the *value,* the investment becomes quite reasonable. No one gets something for nothing. And this brings us to the second point raised at the beginning of this section. Once you've understood your own worth and value to the client, you can establish fees that equitably reflect that contribution. Then, you have to ask for them.

When to Raise Your Fees and What Will Always Happen

No matter what system you're using to set fees, you should periodically evaluate whether they should be raised. If you're using formulas, then your basic needs and aspirations may have increased. If you're responding to market demand and competition, you may find yourself inadvertently lagging. And especially if you're using a value basis, you have to determine *current* value for the client, and your *current worth* to the client.[9]

> **The absolute indicator of when to raise fees is when demand exceeds supply.**

While there are many creditable reasons to raise fees, the most fundamental is that of supply and demand. When you are receiving more requests for work than you can personally handle or subcontract to handle, it's time to raise your fees for new clients. (As a rule, existing active clients should not be raised, and inactive clients returning to the fold should receive only modest raises.)

Every year you should review the appropriateness of your fee structure since, with proposals in the pipeline and negotiations ongoing, it's likely that an increase won't hit your books for 12 to 18 months. For this reason, proposals should always have effective dates specified: for example, "The

---

[9]As a rule, distinctions that are locked into product or strict discipline tend to diminish in worth, because conditions change, competitors move in, and approaches become passé. Distinctions linked to talent and relationships tend to increase in worth, since talent can adjust to changing conditions and relationships are intrinsically valuable.

terms and conditions of this proposal are effective through August 31, 1992. Acceptance after that date may necessitate increased fees or altered conditions." It's not all that unusual for a client to pull out an undated proposal a year after the fact and announce, "Surprise! I just got the budget approval, and I sold the project to the committee." If that work now must involve subcontractors because of your own changed circumstances, your margins could seriously suffer.

Many of the best consultants I know have a multiyear strategy for fees. Let's take something easy, such as speaking engagements:

Activity	Current Fee	In 12 months	In 24 months
Keynotes	$2500	$3000	$4000
Half-day workshops	3000	3500	3500
Full-day seminar	3000	4500	5000

In this example, our consultant wants to gradually raise keynote fees to a significant level, plateau workshop fees, since they are primarily marketing devices for larger consulting projects, and dramatically raise seminar fees, since this is labor-intensive and not a business this particular consultant enjoys being in, although demand will likely continue based on word-of-mouth. These intentions have to be justified by the consultant's growth. In other words, to merit $4000 keynote fees, the consultant has to grow in repute, acquire experiences in a broader array of industries, and develop a wider range of affiliations and alliances. This is why multidimensional growth is such an important consideration. In any case, by projecting your fee strategy, you are able to determine what growth is required on your part to establish appropriate value. You also can work backwards to price your proposals accordingly. There is no such thing as raising fees "next month," even if next month is the January of a new year. Fees must be raised about 12 months ahead of time.[10]

Other Reasons for Raising Fees

You Are Not Perceived As a High-Powered Organization Because You Are So Inexpensive

Don't laugh. Raising fees can *increase* business by forcing your proposals to be approved by higher-level management, which has higher bud-

---

[10]Since we've advocated that 80 percent of your business come from existing clients and fee increases apply primarily to new business, you can see the need to establish high value-based fees at the outset of any client relationship. It is extremely difficult to gracefully raise fees with active clients unless your projects are individually value-based.

getary limits. This is a very effective strategy for the bold-at-heart. I decided to do it after becoming disgusted with a GM training manager who told me he wanted "the cheapest proposal possible" in order to save as much of his budget as possible.[11]

You Are Asked to Do Important Work That Is Personally Unattractive

Higher fees really do offset unpleasant assignments. My wife tells me this every time I miss a social event for an assignment that sends us on another vacation, and I tell myself every time I'm in a town where the restaurants all close at 9 PM.

You Want to Distance Yourself from the Pack

If you find you are bidding on proposals with other firms among which there is little differentiation, you already know that several of them will attempt to bid low. Very few, if any, will deliberately bid high. In so doing, you will force the buyer to examine the value-added dimension you bring to the table. It's your job to ensure that it is distinct from the others.

You Want to Test the Waters

I spoke in earlier chapters of expanding the envelope. Remember the second rule of the prior section: You have to ask for the business. How do you know what you're worth if you don't use the market to try to find out? If clients have been accepting proposals for two years at $75,000, instead of finding new ways to pat yourself on the back, maybe you should be investigating why you haven't been charging $125,000. It's not worth it? Says who? *Only the client can determine worth, and if you don't give the client a chance, you'll never really know.*

To summarize, develop a strategy for fee increases, no matter what system you are using, and particularly if you are basing fees on perceived value. There are several reasons for considering increases, and the most unarguable is "demand exceeds supply."

---

[11]Four years ago I delivered an afternoon speech to Atlantic Electric for $3000, and the *exact same* speech that evening for $300 as a pro bono gesture to the Rhode Island Personnel Association. The utility executives thought it was the greatest thing since cold beer; the personnel association sat there like stumps. Go figure. I'm more convinced than ever that people not only get what they pay for, they *perceive* that they get what they pay for!

When you do raise fees, one thing almost always happens: You lose the bottom 15 percent of your market, both current and potential. But that's okay. We talked in earlier chapters about growing at the top of your market by abandoning the bottom end of your market, and nothing will do that faster than a fee increase. It is difficult at first to turn down business. "Gee," the client will say, "we really want to use you, but we can't possibly afford that amount." There is obviously no conceptual sale here based on value, and there may never be. Some clients aren't interested in value, they are interested only in activity and budget. Those are the ones who will fall by the wayside as a result of fee increases, and that is well and good.

9

Investing in Success

Absence Doesn't Make the Heart Grow Fonder—It Weakens the Memory

Periodic Client Communications

There is an apocryphal story in the sales business about a salesman who outsold his colleagues by 200 percent every year. Yet according to all the tests administered to the sales force, he scored the lowest in sales aptitude and selling skills. His own district manager had thought that the salesman was just lucky and recorded on his evaluation that his potential was limited. After the third year of record-breaking sales, the home office decided it had better discover the secret behind this guy's success, so a corporate psychologist was dispatched.

"Show me exactly what you do in front of a client," instructed the psychologist.

"I place the product manual between us," said the salesman.

"Yes, yes, and then what?"

"Well, I ask the client if he would like to buy the product on page one," said the salesman, as if speaking to an innocent child.

"And what if the client says no to you?"

"I turn to the second page, and ask if he would like to buy that product."

"And if he again says no?"

"I turn to the third page..."

"All right," yelled the Ph.D., "I get the idea. But what if you go through *all one hundred forty-seven pages of products,* and the client has said no to every single one?"

"I turn the book over," said the salesman, clearly explaining the obvious, "and open again to page one and ask the client if he would like to buy that product."

It's amazing what can happen if you just keep talking to the client and asking for the business.

I am now going to share one of the most elemental secrets underlying growth and wealth in this business. It is inexpensive, simple, both tactically and strategically effective, and yet most consultants ignore it completely. In fact, by my estimation at least half of the readers of this book will say, "Of course!" and then proceed to ignore it completely.

Do I have your attention?

You don't get business that you don't ask for. You don't even get remembered if you don't do things that are memorable. If we agree that 80 percent of your business should come from existing clients and that the long-term relationships you are seeking—within which the client trusts the consultant to make key decisions about accepting projects— are dependent on ongoing communications, then you must devise a strategy to effectively remain within your clients' field of vision. This is the essence of the timing strategy we discussed in Chapter 2.

It is actually difficult to contact clients too much. It is easy to fail to contact them frequently enough. If there is anyone, anywhere, who has ever sent you a check for your services, and with whom you haven't communicated in the past six months, then you will never reach your growth potential. The secret is simple: establish an ongoing dialogue with clients. In the worst case, a monologue will do.

There are several options available for continuous client communications:

1. Print
   - Letters
   - Brochures
   - Newsletters
   - Article reprints

- Job aids and checklists
- Posters and sayings
- Cartoons
- Testimonials and examples of assignments completed

2. Phone
   - Calls to "stay in touch"
   - An 800 number and hot-line help offer to encourage use
   - Information relayed on meetings or events of interest
   - Reminders of long-term follow-up responsibilities and dates
   - Introductions to third parties, that is, *customers for your client*

3. Events
   - Interviews with the client for industry journals
   - Attendance at industry and professional meetings that the client attends
   - Hosting periodic conferences on topics of interest
   - Acting as intermediary with other clients for mutual learning

4. Personal
   - Visits to the client without any particular agenda
   - Entertaining key buyers
   - Sending holiday cards or gifts (as permitted)
   - Participating in mutual charity events and fund-raisers[1]
   - Seeking out common community and social events
   - Sending "I'll be in the neighborhood" cards

5. Other
   - Sending fax messages and information
   - Advertising in industry publications the client definitely reads
   - Exhibiting at trade shows that key clients will attend
   - Asking the client to help *you* as a critiquer, adviser, editor, etc.

Some of these might be better-suited to your client base than others, but all of them could be applicable. Are you reviewing a list like this and devising a strategy for *each individual client* for ongoing communications objectives? Once you've done this, you can work on the tactics. Here are some examples from each category.

Every so often I'll send along a cartoon with my name in it. (See those reproduced in Figure 9-1.) A lighter touch is important in communications. As a result of this, one of my clients sent me a cartoon about consultants which I then shared with everyone else on my list, with credit to

---

[1]See the final section in this chapter on pro bono work.

"Of course I can't take all the credit, but it was my decision to hire Alan Weiss..."

"This will just take a minute. It's Alan Weiss with something more important to say."

Figure 9-1. A humorous touch can be very effective. Leo Cullum's cartoon (at top), with its personalized caption, was offered to subscribers to the *Harvard Business Review* for a fee. Stu Heinecke's cartoon, again with a flattering caption, was part of a similar promotional package.

the sender. This creates a *community* of clients, who feel that they belong to a common interest, represented by your firm.

A phone call is entirely justified by your intent in informing a client that an event of interest is approaching. This might be a guest speaker, sponsored by the American Management Association at a breakfast meeting (which is why these memberships can pay such dividends for you). You may choose simply to inform your client that a subject you know is of interest to the client is being discussed, or you may choose to invite the client to be your guest.

Using what I call "events," you might bring two noncompetitive clients together to discuss the problems inherent in managing a diverse work force, or to compare succession planning approaches, or to investigate the efficacy of part-time workers. As the intermediary, you may or may not actively participate in the meeting. But the simple act of creating the opportunity is significant.

Whenever I'm going to be traveling, we review our lists so that we can send cards or make phone calls letting clients (and prospects) know that "I'll be in the neighborhood." It's very common for these people to invite you to see them since they know that your expenses are paid and it's a no-obligation opportunity to get together. Generally, the farther you're traveling, the easier it is to set up the meetings. I'm based in Rhode Island, so when I travel to nearby New York the "in the neighborhood" approach isn't very powerful, since I'm often there, and it's only an hour's trip if a client needed a special visit. However, in Chicago people will usually see me, and in California I can always get an appointment if people are in town. When I go to London, people will usually *change* their schedules to accommodate mine.

Finally, the "other" category includes asking clients to help you. This may take the form of an unpublished article you'd like them to critique before you submit it for publication. Or you might request feedback on a new brochure you're developing. Many firms establish client advisory panels, which convene regularly to discuss trends in business and finance.[2]

These are some of the tactics that apply within the communication strategies. They're really not much different from the salesman who opened the product manual to page 1 and asked, "Would you like to buy this?" Since this is a *relationship* business, we have to keep turning the pages to alternate communications methods to maintain and develop the relationship, but, just like the salesman, we have to be persistent in continuing. Some clients will never respond. However, *no one* will respond if you don't initiate and maintain these avenues of contact. When the client feels the itch to do something, you want your firm in that client's mind. If the client needs something, you want the client de-

---

[2]This is an ideal way to obtain testimonials from your clients to be used on the dustjacket of your books. It is also the opportunity to cite their assistance in the acknowledgments.

pendent on you to provide it. When the client thinks of unsolicited support and valuable information, you want your name associated with the solution.

Ongoing communications are a modest investment. More than anything else, periodic client contacts require the volition to want to engage in them and the innovation required to make them unique and targeted to the client's needs. That volition—to create the strategy and allocate the time—and that innovation—to develop personalized tactics—constitute one of the elemental secrets underlying million dollar consulting. As Huey Lewis says, "It's as simple as that."

Publishing Options

The greatest single marketing device I've encountered is publishing. Putting your ideas and approaches in print immediately does three things:

1. Your own thinking is solidified and your approaches systematized as you work to communicate them. You discover elements of your work that weren't as obvious before you wrote about them.

2. The value of your ideas is validated, in that "selling" an editor requires that you present original and worthwhile ideas for the editor's readers. Editors are besieged with material, so working through that obstacle course can only be accomplished with valuable material.

3. Your credibility skyrockets.

I conduct workshops on how to get published for people who have never written for publication before. The best method is a sequential one that I call the "staircase" approach (see Figure 9-2), beginning with local publications and working up to broader impact and, if you are so inclined, a book. The idea behind publishing is *not* to be blatantly self-aggrandizing, but to let the value of your work speak for you.

As I discussed earlier, my progression included writing articles for no fee for publications such as *Supervisory Management, Manage, Training News,* and a dozen others like them. I moved on to do a column (for a modest fee) for *Training News,* wrote for *The New York Times,* and was interviewed by publications such as *USA Today* and *Success Magazine.* I then began writing for *Success, Human Resource Magazine, Training Magazine,* and others and contributed chapters to two business books. When I approached publishers with *my* first book, I received three offers and accepted one from Harper & Row, which published my next two books after informal discussions, the third with

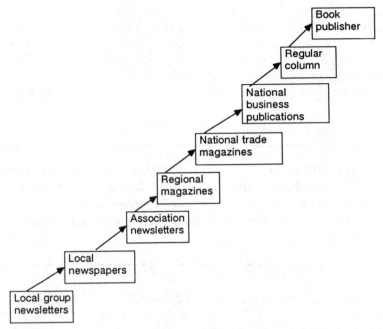

Figure 9-2. The staircase approach to publishing—taking it one step at a time.

an advance. The book you are reading, from the preeminent business publisher in the world, I was asked to write.

I published my first article in 1969. I entered the consulting business in 1972, founded my own firm in 1983, and published my first book in 1988. The period from 1969 to 1988 is irrelevant; the period from 1983 to 1988 is the important one, *because only after beginning my own firm did I experience the growth necessary to provide something worthwhile saying in a book!* So, in five years I was able to gather the material and experiences that allowed me to approach 18 publishers and garner three offers, and I've since published books in 1989, 1990, and 1992. The experiences that make for interesting books—when you are oriented toward multidimensional growth—never stop. Throughout that period I've continued writing articles and columns, doing interviews, and contributing to a wide variety of publications. That is why my phone rings. And although, for expediency, I now have an agent, you don't need one.[3]

---

[3] I recommend the book by Jeff Herman entitled *The Insider's Guide to Book Editors and Publishers*, Prima Publishing, Rocklin, Calif., 1990.

Vanity publishing (you pay someone to print your book) and self-publishing (you print it yourself, often with publicity and distribution assistance) are terrible ideas. These attempts to "have a book" are as obvious as a ham sandwich. Reviewers throw them out, and executives are smart enough to know the difference. *Remember, if you can't convince an editor to publish you, you probably haven't yet developed anything worthwhile to say.*

> *If you write a book for publicity, it will go nowhere but to your head. If you write a book intending to help the reader, it will generate tremendous publicity. Write a book when you have something important to say, not before.*

Here is my brief formula for getting an article into print. This applies to any of the first six steps in the staircase shown in Figure 9-2. You may be able to jump two or more of the stairs at one leap, or you might find yourself on several at once. I continue to write monthly columns at no fee while writing books for considerable advances. These are not mutually exclusive activities. But you have to start somewhere, and if you want to start from scratch and still stand an excellent chance of getting published, here's how to do it.

How to Get an Article into Print

1. Determine what subject you want to write about
   a. Why are you the person to comment on the topic?
   b. How will this subject enhance your business, repute, or standing?
   c. Why is the subject relevant at this time (and for the next several months)?

Don't be afraid to be contrarian. The world doesn't need another piece on left-brain versus right-brain thinking.[4]

2. Determine where you want to publish the article
   a. Who is your audience and what do they read?
   b. Don't be afraid to *ask* your audience.[5]

---

[4]See "Contrarian Consulting" in Chapter 10.

[5]This is the opportunity to involve your clients, as suggested in the section opening this chapter.

   c. Where is it most reasonable for you to be successful?
   d. Research publications and study their style.

I was never published in the Times *until I sent them an article that I realized was just what they needed!*

3. Prepare a professional inquiry
   a. Send it to a specific editor's attention.[6]
   b. Specify what, why, examples, uniqueness, length, and delivery date.
   c. Request specifications.
   d. *Always* enclose a SASE.[7]
   e. Cite credentials—yours and the article's.

This step must be more carefully executed than the actual article!

4. Write it like a pro
   a. Use specific examples, names, and places.
   b. Write it yourself, but solicit critique.
   c. Write it to the specifications.
   d. Make sure you include your own biographical data at the end.
   e. Request free reprints or reprint permission or discounted reprints.
   f. Don't self-promote; let the substance do it for you.
   g. If rejected, resubmit, resubmit, resubmit.
   h. Don't overwrite; write what's on your mind without worrying about the Great American Novel. (When you edit, you'll find the piece is amazingly good.)
   i. Attribute things you borrow, but don't try to dazzle with superfluous references.
   j. Be critical and analytical; readers respond best to provocation and the opportunity to look at things in a new way.
   k. When in doubt, start a new paragraph.
   l. Use graphics when appropriate, and try to load in the metaphors and similes.

Use prior articles as credentials to write newer ones.

Here's my route for getting a book published once you've ascended the staircase. Book publishing is slightly easier when there is a long track record of articles and columns to support it, but these are not prerequisites. The most important aspect is convincing the publisher that your book will sell, and the way to achieve that is to do your own home-

---

[6]The Herman book and *Writer's Market,* both cited earlier, are excellent sources.

[7]Common citation in the trade, standing for "self-addressed stamped envelope."

work, because the editor hasn't the time or inclination to do it for you. It is difficult to get the first book published, but with a targeted, systematic approach it's much easier than most people think.

How to Get a Book Published

1. Determine what it is you have to say:
   a. Your particular expertise from education, experience, training, circumstances.
   b. Your ability to pull together disparate things that others haven't.
   c. Your ideas, concepts, theories, and innovations.

   If you've nothing to constructively contribute, don't write a word.

2. Determine which publishers are most likely to agree with you
   a. Examine their current books in print.
   b. Request their specifications.
   c. Ask people in the business.

   Do not vanity-publish or self-publish — it's a waste of time and no one is impressed.

3. Prepare a treatment for the publisher's review
   a. Why you?
   b. Why this topic?
   c. Why is this topic handled in this manner?
   d. What competitive works are extant, and why is yours needed?
   e. Who is the audience?
   f. When would it be ready?
   g. What are the special features (i.e., endorsements, self-tests, etc.)?
   h. Provide *at least* the introduction and one chapter, a table of contents, and summaries of the other chapters.

   If you can't sell it to the publisher, you'll never sell it to the reader.

4. Write it like a pro
   a. Invite clients and/or respected authorities to contribute.
   b. Use a sophisticated computer and software.
   c. Don't use a ghost writer. If someone else writes your book, why does anyone need you?
   d. Always take the reader's viewpoint.
   e. Schedule your writing sessions just as you would your other responsibilities.
   f. Use trusted others to review, critique, and suggest.

g. *Always* attribute anything that's not yours.

h. Keep it "future-current." Remember, it will be published a year from your submission.

What is published represents your values: are you proud of what you've written?

5. Market it like a pro

a. Don't waste undue time looking for an agent, because most tend to listen only to previously published authors.

b. Don't get discouraged: keep submitting, and find out why you've been rejected.

c. Read contracts carefully because they will specify author's discount, planned promotion, expenses you may incur, and so on. Run it by your attorney.

Remember, a successful business book sells about 7500 copies. Don't expect to be on Oprah *the following Monday.*

Publishing will, at first, require a substantial investment of time. However, that time can usually be found on airplanes and in distant hotel rooms. Once you've broken into the field, you'll find it easier and easier to publish, both because your skills are developing and because your credibility is growing. The staircase method is useful to ensure that you also grow as an author and avoid the "success trap" of publishing repeatedly for a limited audience.

When executives read your books, they may not immediately ask you to consult. However, they will often ask you to speak.

The Speaking Circuit

The perfect synergy for a consultant works something like this:

- An executive reads your book or article and asks you to speak to his or her management staff.

- As a result of the speech, you're asked to consult on pertinent issues.

and/or

- As a result of a speech you deliver, executives in the audience ask for more information, and you send them articles and/or books.

- After reading the material, you are asked to consider several consulting projects.

and/or

- During a consulting project, you provide copies of articles and/or books to key client managers.

- Having read your material and worked with you on your project, they request you to address one of the trade or professional association conferences.

These sequences can occur all the time if you are in a position to exploit them. If you have written nothing, or if you don't "do" speeches, then such potential synergy is academic. In that case, your marketing is also academic.

Making speeches before in-house management conferences (i.e., *The New York Times* Regional Newspaper Group), industry trade associations (the American Bankers Association), business associations (American Management Association Conferences), professional specialty groups (annual conference of the American Society for Training and Development), personal development groups (the Business Roundtable), and university management extensions (Case Western Reserve University's Weatherhead School of Management) provides high-impact marketing. The visibility is excellent, the opportunity to promote your approaches is ideal, and you earn immediate credibility merely by dint of having been invited to speak.

Here's some valuable information: the Credit Union National Association has 52 state credit union leagues as members and an annual budget in excess of $5 million; it publishes seven different periodicals and holds meetings once a year (the next three, at this writing, are in Nashville, Denver, and Cincinnati).[8] The American Chemical Society has 140,000 members, also a $5 million budget, costs $82 a year to join, publishes 27 periodicals, and holds two meetings a year. I could tell you similar things about the Broadcast Promotion and Marketing Executives, the National Association of Jai Alai Frontons, or the Shoe Service Industry Council. I can do this because the appropriate source books are available each year for less than $100, and they also contain the name of the executive director, addresses, and phone numbers, and information about the history of the association.

Once you break into these groups, you have the opportunity to capitalize on word-of-mouth publicity. The best strategy is to begin with modest regional groups for little or no fee, then work your way to their national parents. Another sound approach is to gain entry from your clients. A banking client can introduce you to contacts in the American

---

[8]All citations in this section about associations are from *National Trade and Professional Associations of the United States*, Columbia Books, Washington, D.C., 1991.

Bankers Association and even recommend you for a speaking slot (members are frequently asked to nominate speakers).

How valuable are speeches? In June of this year I already have eight booked and another pending, ranging from 45 minutes to three hours. *Every one* was a result of a request to me based on prior speeches, consulting work, or my books and articles. Seven of the speeches are "repeats" for satisfied groups; the eighth and the pending ones are new associations for me. The groups range from Mercedes-Benz dealers to the American Press Institute and the Pharmaceutical Manufacturers Association of Canada. My goal is to generate additional business from all eight.[9]

An attorney friend of mine recently made a transition into full-time consulting, specializing in dental practice buyouts, mergers, and partner financing. After several harried weeks trying to decide on advertising, direct mail, and other options to reach his potential audience, he came to me for advice. I suggested that he approach every state and regional dental association with a proposal to speak on his topic. After his first few efforts were accepted, he is now in great demand and will be appearing before national groups with considerable fanfare (and considerable fees — people will pay you handsomely to market your services on the speaking circuit). If this strategy works so well for an attorney pursuing business from dental practices, how well might it work for consultants with a broader-based constituency and, consequently, more options?

There are plenty of courses, books and seminars on how to speak. The venerable Toastmasters International is still superb, as are membership organizations such as the National Speakers Association.[10] Private firms such as Communispond and The Executive Technique are also high-quality alternatives. It's not my goal here to teach you how to speak, but it is my hope to convey to you *how to get speaking assignments*. This is as good a place as any to explain what should be in your press kit, which has a variety of uses but is particularly helpful in pursuing speaking opportunities.

Figure 9-3 shows the contents of a professional press kit oriented toward obtaining speaking assignments. (These should be preassembled but tailored each time for the particular client and use, so the articles included, testimonials, and personal experience may differ in each case.) The kit should be in the form of a professional presentation folder, with pockets for material, room for books or cassettes, and a place for a business and Rolodex card.

---

[9]Upjohn, Boehringer, Ingelheim Pharmaceuticals and Bristol-Meyers Squibb have since become clients as a direct result of the speeches.

[10]See the appendix for addresses of key resources and an annotated bibliography.

■ Corporate brochure	■ Third-party articles validating your work
■ Black-and-white glossy photo	■ Personal biographical sketch
■ Personal experience in the subject area	■ Testimonials from clients
■ Interviews conducted with you	■ Articles you've written
■ Audio- or videocassettes of prior speeches	■ Book reviews or similar notices
■ List of clients	■ Fee schedule for speaking
■ Examples of specific work in the industry	■ List of references
	■ Professional affiliations
	■ Honors or awards you've won

Figure 9-3. The contents of a press kit. A professional press kit denotes a professional speaker.

Circulate your press kit to the association executives in the fields that are relevant to your work. Send it to independent meeting planners.[11] Provide it for clients who are in a position to pass it on to their professional affiliations. Make it a habit to send out three press kits a week in targeted mailings. (This is something a secretary can do even while you're traveling. It's the essence of marketing productivity.) Follow up with phone calls. And mail repeatedly. If people are deemed worthwhile to receive the press kit, place them on your mailing list for your regular client mailings, and send a new press kit to them once or twice a year.

There are speaking bureaus that book speakers for a commission based on the fee. I am here to tell you that I would rather deal with door-to-door used-car salespeople who are collecting money for an obscure self-awareness religion in the form of whole life insurance. Speakers' bureaus generally only help when you don't need them; that is, they disdain speakers without a national reputation and embrace those who are already well-known. They are often demanding and unreasonable in their working relationships, and some of the most unethical stories I've heard in our profession emanate from relationships with speakers' bureaus. I'm reasonably sure there must be some good ones. But I

---

[11] In all cases, send it only to a specific person by name, with a personalized letter; for example, "I've been told that you are arranging the Miami conference with an emphasis on productivity..." While it takes some work to find names and specific items of reference, that investment is paid back handsomely by the fact that the odds of the recipient reading the material are enormously improved. Blind mailings are never worth the effort, because meeting planners and association executives are flooded with them.

haven't encountered them yet, and I'm absolutely sure that you don't need them. Other than that, I don't feel strongly about it.

> **Million dollar consultants are passionate about what they do and how they do it. There is no more natural forum than a speaker's platform to disseminate those views and share that passion. This is known as painless marketing.**

I have not yet met a top consultant who does not take to the lectern as opportunities develop. And make no mistake, a consultant with practical experiences in improving client conditions is a valuable speaker and in great demand. A professional speaker who is not really a consultant (remember the definitions of Chapter 1) but who talks on "inspirational" topics or repeats a standard performance on the podium is not as much in demand. Buyers, and audiences, are requiring practical, results-oriented business advice more than ever before. There is a wonderful opportunity awaiting any consultant who takes the time and invests the energy to learn to speak well, organize experiences and approaches, and seek out the people who can arrange the audiences that will lead to increased business.

Pro Bono Work

Pro bono work is work done for free. Chapter 14 will deal with such no-fee work in the context of contributions to the environment and ethical issues. Here, I want to deal with it as an investment in your future success, because pro bono work can rebound into lucrative fee-paying opportunities.

And let's be clear on another thing: pro bono work is work done without fee at your initiative or as a result of someone else's request and your unhindered decision to comply. It is *not* work done for free because the client has refused to pay your fee but you still want to complete the project (to keep it from a competitor, to be in position for a legitimate project, etc.). That situation isn't pro bono; it is desperation. *There are no chapters in this book on desperation, because you must always deal from a position of strength if you are to be successful and to grow in this business.*

There are obvious candidates for pro bono work: the local Boy Scout troop, your children's school (public or private, at any level), business associations (e.g., the chamber of commerce), hospitals, religious institutions, and so on, depending on your areas of expertise and local need. I've found that by helping a school fund-raising drive to set its strategy, or by offering organizational diagnosis to an arts council, or by critiquing the decision-making processes of a charitable board, or even by discussing leadership skills with volunteer association officers, your name and talents become known. These organizations are often excellent laboratories to apply your skills and are equally often *valuable learning opportunities, since nonprofits sometimes perform more effectively than the for-profits!*[12]

As your talents and contributions become known—and they should, because your contribution is a rare one to these organizations—you will find that your colleague volunteers often hold key positions in attractive, potential clients. They'll often solicit your advice about *their* organization's problems while working with you in the volunteer activity. This places you in the appealing position to (1) give them some advice, and encourage them to contact you for more, (2) send them some of your materials which address the issues they've raised, and (3) put them on your mailing list for periodic communications. Sooner or later the timing approach will work and they will feel an itch that prompts them to think of you.

Ironically and shockingly, the greatest impediment to pro bono work of this sort is that many organizations will opt not to utilize the help! I've been turned down by school boards, business recovery councils, and volunteer groups of many types, despite my credentials and references, and despite their clear need (and often appeals) for help. The reasons vary, but they are usually two-fold: First, an outside consultant can create fear among those who know they have been performing poorly but have been able to conceal the fact through lack of scrutiny. These people often want to control the consultant's intervention, and that is ethically unacceptable to me. Second, there is sometimes a bureaucratic requirement of one type or another that is unattractive or impossible to meet. (Volunteers must contribute financially to the cause; 40 hours of background instruction is required; you must reside within a certain geographic area.)[13]

---

[12]See "Do Good and Good Will Follow," pages 183–196, from my book *Making It Work: Turning Strategy into Action Throughout Your Organization*, Harper & Row, New York, 1990. Consultants can learn a great deal from nonprofit structures and operations and can impart this wisdom to conventional private sector clients.

[13]A joint Providence Chamber of Commerce and Council of the Arts endeavor aimed at securing management consulting help for art institutions is my favorite boondoggle. After advertising for business executives to serve as consultants—whom they would "train" in consulting techniques—they turned down my offer of help because I wouldn't commit to their rudimentary and tedious "training" process. In other words, I wasn't a consultant until they told me I was! Bureaucracy, of course, is the triumph of means over ends.

Thus, it's important to volunteer frequently and diversely until you establish a win-win relationship with groups of your choice. Don't be discouraged by being brushed off. It's an occupational reality for volunteering consultants.

In volunteering your services, underpromise and overdeliver. Unlike the normal client relationship, it's important here to be regarded for what you do, and for what you say.

Here are the guidelines I've found useful for considering whether or not to undertake a pro bono relationship:

- Can I commit the *total* time required by my promise and by the expectations of the organization? Just because I'm volunteering doesn't mean I don't have to live up to my commitment. If I can't appear at every meeting and perform every task, I won't accept.

- Is the group organized in such a way that I'll be able to make the contribution I'm capable of? If there's a "veto" power held by a politically oriented officer, for example, the group probably can't make the best of my talents.

- Is the group involved in a public good? The legions of lemming-like volunteers for the defunct est organization were certainly doing something for nothing, but it was to enrich the coffers of an individual and his organization.[14]

- Is there an impact or outcome to be made, and can my contribution be recognized as supporting it? Any local school fund-raiser, charitable event, or chamber of commerce undertaking would seem to fill that bill. The 1990 California commission investigating self-esteem, parodied so well in the comic strip *Doonesbury*, did not.

- Are there other people involved directly or indirectly with whom I would want to establish a relationship? Will I work side by side twice a month with the presidents of two state banks? Will I present the report to the governor at the quarterly progress meetings? What kind

---

[14]est stands for Earhard Seminar Training, one of the first and, in my opinion, most dubious of the self-awareness, guru-school movements.

of networking will I be able to establish? "What's in it for me?" is not the primary reason for wanting to do good work, of course. But when you consider pro bono projects within the framework I've defined in this section, it's quite reasonable to analyze what benefits might emerge for you.

■ Will the nature of the particular pro bono opportunity appeal to a client or prospect who may be involved with that cause? Health care prospects will look more favorably on a firm which, although it has no current health care clients, has done volunteer work in setting strategy or evaluating personnel for community health care projects. If one of your client CEOs is a chairperson for the Red Cross, for example, and you're considering volunteer work anyway, the Red Cross certainly has a built-in attraction.[15]

Volunteer consulting work should never be done if it conflicts with your client responsibilities; nor should it be done as a substitute for an orthodox client relationship. However, I believe it should be a normal and ongoing part of your investment in your own success, a low-key marketing approach that will do good for you as you do good for others. It's often overlooked. I find that I'm almost *always* the sole consultant involved in volunteer efforts, amidst bankers, retailers, educators, insurance professionals, and utility executives. It's more than slightly ironic that one productive path to million dollar consulting pays no immediate fees, which may be why so few venture into it.

Despite the best investments in success and the greatest diligence in trying to develop your business and your personal capabilities, uncontrollable events can intervene. Let's see how even bad times can become good times if you'll let them.

---

[15]This fits in with the communications tactics under "special events" discussed above.

10
Turning Change into Opportunity

Bad Times Can Be Good Times If You Play Your Cards Right

Early Warning Signs of Business Decline

This section is concerned with your business, not the general economy, which will be covered in the next section. I'm not suggesting that you should be an economic prognosticator, which is a rough equivalent to the astrologers I mentioned in the introduction. But I will suggest that you be prudent in assessing your own cards and realistic in deciding how to play them. A lot of people have lost the farm pulling for an inside straight.

There is a tendency in our business to look no further than the latest client check. Those with great foresight sometimes look all the way to the longest-term signed contract. But you have to look past all the "guaranteed" stuff and into the realm of the uncertain. You have to know what's at the other end of your pipeline.

The pipeline approach to sales forecasting and early warning of business decline is illustrated in Figure 10-1. At one end of the pipeline are your current implementation assignments, and within the pipeline are your contracts waiting to be implemented, moving up to their turn in

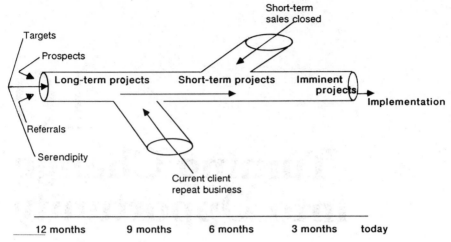

Figure 10-1. The business "pipeline."

the flow. At the opposite end of the pipeline are the prospects and targets that you would like to induce into the flow. Along the way are the repeat business deals with current clients and short-term proposals that are accepted (these are wonderful but rare, like the inside straight).

Long-term contracts are those due to conclude in about 12 months. This means that they are assignments requiring a long time period for completion, or they are projects which you won't begin until several months hence, owing to the client's schedule or yours. In either case, you know you'll be working and receiving income "out there" which, for my purposes, is about 12 months. As the due dates approach, these become short-term projects, with implementation responsibilities about six months or so away. Finally, they become "imminent," meaning you'll be starting the implementation at any time.

Now, here is the snag that trips up most consultants who try to forecast their business and, consequently, their cashflow. *Everything in my pipeline is signed and sealed.* In almost all other cases, however, consultants use prospects and potential business as the flow in their pipeline. This "potential pipeline" creates several instant hazards:

1. The pipeline will not be a predictor of guaranteed business. It is a predictor of *potential* business. In actuality, if none of the potential materializes, the pipeline could be totally empty at any given moment.

2. If the potential is realized, it is often imminent business. That is, the consultant calculates that a potential deal will require 12 months to close. If accurate, when it does close it's now due to be delivered. What of the shorter-term business, repeat business, and other immi-

nent business? How does one coordinate all this? Is it really feast or famine?

3. Marketing activity should be aimed at the other end of the pipeline, to create contracts within the pipeline. If the pipeline is filled with potential business, where is the marketing effort to be focused? Wouldn't you have to market *within* the pipeline as well, since this business is pending and could go either way?

4. There is a false sense of security in having a great deal of potential business lined up. One tends to ease up on marketing at the source of the pipeline to concentrate on the "sure things" within it. If these things fall through, there is little entering the system.

The area I designate for prospects considering proposals is *outside* the entrance to the pipeline. I focus my marketing efforts there (mailings, speeches, articles, and books) and place referrals there as well. Only after an agreement is signed do they enter my system. In this manner, any adverse effects—prospects rejecting a proposal, the competition beating me out for an assignment, a verbal approval being overturned, etc.—are outside my pipeline. Thus, I can look about a year out (often with my bankers at my shoulder) to see a realistic view of cashflow and profit.[1] And I know that I must continually corral business into those pipeline openings. This is much easier to do at the long-term end than the "imminent" end, since I have time to work on the prospect and don't feel a desperation in trying to close the business. When the pipeline is dry, the pressure builds to create business that is virtually ready to be delivered, and this is usually poor business at poor fees.

These are the red flags that will indicate that you may be looking at some business economic problems in terms of flow and volume:

1. The pipeline is filled with potential, not signed business.

2. The business in the pipeline is not evenly distributed, but is clumped together at one period.

3. You have no idea who the prospects and targets are that constitute potential entries into the pipeline.

4. Every organization in or around the pipeline is an existing client: there are no new prospects represented.

---

[1]Even if clients avail themselves of discounts for payment on signing, I still allocate the revenue stream according to the implementation dates. In this way, I know that a $125,000 project is to be implemented in three months, regardless of whether the client has already paid the invoice.

5. Repeat business from current clients is absent from the pipeline.

6. No referrals appear or make it into the pipeline.

7. All business enters the pipeline at the same entrance, for example, two weeks out or three months from now.

If these or similar conditions occur, you can bet that your cashflow and stability will suffer in the months ahead. While it's always possible to deal with those conditions on a contingency basis—borrow money, go after short-term business, scramble for subcontracting work—it's far better to prevent those desperation measures by examining your flow for the red-flag conditions and taking appropriate preventive measures.

This is a paper exercise, which can be done on a plane or while waiting for an appointment. There's really no excuse to be surprised by assignments drying up. Yet so many of us, caught in the euphoria of current business and its delivery, blandly assume that there's more where this came from. The only real measure of whether there *is* more is in scrutinizing the pipeline for real business and lining up enough prospects to "clog" the entrances to the pipe. I don't want to see the light at the end of this tunnel. I want so many prospects lined up that all I see are bodies clambering to get in.

Avoiding Down Times:
The Five "Up-Time" Rules

I once watched a speaker pitch his cassette series, which I'll call "How to Think Positively and Grow Rich." He had explained all of its benefits, cited the cost as an unbelievably low $495, and told the audience they could buy the series right then and there and receive a 10 percent discount off the unbelievably low price. He wound up his spiel by asking, "Can anyone cite a reason *not* to buy this invaluable set of tapes?"

After handling some routine questions, the speaker acknowledged a man with hand raised in the middle of the audience. "I think your approaches are wonderful," said the man, "but I have a perfect reason not to buy. I can't afford it." There was an unmistakable murmur from the crowd, which was cut off by the speaker with what, to me, was an extraordinary retort.

"That's exactly why you should buy it!" he yelled. The crowd—and I—were confused.

"Tell me," continued the speaker, "how old are you, sir?"

"Thirty-one."

"Did you graduate from high school?"

"Yes."

"Did you graduate from college?"

"I have an associate's degree from a junior college."

"Have you been continuously employed since graduation?"

"Yes. I've worked for three firms."

"What's your current position?"

"I'm a payroll supervisor for the local hospital."

"So," summarized the speaker, moving toward the man, "you have an associate's degree, have never been unemployed, and at the age of 31, after over a decade of continuous employment, *you can't even afford to purchase a set of tapes that you think are wonderful! That's why you need them—because you haven't been thinking positively and you certainly haven't grown rich!*"

After the meeting, the crowd surged around the product booth, frantically waving money and credit cards. I had never seen anything like it. It was, quite simply, brilliant.

If you believe that times are bad for you, they will be, because your actions will be predicated on dealing with bad times. If you believe that all times can be good for you, they will be, because your actions will be consistently supporting your growth, despite conditions around you.

Rule 1: Use Down Times As a Spur to Taking Action

Often, the very objections that people raise also hold the reasoning to convince them that they should agree. In down times, consultants often hunker down and assume the worst. Sometimes they actually put themselves out of business (see the advice about not selling the conference table that concludes this chapter). But there are some clear actions that enable you not merely to avoid down times, but to continue your growth despite them.

We've established that the conceptual sale is the key to selling new business. This is more important than ever in down times.

If a client says, "I couldn't agree more that we ought to undertake this project, but we just can't afford to," you are in the position of the speaker above to reply, "That's *exactly* why you have to begin now. The longer you wait, the more you'll fall behind and the more expensive it will be to catch up. The sooner you make the investment, the more money you'll save. If money is the only thing stopping you, let's work out a payment schedule that alleviates that pain as much as possible, and let's start generating the payback immediately."

If prospects persist in stating that money is the hang-up after stating that they need what you're suggesting, you haven't really made the conceptual sale. Once the conceptual sale is made, the prospect will see the cost in terms of an investment on a future return, and the mechanics of a payment schedule are easily worked out.

Rule 2: Diversify Geographically

During the early 1990s, while most of the country experienced some degree of recession, New England had actually been in a depression. Many of my colleagues in the consulting and speaking professions had been severely affected, often to the point of pursuing traditional jobs in sales or administration, hoping to go back to consulting when things improved. (Of course, this means they aren't really consultants, but people whose hobby is consulting. Can you picture an attorney going into insurance sales because business is poor?)

I have continued to grow during these tough times. Revenues increased by 45 percent from 1989 to 1990 alone. You see, I have only five clients in all of New England. The rest of my business is all over the country, with some in other countries.[2] You cannot allow your business to be overly concentrated geographically, not just because of regional economic conditions,[3] but also because a strong regional competitor can sometimes overwhelm you.

Rule 3: Don't Let Yourself Be Vulnerable to the Same Economic Conditions Threatening Your Clients

The economy is like a hydraulic system. Even in the worst of times, *someone* is doing well.

I've found that some industries do well, regardless of the economy, as long as they're well managed. The pharmaceutical industry is one example. There are others that do well in bad times—self-help, for exam-

---

[2]See Chapter 14 for obtaining international clients.

[3]Periodically, states like Florida have attempted to pass a sales tax on service firms, which would make consulting services more expensive for the client (or decrease the consultant's margin, if absorbed). If you are an executive search firm operating solely within Florida, this tax liability poses a significant threat to growth.

ple, because people are more prone to make repairs or build some things themselves rather than buy new. And then there are the industries that thrive when the economy rebounds, such as air travel and hotels.

If you're a content specialist, it's somewhat more difficult to diversify industrially. However, my advice to all is to diversify by industry and sector to the maximum extent possible. Try to obtain clients who do well consistently, clients who thrive on downturns and clients who thrive on upturns. The outplacement business thrives on economic downturns, executive search on economic upturns. A true consulting business thrives during both.

Rule 4: Increase Personal Productivity

Every week you have approximately 40 hours to invest in your growth. In the worst times, you won't use any of those hours to deliver client projects, deposit checks in the bank, or close business. So during these worst of weeks, what is the opportunity for you?

Figure 10-2 shows a suggested 40-hour "down-week" schedule that is consistent with pursuing multidimensional growth despite conditions around you.

The more astute among you have noticed that there are more than 40 hours represented. That's because some items might not apply to you (although if you're following my advice, they should), some of you will invest more than 40 hours, and some of you might be able to move more quickly than the time I've allocated. No matter. The point is that there is *plenty* to do even when there's no client work to be done.

Rule 5: Watch the Company You Keep

Finally, I've always tried to work solely with companies with which I'm proud to work. I don't accept assignments that require drastic cost cutting through the ranks in order to fund lucrative executive bonuses; I won't lie to or deceive client employees; I won't assist a company that is treating its customers badly or selling obviously inferior products or fraudulent services; and I won't work with executives whose orientation is bigoted or crude.

Quite simply, clients who treat their employees and customers shabbily will treat their consultants shabbily. In poor times they will refuse to pay the bill and honor commitments. They will make unreasonable demands, take credit for your contributions, and blame you for any short-

Activity	Hours per week
Call two "old" clients a day to maintain communications	5
Call two prospects a day to follow up on proposals	2.5
Send letter/package/press kit to five targets a day	5
Network by phone with colleagues, once a day	2.5
Research or write article for magazine publication	5
Research speaking possibilities in associations	2.5
Volunteer or perform pro bono work locally	3
Read professional literature for personal growth	3
Attend an association meeting or conference	3
Create/upgrade your press kit and examine others' kits	2
Plan a client conference or select advisory board members	2
Plan "in the neighborhood" mailings for future trips	1
Call subcontractors to review current or planned work	2
Spend time with or develop an alliance partner	2.5
Plan the next mass mailing to your list	2
Take your banker to lunch or pay a courtesy call	2
Follow up on résumés you've received	1
Examine and upgrade your professional listings	1

Figure 10-2. Eighteen actions to take during a down week.

comings. Companies and managers who act poorly in good times will act horribly in bad times.

My rule of thumb for evaluating the acceptability of a client is very simple: Would I purchase stock in this firm? Would I invest my own money and future in the quality of this firm's management, strategy, products, services, and employees? If I'm not certain—or certain I wouldn't—why on earth would I want them as a client?

Contrarian Consulting: Swimming against the Current

Changing times are often interpreted as "bad" times. Changes can threaten consultants because their precious matrices, formulas, and models may no longer be applicable or embraced. Is anyone out there still enamored by transactional analysis as a management tool[4] or applying Maslow's hierarchy of needs as a pragmatic method to motivate people? "Left-brain/right-brain thinking" has been debunked, thank goodness, and the current fad will also give way to its successor in good time.

Million dollar consultants welcome change because it represents *opportunity,* not threat. Change provides the possibility of demonstrating new talents, helping clients in new ways, and embarking on entirely new approaches. Change is essential for dramatic growth to be possible. And one excellent way to exploit change—indeed, to *create* change—is what I call *contrarian consulting.*

The speaker mentioned earlier who took an objection and turned it inside out by using it as a validation was being contrarian. "I can't do it" is followed by "that's why you should do it." I open many executive conferences by asking, "How many of you truly believe in training?" Every hand always shoots up. After looking around the room, I tell the audience that I don't believe in training. "You train animals," I explain, "but you must *educate* people." That comparison and immediate challenge to traditional clichés rivets attention and creates quite a stir. I am instantly different from other consultants they've worked with or considered.[5] The first article I ever wrote for a publication that eventually paid me to write a column for three years was entitled "The Myth of QC [quality control] Circles," and was written during the peak of the popularity of those employee participation programs. (My point was that management often used the program as a substitute for its own responsibility for quality and didn't follow through on participants' suggestions, making the situation actually worse than before the program's implementation. This turned out to be the rule, rather than the exception.)

My advice to clients is often to *reduce* "training" and invest more in education. Learning should be as close as possible to the application of what's learned, and seminars are notorious for sterile learning, which is quickly forgotten because it can't be readily applied. Now, how many consultants do you think have been telling their clients and prospects that there's too much training going on? Many organizations believe that quality is what they think it is, which usually means "zero defects." I tell them that what they think is irrelevant. It's the customer who will determine what quality is, and what I can help the organization learn and apply is just what criteria the customers are using! Quality, I pa-

---

[4]It's still used among eclectic therapeutic approaches, as it should be and was always meant to be.

[5]This is consistent with the strategy outlined in Chapter 4 of distinct service and breakthrough relationships. Contrarian positions are wonderful tools to implement that strategy.

tiently explain, is not the *absence* of something in management's eyes, i.e., "defects," but the *presence* of something in the consumer's eyes, i.e., "value." If you don't think that gets attention, then you just haven't tried to stray from the beaten track. Most quality approaches I've seen — with six- and seven-figure investments — are all backwards, in that they focus inward and not outward.

> *A unique approach is required if a small consulting firm is to win the same type of major, lucrative contracts won by larger firms. You don't become unique by trying to do what the larger firms already do. You become unique by beating a new track—a contrarian track.*

How much mileage does contrarian consulting garner? Well, how about a featured article in *The New York Times*? Here's a headline that caught my eye:[6]

Scrap Consensus, Try Diversity

The author, a consultant by the name of Allan Cox, took the position that the last thing corporations need is Johnny-One-Note thinking and that competing opinions and diverse options are what really lead to the highest-quality decisions. Does it fly in the face of current thinking about teamwork, unanimity, and conflict resolution? Yes. Does it make sense in its own right? Yes. Is it a distinct approach that will make an executive say, "Hey, this guy's onto something. Maybe we've had the wrong approach here." Absolutely.

I've found that in bad times and in times of uncertainty and change (which is most of the time these days), executives are not falling back on the tried and true. They are receptive to new approaches and are willing to swim upstream if there is someone credible to guide them. I have no intention of trying to develop a competing strategy matrix to that of the Boston Consulting Group. But I'm happy as a clam to offer clients a strategic approach that places strong emphasis on values at two differ-

[6]Allan Cox, "Scrap Consensus, Try Diversity," *The New York Times,* April 7, 1991, section 11, page 3.

ent levels in the organization, which most of them have never even thought about. I don't want to compete with Drake Beam to design outplacement programs in times of staff reductions. Instead, I gain entry and attention by explaining how to *add* superb talent, which otherwise would be out of reach, during down times. And I won't touch merger and acquisition work for firms in excellent shape seeking to expand. But I will implement a program for them to *reduce* their work force over time, since smart management should always seek to stay as lean as possible, and the best time to ensure that is from a position of strength, not out of the desperation of economic problems.

Are you getting the picture? If you take nothing else out of this book, understand that a central element in achieving wealth is to acquire the same large contracts that major consulting firms do with a small firm's smaller overhead and better economies of operation. But it's virtually impossible to do that by trying to outperform the big firms at what they do so well to have grown so large. You must seek out different paths that aren't always in the mainstream, but that you can justify and substantiate as being of tremendous value-added in improving the client's condition. This is what I call contrarian consulting. It will get you speaking engagements, it will get you published, it will get you noticed, and it will get you rich once you become good at it.

Sign on the office wall of one of my clients: "If you're not the lead dog, the scenery never changes."

I'll conclude this section by offering a few of my choices for those organizational issues that justify trying to swim against the current (see Figure 10-3). But remember, these are my observations based on today's conditions. They may all be mainstream by the time you read this!

We've now examined what to look for in terms of your personal business down times, what to do to be productive in general economic down times, and how to swim against the current to create opportunity in down times or up times. But what happens when things get really bad? What do you do when you look up and see deep sea creatures swimming in the waters *above* you? Don't panic—I'm here to tell you that we've all been there, and that you should do what you've been doing all along.

Issue	Contrarian View
Managing employee diversity	Assimilating employees
Daycare for employees' children	Aged parents (at home) day-care
Problem solving	Innovation
Succession planning	Boosting high-potential people
Merit pay for individual performance	Merit pay for team/organization performance
Handling complaints	Preempting complaints
Formulating strategy	*Implementing* strategy
Managing tasks	Managing outcomes
The employees serving customers	The employees *as* customers
Conflict resolution	Encouraging conflict

Figure 10-3. A contrarian view of contemporary business issues. Too many consultants simply try to follow the pack.

The Myth of Cutting Expenses (Don't Sell the Conference Table)

One of my friends runs an international training firm. When he gathers together his partners from around the world he often hears lamentations of woe from areas where the economy has gone sour or a large client has defected. Invariably, his partners would recommend cutting expenses, cutting staff, and adopting a lower profile. After the cutback alternatives are exhausted, my friend gives what I call his "last dollar speech."

"If you had only a dollar left," he asks, "would you try to stretch it out for as long as possible to feed your family increasingly meager meals each day, or would you invest the whole amount in a marketing plan that might create enough business to feed your family in proper style for a year or more?" I'm always impressed by his logic whenever my prospects are dimmer than I'd prefer—after all, the dollar will eventually be gone, but the marketing effort can perpetuate itself.

There is a centrifugal force in our profession which pulls people toward conservatism when times seem bad. Risk is one thing when there's a hundred grand in the bank and clients knocking at the door, but it's quite another thing when your banker is a stranger and your door is silent. Yet the last thing to do in bad times is to pull in your horns and try to eke out an existence by reducing expenses "until things get better." In most cases, things don't get better unless you do something to make them get better, and you don't make things happen by doing less. You must do more.

Can you picture a professional sports team that has finished a mediocre season of .500 ball announcing at a press conference: "In view of our uninspired past season, we've decided to cut back on the coaching, staff, reduce practice time, eliminate recruiting efforts, and halve the size of the conditioning area. We think that will substantially improve our position for next year." The press would have a field day, season ticket holders would forsake the team, and the general public would lose interest after a good laugh. Now, substitute publicity for press, clients for season ticket holders, and prospects for the general public, and you'll begin to see what even tacit plans to cut back your operation will create: loss of repute and relationships.

In the next chapter we'll discuss credit lines and banking relationships in some detail. The point for now is, do not panic when things look tough. If you reduce your expenses by eliminating client mailings, attending fewer meetings and networking events, putting in an answering machine to replace office staff, and the like, you are panicking. No matter how much you save, the "dollar" will eventually run out.

How do tough times become good ones? For starters, remember that the times are tough for others as well, and *they* are probably cutting back. That means that the same, continuing investment on your part for marketing and publicity *will carry even a better return,* since there is less perceived competition. Also, clients are impressed by consultants (and any outside professional or vendor) who act consistently in good times and bad and whose service and quality performance do not vary. Thirdly, no one knows anything of your personal successes and failures except what you choose to reveal. A cutback in your market profile and uncharacteristic behavior (i.e., refusing to extend credit, demanding expense reimbursement for trivial items, arbitrary fees) will tell clients and prospects exactly what you don't want them to know.

> *You are never alone in tough times, but you can be alone in exploiting them for opportunity. Your attitude must be: "Everyone else has it tough. How can I exploit my position?"*

One group of partners I know had periodic meetings about the hard times that had beset their firm. Two of the three continually sought increased visibility and better marketing avenues, and a generally more aggressive role in client support. The third, Carl, repeatedly argued for drastic cost reductions, which the other two sometimes acquiesced to for "consensus" reasons. Finally, when things were at their nadir, Carl once again asked for cost cutbacks. When asked what was left to cut back, he suggested selling the large maple conference table in the firm's lone meeting area.

"It's worth about 500 bucks," he explained, "and that will pay the rent next month."

"And our clients and prospects," responded one of the others, "will sit on the floor or remain standing!?"

The conference table wasn't sold, the partners stopped trying to reduce expenses, and Carl eventually became a subcontractor for them. He wasn't cut out for taking risks, and he never again earned significant reward.

It is a terrific temptation in tough times to stop spending and treat each dollar as if it were a vanishing resource that would never be seen again. There are at least seven things wrong with this philosophy:

1. You will cut back on your marketing just when it can deliver the biggest return since the competition is cutting back.

2. Clients will immediately detect any reduction in service commitments, jeopardizing the relationship that required years to build.

3. Prospects are not impressed by firms that stint in the acquisition process; they are impressed by firms that send several people to initial conferences and don't attempt to charge back expenses for exploratory meetings.

4. Your bankers are not nearly as concerned about expense control as they are about income. In fact, bankers lend money against some reasonable payoff. A marketing campaign, new product, or publicity trip can provide payoff. A reduction in expenses does not provide incentive to an investor.

5. You will effectively blunt your multidimensional growth. Networking, memberships, pro bono work, and related activities all take a hard hit when expenses are reduced.

6. You will not be attractive to recruits, subcontractors, or alliance partners. No one is comfortable with someone attempting to work on a shoestring, someone who pays their bills late or doesn't invest the proper resources to get a job done in a quality manner. These sources of income and assistance to your firm will evaporate.

7. You will become totally reactive because your ability to invest in proactive measures will disappear. Consequently, you will be too

late, too often, with too little. It is virtually impossible to practice contrarian consulting, for example, in a low-profile, reactive mode.

We talked in Chapter 3 about the "success trap." Here, we're talking about the "failure trap." You can only fail in this business if you allow yourself to fail, and one of the surest ways to do that is by adopting a failure mentality when times are tough. Cutbacks and cost reductions are symptoms of failure and self-defeat. Consistent relationships and activities, during all times, are signs of a success mentality. You establish the image that you convey to the client, and these images are notoriously transparent.

I've never met a consultant who wasn't doing "fabulous" business. Every one I meet in the business tells me how great he or she is doing. And that's funny, because I meet a great many consultants who double-bill clients for expenses,[7] are dressed poorly, don't have any current literature, never attend industry or trade conferences, and haven't tried anything new or adventurous in years. They are as obvious as a ham sandwich, and if they think their clients and prospects can't see what the rest of us can, they are about as intelligent as a ham sandwich.

Bad times can be especially good times if you allow them to be, if you step away from the pack and the panicky responses. What would you advise a client in a highly competitive industry when economic conditions seem bleak? If you would advise that client to do anything *other* than to exploit the opportunities that others are unprepared or unwilling to address, not only are you lacking the stomach for this business, but you're lacking the mind for it, as well.

---

[7]This is a practice of visiting two or more clients during a single trip, but billing each one for the total expense rather than a pro rata share. Not only is it unethical, it is stupid.

PART 3

Success: Achieving Self-Realization

11
Managing Capital

Borrow $1000 and They Own You, but Borrow $1 Million and...

Establishing Credit Lines

Once you've created what the accountants like to refer to as a "going concern," it's time to start acting like one. Treat your bankers as you would your clients – as partners in a relationship business.

The easiest and most practical credit source to tap for your growing firm is home equity. However, the credit lines you arrange should be business credit lines, in the name of your business.[1] I'm very partial to this form of credit because:

1. Most banks will allow for interest payments only, meaning you repay principal at your leisure. This is a considerable cashflow benefit during lean times.

2. The money is immediately accessible, either in the form of checks drawn against the credit line or a phone call to transfer funds into the

[1]If you need a personal credit line, too, that's fine. You can split the equity the bank allows you in your home between the two. For example, if the bank's appraisal provides for $200,000 in credit, you can allocate $150,00 for personal purposes and $50,000 for business purposes, or vice-versa. However, don't regard them as interchangeable, because business credit used for personal reasons must be allocated as some form of compensation or loan, both of which will increase your tax liability.

business account. This provides the flexibility to meet unanticipated, short-term needs (for example, paying a subcontractor to help with an unexpected project even though the client won't pay you for at least 30 days).

3. As you borrow against and repay this line, your credit standing continually improves. Banks despise people who don't pay their debts, but they aren't enamored of people who never borrow, either. Their favorite people are *customers*—people who borrow money and faithfully pay it back with interest. This relationship has been in place for only about 2000 years.

4. It gives you peace of mind, and that is invaluable. If you are worried about how to pay the bills each day, you are spending that much less time developing the business. All professional firms have credit with banks. One absolute sign of your growth and professionalism is one or more bankers whom you can call at any time.

5. You are not surrendering any aspect of ownership or control of your business by borrowing and repaying in this manner. Assuming that you use the credit only as required and responsibly, and your overall personal money management practices are sound (that is, you don't buy a new Mercedes after every sale), you will remain in complete control of your destiny.

An important precursor to the following system is to build credit references by acquiring the standard travel cards such as rental car firms and airlines offer, as well as telephone and commercial credit cards *billed to your business.* Even gasoline or store credit is useful. Also develop local credit accounts with the stationery stores, printers, office suppliers, and other vendors with whom you do regular business. These will all help with the bank. Use the credit—even if you don't need it—and pay it off promptly to establish a payment record.

I'm going to suggest a process to establish or increase your credit resources using home and/or business asset equity. This should work for the professional who has no current credit lines with a bank and will also (and, perhaps, even more dramatically) increase credit opportunities for those with modest arrangements already in place. (All of the following assumes that the advice in the preceding two sections of the book has been taken to heart. That is, you are growing from a lone wolf to a thundering herd. If you haven't the confidence to use home equity to fund your business, then you're in the wrong business.)

Step 1: Get Your Business Finances into Shape

You should arrange to have a monthly balance sheet and ledger. There are excellent computer programs that will turn out professional documents if you choose to do this yourself. I choose to use a bookkeeper on a monthly basis because:

- She proactively suggests improvements in my reporting.
- She is another source to catch errors and reconcile problems.
- I can use her as an independent reference if needed.
- She is cost-effective, since less than 30 minutes per month of my time is required.

Shop around for bookkeepers, asking clients and colleagues for references. You want one who uses a computer (otherwise chances of error are increased and you're paying an hourly rate for someone posting entries by hand) and one who will come to your office as needed. In my experience, you can acquire excellent help for as little as $18 an hour (though many charge $50 and over), and your affairs can probably be handled in 5 to 15 hours a month, depending on the number of employees and complexity of transactions.

Obtain a payroll service, such as Paychex, which will provide you with salary checks and tax notices and documentation. Even if you are the only one on the payroll, the ease and accuracy of the system make it a must. You'll be issued checks on your existing business bank account, be notified of tax bills due and amounts withheld, and have an excellent tie-in to your bookkeeper. These services are available around the country and can cost as little as $26 per month, which is more than paid for by your freed-up time. The services call you weekly or biweekly for payroll amounts and usually provide next-day check delivery, drawing on your existing accounts.

Finally, find yourself an excellent financial adviser. By "adviser" I mean someone who will sell you nothing other than his or her expertise (sound familiar?). Ideally, the adviser should have an array of diverse professional clients so that your circumstances are not pigeon-holed into a "model" financial approach.[2] The adviser should *not* be a lone wolf; he or she should be part of a firm and, preferably, should be one of the principals. *In this manner, the adviser is in an empathetic position*

---

[2]Consultants' businesses aren't readily understood by someone specializing in medical practices or small law firms, for example. You need someone who understands the entrepreneurial nature of your business.

to your own! Your adviser should handle your firm's business taxes and affairs, *and* your personal business taxes and affairs, because they are so intertwined in the ownership of a personal services company. Ideally, in addition to an empathetic understanding of your business and your strategy, your adviser should have these attributes:

- Strong ties with local banks to assist in obtaining credit lines
- Strong ties with local business to assist in getting leads and publicity
- Sufficient staff so that your questions are immediately answered
- Computerized tax-reporting documents and planning guides
- Contemporary, in-depth knowledge of small business tax regulations

> *In selecting a financial adviser, professional credentials are a secondary requirement. The primary requirement is the chemistry. Does the adviser appreciate your business and its intent and empathize with your growth plans and challenges?*

If you are aggressive about taxes, find an adviser who is similarly disposed. If you are conservative, find a soul mate. Expect to pay anywhere from $3000 to $10,000 a year for first-rate help, depending on your firm's size and your personal requirements.

The combination of a professional financial adviser, bookkeeper and payroll service will create a financial picture of your company that is comprehensive and impressive. Figure 11-1 shows how they relate to each other and to your business.

Step 2: Sweat the Financial Details Yourself

Once the system is in place, you must have quality data for it to polish. Consequently, keep careful records of receivables, contracts, prospects, and all other items that bear on your fiscal health.[3] These should be

---

[3]The pipeline approach of Chapter 10 can be a key input.

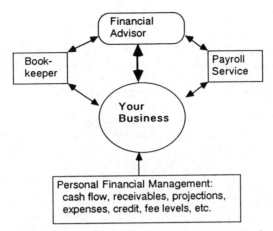

Figure 11-1. A financial management system: the financial professionalism of a going concern.

computer-prepared and updated weekly, as required. The objective is to demonstrate that you have your business finances well-managed and under control. *Bankers don't like to do remedial work. They like to work with people who are already in excellent condition.*

Use these documents to construct a rolling, one-year forecast. The forecast includes booked business, advance payments, scheduled payments, proposals submitted, targets of opportunity, and probabilities of success with each of them. These aren't matters to delegate to the bookkeeper or adviser because they are qualitative assessments that rely upon your knowledge of your client base and judgment about your prospects.

If your banker can see the financial documentation prepared by your adviser for the preceding year (or more, if available), he or she will be much more amenable to giving credence to your projections for the next year. Without that professional backup, however, and a reasonable growth predicated upon it, it's hard to convince anyone that forecasts are anything more than aspirations.

Finally, construct a personal financial statement that shows your current assets, liabilities, and net worth *including* the worth of your business and its prospects. If done well, this can be the most powerful document in convincing the bank to provide credit. Banks love to see two things side by side: ability to pay, meaning strong cashflow and reasonable debts; and appropriate net worth, meaning sustenance in case cashflow suffers temporary interruptions.

Step 3: Court the Banker
As a Partner

Working with your adviser, references from colleagues, and knowledge of your business community, you should pursue those banks that

- Offer credit lines based on home and business equity
- Provide personalized services for key customers
- Have established similar relationships with professionals
- Are sound, stable, and convenient[4]

In a larger community, this is fairly easy. For example, in Providence, with a population of 400,000, I found three excellent candidates. In smaller communities, you may have to go further afield and sacrifice the convenience aspect.

Approach the right person. This is usually a full vice president (everyone else in a bank is an assistant vice president, a title apparently given out in lieu of raises) in a department such as "personal banking," "professional lending," or the like. An introduction from your adviser shortcuts the process. If you don't have that luxury, find the specific name, write a letter explaining that you'd like to meet to discuss your business and a possible banking relationship, and follow with a phone call for the appointment.

Your attitude should be that of a careful *buyer*. The bank will be lucky to have you, so you want to make sure you choose the right bank. Provide the documentation from your adviser and your own rolling projections and financial statement. Make it clear that you intend to move *at least* your business accounts to the bank you select, and probably a great deal of your personal business, as well.[5] Share your business strategy in detail, preferably in writing. Show the banker the articles you've published, the clients with whom you work, and examples of your projects. Provide specific client references and a press kit, just as you would for a prospect. And bring the last several years' tax returns for yourself and your business.[6] Illustrate the

---

[4]If, for any reason, you are not familiar with the stability of local banks, use a bank rating service for an in-depth analysis of their strength. The cost is modest—less than $100 in most cases—and in an era of closed banks and frozen funds you will sleep much better at night.

[5]Minor digression: You don't want all of your business at one bank for pragmatic economic reasons. Maintain a small, second business account elsewhere, and divide your personal accounts as well. Your financial adviser should provide an intelligent diversification of funds for you locally.

[6]My experience is that you are in a stronger position if you have formed a regular corporation, as discussed in Chapter 3.

growth you've achieved, and the growth you've projected for the next few years, backed up by the figures and projections.

Then settle back and ask what the bank can do for you. Don't be anxious. Explain that you're exploring several alternatives. Ask about key services, such as overdraft protection, cashing foreign checks if and when you do business internationally, wiring funds, notarizing documents, and so on. You are not looking for a loan. *You are seeking a relationship that will support your growth.* Let the banker sell you.

You should work at establishing this relationship as hard as you would with any client. After you establish it, keep your banker on the mailing list you use for promotion. Have lunch together once every other month. Provide yearly tax returns and financial statements, as well as updates on your rolling projections, without being asked.

Depending on the size of your business and the nature of your collateral, try to begin with a minimum of $50,000 dedicated to your business credit line. Always try for the upper limit. Remember, you don't have to use it, but it's difficult to increase it under desperate circumstances. Every year, when you submit updated financials to your banker, explore the possibility of raising the limit.

When you are trying to borrow $1000 at a time, bankers will regard you as a minor bureaucratic fact of life and demand that you jump through hoops. But when you have the capability of borrowing hundreds of thousands of the bank's money, representing a sizable risk and a sizable piece of business, you and the bankers are in it together. Ironically, the more you borrow, the more you're in control.

The first thing I did when I received a $100,000 credit line was to borrow $25,000 against it for a month and pay it back along with the interest charge. I wanted my company and my banker to get used to the process.

The Rules of Incoming Cashflow

The rules of incoming cashflow are as follows:

- Rule 1: Cash must flow *in* at a rate in excess of cash flowing *out,* and that excess must represent sufficient funds to cover your total personal and professional needs.

- Rule 2: If you adhere scrupulously to rule 1, there are no other rules that mean a thing.

Are there any questions? Well, there must be, because small businesses fail at an alarming rate, and consulting businesses are no different.

The most direct way to manage the "flow-in" portion of our equation is to meticulously monitor receivables. A receivable is, quite simply, a payment due from a client that has been billed but not yet paid. If it is never paid, it becomes a bad debt and disappears from your revenue column. In nine years and millions of dollars of business, dealing with the largest firms on the planet in long-term consulting relationships, and dealing with tiny businesses that purchase my books and cassettes, *I've never had one unpaid bill of any type or any amount.* None. Not one. *Niente.*[7]

Collecting Receivables

Here is the time range for collecting receivables, in order of priority:

Prior to work commencing

  In full on commencement

    Partial on commencement, balance in progress

      In progress

        In progress and at conclusion

          At conclusion only

            Delayed after conclusion

              Contingent upon certain results

                Never

Prior to Work Commencing

We've discussed in earlier chapters the benefits of offering a discounted fee for early payment in full. If you are signing a contract that requires about nine months of elapsed time for implementation at $100,000, for example, a 10 percent discount nets you $90,000, 30 days prior to commencement. The compounded interest earned on that money over a year at a 5 percent rate of return would be about $5000, not to mention the far greater flexibility in your cash management and less administrative work in billing and follow-up.[8] Finally, *if the money is in your bank account, no amount of client reorganization, buyer departure, or eco-*

---

[7]My greatest challenge was a $50 bill for abstracts sent to a department in Rutgers University. After six months, I wrote directly to the president and got my money. The purchasing department hadn't appreciated that I am an alumnus and still had some connections.

[8]Even if the full amount isn't banked for the entire term, its presence prevents you from having to use other funds — or, worse, credit lines — that would cost you interest income or interest payments.

nomic downturn can threaten your payments. This is simply a wise move every time.

In Full on Commencement

This is a highly desirable arrangement, which may be worth a 5 percent discount in your fee. You are losing a month's interest based on the formula above, and if the check isn't ready you will probably have to begin implementation anyway, since your time and resources are committed. (When paid prior to commencing, you have at least 30 days to communicate with the client that the fee has not been received per agreement, and the discount may be withdrawn.) There are some clients that pay in this manner without a discount, because it's easier for their financial administration, because of excess budget remaining at year-end or canceled projects that have created a budget glut. You don't know unless you ask. I've often been requested to accept partial or full payments early as a favor to the client. I always manage to comply.

> *At fiscal year-end, many organizations have systems that force units to spend unallocated budgets or face a reduction in the following year's budget. In these cases you can be paid well in advance without any discount because you are actually doing your buyer a favor. Always be cognizant of your client's fiscal year and remaining budget.*

Partial on Commencement, Balance in Progress

This is by far the most common form of payment option. You should request at least 50 percent on commencement, since your expenses will be borne by your cashflow (you won't be billing expenses until the end of each month, and the client will likely take at least an additional 30 days to pay them). I favor billing the remainder in two portions of 25 percent each at 30- and 60-day or 45- and 90-day intervals. You want to avoid payment on completion whenever possible, since too many events outside your control can interfere with "completion." (I once had an entire operation burn to the ground.) Set *calendar dates,* not *activity dates,* to determine the payment schedule. Explain to the client that you have to manage cashflow just as the client does, that unanticipated events can occur, and that you're sure the client doesn't want to establish an incentive to finish rapidly rather than thoroughly.

In Progress

We now enter the portion of the range that represents danger in cashflow management. If you collect your fees only in the course of the project's progress, then try to collect a healthy portion as soon as possible. Also, don't establish relative dates, such as "in thirty days." Always establish absolute dates: "due on or before July 9." Otherwise, someone in accounts payable will inevitably claim it was due 30 days from some point two months later than you had meant. If you are forced to collect in progress, try to avoid any portion of that on completion, for the reasons stated above. Keep the number of payments to a minimum (five of $20,000 is far better than ten of $10,000) and always send your statements 30 days *in advance* of the due date.

In Progress and at Conclusion

A double whammy—the last payment is subject to the problems of determining "completion." The danger with "in progress" and "in progress and at conclusion" is that too many variables can change within the client company that can jeopardize your outstanding payments. Try to establish calendar dates if you're stuck with this option.

At Conclusion Only

Never, ever accept such a contract for consulting work. Even if you trust the client implicitly, it is unprofessional and antithetical to the collaborative, relationship-oriented business we've espoused. These tend to actually become contingency contracts (see below), which have no place in intelligent cashflow management. The only exception for this option is when you are delivering a speech, workshop or seminar, or some similar short-duration service. In those cases you may well bill after the fact, including your expenses in one statement with your fee. But this is not consulting work, *and I try to get paid in advance even for these brief assignments.*[9] (The briefer the assignment, the easier it is for the client

---

[9]Even for 45-minute speaking assignments, I demand a 50 percent nonrefundable deposit to hold the date and offer 10 percent off the fee if paid in full at time of booking. The entire fee is payable if the speech is canceled within 30 days of the scheduled date. Generally, the balance is due on the presentation date.

to cancel it owing to other priorities, which means you've sacrificed several days of your time in preparation and allocation for delivery.) As a rule of thumb, if the assignment is over $5000 it's worth arranging a favorable payment schedule.

Delayed after Conclusion

This implies either that the client wants to see "how things are working" or has serious cashflow problems of his or her own. Don't accept this for *any* kind of work. At best it is a contingency agreement.

Contingent upon Certain Results

Contingency fees have become more popular of late. The proponents claim it's simply payment for performance. I believe that it's the result of desperation. Essentially, a contingency fee means that you get paid if certain mutually agreed upon measures are met. This can be something as objective and measurable as a written performance evaluation system, or as subjective and nebulous as a reduction in controllable turnover. Although there are those who claim contingency fees are higher than typical fees because they enable the consultant to have a piece of the action, I think they are inevitably lower and harder to collect and seriously undermine cashflow. *The acceptance of a contingency fee really means that the consultant has never made the conceptual sale, and has never demonstrated how the client's condition can be improved.* The client is certainly willing to take a "flyer" that might not cost anything, however, and the consultant badly wants the work. Hence, you have not a collaboration but a potential confrontation. Not only must you justify that the results have been achieved, but you must convince the client that you alone were responsible ("Come on, it would have happened anyway!"). Whenever I see lawyers advertising about taking on personal accident claims with no payment "unless they win," I picture mercenary soldiers. That's not the business I'm in.

Never

If you are not getting paid, and your billing arrangements call for advance payment or in progress payments, you certainly have the leverage to stop the project and resolve the situation. You're better off losing the assignment than losing the assignment *and your time and contributions*. However, when you're not scheduled to be paid until late in the game or after it's over, you may find that you're at risk to lose everything. (If your payment is 90 days late, assume that you're not going to get paid at

all. That's not a harsh assessment. You are being treated unprofessionally.)
Since you have nothing further to lose, fire your heavy guns:

- Approach the CEO of the entire organization directly, by phone and
  certified mail. Request an immediate response and let the CEO know
  that you intend to seek legal recourse and publicize the difficulty.
- If the contract is large enough to warrant it, have your attorney at
  least "fire a shot across the bow" to the client's legal department and
  again to the CEO.
- If the contract warrants it, sue. In my opinion, if you can sue in an
  amount in excess of the unpaid bill, do so. If the client wishes to settle
  merely for the actual amount due, accept *but insist that the client pay
  for legal fees*.

I have never been in any litigation with clients at all. This is mainly due
to the quality of my clients and the quality of my work. But in a couple
of instances, at least a partial reason for this was my clear, written billing
procedures and payment schedules.

If you arrange intelligent billing options and work with the client in a
partnership orientation, you can avoid the major pitfalls that endanger
cashflow. The way you establish the relationship will determine how
much money you collect and how early. Most consultants are their own
worst enemy. The only worse thing than having no business is having
business that doesn't pay the bills.

Remember, you don't develop the business by reducing expenses,
you develop it by maximizing income. The "velocity" or speed at
which you receive income is as important as the volume that you generate. Never tolerate a client who owes you money beyond the
agreed-upon terms, and always make those terms as favorable for
you as possible. You are a consultant, not a banker.

Ten Expense-Management Tactics

While you don't develop your business through Scrooge-like attention
to expenses, you can increase your ability to invest in growth strategies
by avoiding unnecessary drains on capital. The best time to examine expense controls is in *good* times, from a position of strength, and not in
bad times from a position of desperation. Remember, selling the conference table is never an appropriate decision.

I've assembled 10 techniques to help build expense management into
a source of growth funds for your business strategies. Some might seem

old hat and others unreachable, but as you grow all will apply at one time or another.

1. Maximize the Number of Bills You Pay on Credit Cards or Business Accounts

This enables you to refuse payment if goods or services were not delivered as promised or if charged items could not be used. The credit card laws of this country are excellent: you have a legal right not to pay American Express or Visa if the business which accepted your charge card did not provide their product or service to your satisfaction.

How dramatic can this be? Well, anyone who charged tickets on Eastern Airlines and was unable to use them when the company went under *did not have to pay for them if they were charged on a credit card*. But those who paid cash, or paid their travel agents, or used some other forms of payment were stuck. I often return airline tickets already billed to my credit card accounts because my plans change abruptly and it's easier to buy entirely new tickets. When the charge for the unused tickets appears on my bill, I simply ignore it (and inform the credit card company of the return). But if I had paid for them, I'd have to file for and await a return of the funds, which can take more than 90 days.

Don't let anyone talk you into the "wisdom" of paying cash, unless you intend to sell consulting services from a pushcart in the street. Establish local accounts with printers, office supply stores, travel agents, and anyone else with whom you regularly do business, and keep at least three major credit cards.[10] At year-end, many provide a complete summary of the year's expenses, which can be invaluable at tax time.

2. Pay All Local Vendors Promptly

If you find yourself in a cash squeeze, don't put off the local suppliers. These are the people who can least afford disruptions in *their* cashflow and whom you will often need to provide last-minute frenzied help with a project. I'm often told that I'm a pleasure to do business with, not because of any special charm, but because I scrupulously pay bills on time. As a result, I've often been able to jump the line at the local printer to get a rush project out or get a special date from a video production house. Simply paying on time has become a sterling character asset

---

[10]Hold at least three because not all credit cards are accepted in all places, sometimes there's a computer snafu with one, and it's also good for your overall credit rating. Try to have at least two corporate cards, and insist that your employees use them for all travel-related expenses.

these days. If you must, put off Hertz or pay only a portion of the MasterCard bill, but always pay quickly close to home. (And it doesn't hurt to send a present at the holidays, either.) That's why you have the bank credit lines, right?

3. Make an Expense Budget and Compare Your Actual Expenditures Quarterly

Use major categories such as travel, office supplies, insurance, telephone, memberships, etc. After two or three quarters you should be able to arrive at your average expenses in these areas. Subsequently, comparing your actual outgo can provide you with critical expense-management information. For example, you may well find that your renewal and membership category is inordinately high and realize that you've joined five airline clubs (which run about $150 apiece nowadays). How many have you used in the last six months? If you never fly two of the airlines, drop them. Similarly, you might find overlapping insurance coverage, travel expenses you neglected to bill for reimbursement, or fax charges that aren't yours.

If you don't have a budget, you're at a disadvantage when trying to compare the actual expenses against reasonable criteria. When you're growing, it's easy to overlook the "budget bloat," so make it a point to build such scrutiny into your quarterly activities. (I most frequently find errors in rental car bills, local limousine bills, and any billing that covers a period in excess of one month.) There are several excellent computer programs that allow you to track and compare expenses at minimum effort, often keyed to your checkbook.

4. Use a Travel Agent, and Make Your Travel Preferences Clear

Don't waste $500 of your personal time trying to save $25 on a hotel rate. Tell the agent how you prefer to travel (first class, first class but only with free upgrades, best coach fare nonpenalty, best coach fare no matter what, etc.) and where you prefer to stay (closest hotel to client, only in Marriotts, in the least expensive place within 5 miles, etc.). Give the agent all of your club membership numbers and sit back and run your business. The agent is being paid commissions to pamper people like you. Not only should you be able to simply give the agent a general itinerary; you should expect periodic perks that the agent is capable of providing, such as free upgrades, discounted travel opportunities, and so on. Use only one agent and expect excellent service. Keep moving until you find one with whom the chemistry is perfect. My travel agent saves me tens of thousands of dollars of my time and my money each year, and gives *me* a gift at the holidays.[11]

5. Pay Your Bills Twice a Month at Single Sittings

If you pay them more frequently — for example, as you receive them — you tend to lose track of the big picture in terms of total outgo each month. (Firms such as Hertz and Federal Express will bill you each time you use their service, so you might have several bills from each every 30 days. It's nice to know the *total* you're paying, and it's less hassle to pay twice instead of five or six times a month.) If you pay less often, you're likely to miss some due dates, especially if your travel schedule takes you away during your normal bill-paying time. Also, a single session can be onerous if a great many bills pile up.

Match up credit card receipts against the billing statement (I've found unauthorized use of a commercial credit card and telephone credit cards). Minimize your bill-paying legwork: If some firms accept direct bank transfers, you can reduce your paperwork; at least have address labels prepared for those that don't provide return mailers; the more you can arrange for expenses to appear on a single or a few major credit cards, the easier it is to write a single check instead of dozens.

6. Try to Buy Equipment (Rather Than Lease or Rent It) and Pass Up Long-Term Service Contracts

If you buy your computer, fax, copier, phones, and other major equipment, you can take certain business deductions (or depreciation, depending on amounts and your accountant) immediately and avoid long-term payments which eat into cashflow. (If you must, use your bank credit line to purchase that expensive copier that will increase your productivity, and pay it off as cashflow permits.)

Purchase service contracts or insurance only in those cases that make sense. For example, my postage scale calculates rates based on

---

[11]Always carry the pocket version of the *Official Airline Guide* (2000 Clearwater Dr., Oak Brook, IL 60521) in your briefcase for midtrip reservation changes that must be made immediately. You can subscribe to it for less than $100 per year and receive each month's airline schedules. There are also international versions available. This is one of the most effective devices for time management in a traveler's repertoire.

class of service, weight, and prevailing rates. I'm insured against rate changes in that Pitney Bowes will send me new software to reflect any changes in return for my yearly premium. Otherwise, the cost could be excessive in the case of multiple rate changes. But we don't carry a maintenance contract on the postage meter because the chances of a problem are remote in my experience, and the repair costs aren't excessive anyway.[12] What you don't want to allow to develop is a procession of monthly bills representing payoffs on a dozen pieces of office equipment.

7. Request Prepayment of Expenses As Well As Fees

With certain set arrangements (for example, you are delivering six workshops a year at the same site in exactly the same manner), you can predetermine expenses and request payment in advance. While airline fares can vary, an alert travel agent can usually protect you, and if the client pays in advance you have the luxury of advance purchases or interest gathering in the bank. Unlike fees, you can reach an agreement with the client that any project cancellation will generate a return of the prepaid expense reimbursement.

> *You have no idea what billing terms are acceptable to a client unless you ask. The answer might surprise you.*

With such "set situation" work, over half of my clients will pay the fee *and* travel expenses in advance, especially if I make my reduced fee offer contingent upon payment of full expenses in advance as well. You simply don't know what the client will accept unless you ask. (I recommend that you deposit all prepaid expenses that are not immediately expended on advance purchases into a separate, interest-bearing account that you do not otherwise access. "Success" in this technique has a pitfall, in that you can spend thousands of dollars in advance expense

[12]As a general practice, find a quality rental source for key office equipment in the event of breakdowns. The time for that search is when you *aren't* experiencing breakdowns. Your computer printer will fail, as a rule, exactly when your most critical client report is due. You'll want to be able to reach for the Rolodex and call the rental people immediately, and not waste time trying to determine if such services exist.

reimbursements months before you incur the actual debt, resulting in disproportionate outgo later on.)[13]

8. Don't Forget to Ask, "What's the Absolutely Best Rate (or Deal) You Can Give Me?"

Not only do airlines, hotels, and rental car companies have bewildering hidden deals that you can mine with a good shovel, but local vendors will often negotiate if you simply ask the question. In those cases where you don't use a travel agent, ask the reservations clerk what the absolute best rate is—*not* what you might qualify for. Then work with the clerk to determine how you can qualify for it. I've called the same airline four times, spoken to four different agents and received—you guessed it—four different rates. I "accepted" the best offer.

If you merely ask the local printer or graphics artist or computer store manager, "How much?" they will understandably give you the best rate *for them.* But if you ask, "What's the best you can do for me here?" they will tend to give you the best rate *for you.* The more you patronize the business, the better deal you should expect.

On a recent trip, I flew first class on American Airlines, stayed in a suite at a Hyatt Hotel, and drove a full-sized Hertz car, all without coupons or frequent traveler awards. The air fare and hotel cost me no more than full coach fare and full rate on a regular room. Only the car cost more than a smaller one, but it did come with a phone at no additional charge.

9. Don't Prepay Your Own Bills

Certain otherwise excellent institutions will bill you months in advance. While I admire their intent, I have no intention of helping them out.

For example, the very worthwhile American Management Association and the American Society for Training and Development will bill your renewal membership about *four months* in advance. Either stick the bills in a tickler file for the appropriate month or throw them out. Rest assured you'll receive others. Business publications will also bill far in advance to ensure "uninterrupted service." My experience is that even publications I drop keep sending me issues after the expiration date in attempts to lure me back.

---

[13]I can calculate rental cars, hotels, and incidentals in addition to air fare with significant accuracy. If I'm $100 or so worse off, it's still worth it to have received early payment. If I'm $100 or so to the better, I return it to the client with a note of explanation. This generates substantial good will.

You might want to drop a membership (such as the excess airline clubs mentioned above) or change some provisions. It's tough to do that once the check has been cashed. Pay bills on time, not before time.

10. Establish a Clear, Written, and Signed Expense Policy with Your Employees and Subcontractors

Specify what you will pay for by type (Holiday Inn or equivalent lodging), amount (daily meal charges, a maximum of $40), and policy (taxis to and from airports and clients unless rental car rates are less). Demand that expenses be turned in monthly (or more frequently) with complete receipts, and promise reimbursement within a reasonable period. (I find 10 days to be reasonable, and "when the client reimburses me" to be unreasonable.) While using your corporate credit card and travel agent is helpful, you also want to avoid inappropriate charges on those cards, so make sure there are criteria for the card's use (always for air travel, never for incidentals). One subcontractor kept calling her lover on my credit card, and when they quarreled, my phone expenses tripled.

I find that subcontractors and employees are rarely dishonest but that there can be large areas of misunderstanding. You are protecting all parties by specifying the policy on phone calls, local secretarial services, weekend travel, and so forth. My practice is to have anyone who travels on my behalf sign a brief statement of expense reimbursement policies and their agreement with them. In return, I pay promptly and always give the benefit of the doubt ("The personal calls were to my husband whom I forgot to tell about the baby-sitter being rescheduled so that....).

In managing capital, it's not what you make, it's what you keep. If you're successful in keeping most of it, you can invest in accelerating your growth to dramatic heights.

12
Accelerating Growth

Growth Does Not Always Equal Expansion

Seven Techniques for Intensifying the Firm's Profile

In 1990, the world's 39 largest consulting firms had combined revenues of about $13,945,000,000.[1] Although I believe these figures are artificially high because they probably include some financial work—which I wouldn't consider consulting—from firms such as Andersen Consulting (number 1), Ernst & Young (number 2) and a half dozen others like them in the top 10, they are as accurate a number as is available from a highly reliable source. Those same firms employed about 103,000 *professionals* (we are not including administrative and support staff).

A simple calculation produces revenues per professional within the industry leaders of $135,390! We are not talking about profit here, we are talking about *gross revenues*. I don't think we need a financial consultant to tell us that *profit* per professional would probably be somewhere between $10,000 and $30,000, depending on overhead, although I believe that some of these firms lost money that year. (And several firms from the 1989 list dropped off the 1990 list.)

---

[1]Source for this and following statistics about these firms is "The World's Largest Management Consulting Firms," *Consultants News*, Kennedy Publications, June 1991, page 4.

> *How much you make is never the issue. It's how much you keep that counts. Yes, I do tend to repeat this.*

Unless you have a personal objective to build a large firm, surround yourself with the accoutrements of size and mass, and build the equity in the company to the point where you own a valuable business (or share), there is no intrinsic personal financial benefit in linear growth. The highest revenue per professional on the list was $333,000, and that was from McKinsey, which has the most recognizable name in the business. Many firms were under $100,000 per professional. How do you adequately reward people for their talents at that level of productivity, let alone compensate for unceasing travel and long hours, once overhead and related expenses are deducted? I have always been of the view that the sole reason to work for a major consulting firm was the opportunity for partnership and equity, and if that is your personal and professional goal, then go to it.

But if your objectives are to earn a high income while helping clients to improve their condition—in other words, support your family and your aspirations while engaging in constructive and valuable work—then your chances of fulfilling that goal are immeasurably greater in running your own small firm ("small" as compared to the giants). You don't have to wait years for a portion of the ownership because you already have all of it. You are not reliant upon colleagues' productivity or management's strategic decisions, and you control absolutely how much money you keep. Ask virtually any professional—doctor, attorney, CPA, architect, musical director, writer, etc.—and they will all tell you the same thing: It's far better to earn $75,000 working for yourself than it is to earn $100,000 working for someone else. And when you begin to earn $300,000 or $500,000 or $1,500,000 working for yourself, the opportunities increase geometrically, because the discretionary income of your firm and yourself becomes so powerful.

The firms on that "top 39" list include names such as "Martin E. Segal," "Bossard Consultants," and "C&B Consulting Group." Have you ever heard of them? I haven't. Yet their gross revenues in 1990 ranged from $60 to $112 million. The general business community probably hasn't heard of you either, but all you're interested in for the moment is growing to $2 or $3 million.[2] How can you intensify the firm's profile so

---

[2] I've found that 9 times out of 10, people to whom I'm just introduced who tell me that they've heard of Summit Consulting Group, Inc., are either confusing us with someone else or under the impression that they *ought* to have heard of us.

that such revenue goals are realistic and your key prospective buyers begin to perceive you as a "million dollar business"?

Here are the major methods I've found to intensify your profile. As we see in Figure 12-1, your perceived profile will inevitably be *a diminution of what your firm actually is* unless you actively manage and intensify that image. You may call this public relations, or image building, or marketing, or exposure. I call it million dollar consulting.

1. Author or Coauthor
Scholarly Research

We've discussed in earlier chapters the merits of publishing articles. In this instance, I'm concerned more with academic work that will validate your approaches and sanction you as an authority. One of the methods I utilized was to pursue my doctorate in organizational psychology, recruit several key clients as "laboratories," and keep all of my clients abreast of my progress and ultimate degree. Excerpts from the disser-

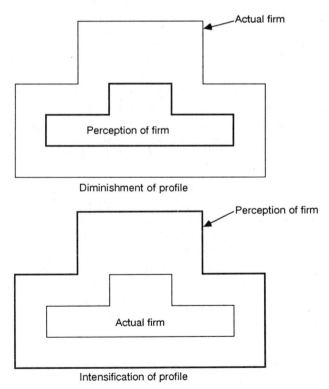

Figure 12-1. Market perceptions of the firm. Public perception of your profile will be what you determine it to be.

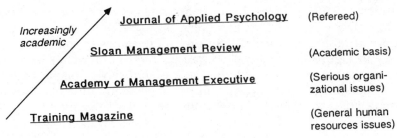

Figure 12-2. Different publications have different appeal.

tation have been published or cited in the popular press, and I make copies of it available to any client or prospect who is interested (or whom I can make interested).[3]

There are other, somewhat less grueling methods to produce work in this arena. It is usually highly attractive to university professors to collaborate with consultants on research papers. In fact, it's often a marriage made in heaven. The professor must publish anyway, and he or she has a raft of theories and beliefs honed from years of reading, research, classroom discussions, and—heaven forfend—part-time consulting. You, on the other hand, aren't well-versed in the rigors of scholarly research, but you have clients who can serve as laboratories or data bases, as well as observations and theories based on pragmatic, real-life observations and the time and motivation to collaborate with the professor. These collaborations often produce work that appears in refereed journals, which constitute one of the most serious and validated publishing outlets. (Figure 12-2 shows examples of the journalistic hierarchy.)

The purpose of such publishing, whether solo or in partnership, isn't to establish yourself as an academic. In fact, you don't want the profile to be one of lofty theory without practical application. It is, however, to establish you as a *recognized, credible source* within a community with strict standards for intellectual honesty and disciplined research. That kind of profile will attract and impress executives; it is also useful in winning over the occasional academic who happens to be sitting in the top human resources chair of a prospective client.

---

[3]We'll be discussing international expansion in Chapter 14, but I want to mention here that advanced degrees—and particularly Ph.Ds—are virtually *de rigeur* to secure work in the Far East and other places.

2. Present Papers, Theories, and Findings at Conferences

This, too, is different from the public speaking we advocated earlier. Those were paid speeches before groups that constituted high-potential buyers of your services. In this case, we are speaking about professional conferences that might not have a potential buyer within 50 miles.

There are thousands of major conferences held every year on behalf of every imaginable professional group.[4] They usually pay very little or nothing for most presenters, and you'll often have to foot the travel bill as well. But the opportunity to present your firm's work on "Strategic Planning for the Commercial Banking Industry in Recessionary Times," or "Motivation of the Work Force through Nonparticipative Management" (remember contrarian consulting from Chapter 10?) will significantly enhance your profile. These proceedings generally produce papers, recordings, reprints, summaries, news accounts, and similar summaries of their output.

You will have to appeal to the organizing committees of these affairs up to a year in advance. It's a good idea to put all of them that are relevant on your general mailing list (see Chapter 6) so that they can call you when they happen to see that your work lends itself to a future theme of their conference. The work is well worth it, because it is highly credible to cite these presentations in your firm's materials and the various summaries of your material can be reproduced and distributed as part and parcel of your press package, as appropriate. Moreover, there is a centrifugal force at work that will tend to retain you within the orbit of these conferences once you have presented to strong response. You will find yourself on *their* mailing list, requesting papers and future presentations.

3. Appear on Radio Talk Shows (and Television If You Can)

"Appear" in this sense is a misleading phrase. There are public relations, media, and "image-building" firms in this land that can place you on radio talk shows with considerably more ease than you imagine. For a modest fee, which can range from as low as $200 for a local-exposure talk show to $500 for a syndicated, national show, the firm will arrange for a brief (5- to 20-minute) interview, which may also include some lis-

---

[4] I attended an awards banquet one year for exceptional service in the water treatment industry, and the top honoree of the evening, after acknowledging prolonged applause, began his acceptance speech by deadpanning, "It's true, sludge is my life."

tener call-in questions. In most cases, you provide a synopsis of the type of work you do (that is, whatever you want to promote at the time: your strategy work with large companies, your motivation work with small firms, your newest book on leadership, etc.) and a list of a dozen or so questions that the host should ask you. This serves the dual purpose of making the talk show host appear to be knowledgeable about your business and approaches and focusing the conversation on your highest-profile potential.

And now the "appearance" part. Most of these shows conduct the interview — no matter where the station and host are located — with you sitting in your office (or at the pool) over the telephone. Through the magic of modern communications, your interview and any questions and answers with listeners are completed without so much as bus ticket required. Although many of these shows may have only local appeal and/or poor demographics for your work, by choosing a good media firm, carefully selecting the shows, and being very patient, you can achieve some penetration of relevant markets.

However, the most important benefit is the ability to cite your appearance on the *Minneapolis Today* radio show specifically to discuss your work in conducting customer focus groups or your interview by WWXR in Chicago which focused on your work in increasing sales force productivity. These are highly beneficial instances to include in your literature and to politely drop into conversations with prospects.

These firms can also place you on television talk shows. The investment is still less than you'd expect — perhaps around $1000 per placement — but the key is that you must have a dramatic and unique story to tell. Don't despair. If you watch the TV talk shows during any given week, you'll find that they desperately need people with decent stories to tell, and there's no reason why yours can't be one of them.

4. Place "Nonadvertisements"

I don't advocate advertising as a useful promotional tool for a consulting firm, although I do believe in appearing as an endorser or supporter. ("Summit Consulting Group, Inc. proudly supports the efforts of Save the Bay.") However, there are occasions when a "nonadvertising" advertisement can make sense.

I look at these as informative efforts, as opposed to promotional efforts. You are, in fact, informing the reader that "this is the profile of our firm." One good instance occurs on anniversaries: "The Delpha Consulting Company wishes to thank all of its clients and friends for their continuing support on this, our tenth anniversary." A display ad of this type in magazines most relevant for your targeted demographics helps to create a perception about your profile. Such an ad is often accompanied by a client list, examples of projects completed, or fields of expertise. You can include a photo of your staff or you at work on a client site.

Another appropriate reason for an ad is to announce something. You might announce:

- That you are the recipient of a particular award or honor
- The addition of a notable professional to your firm
- An alliance you have formed with another organization
- A new toll-free number or additional office location
- Congratulations to a client for a certain achievement or honor
- An annual conference or meeting your firm is hosting
- Sponsorship for a charitable or nonprofit undertaking

These types of ads shouldn't be frequent, or they will be perceived as promotional advertisements despite their content. They are usually most effective when done once or twice a year and without pattern. You are simply being your own press agent in a low-key manner and influencing the perception of your firm.

5. Seek Out and Apply for Awards and Honors

If you actively inquire, you'll find a plethora of awards and honors in our profession, ranging from client interventions to papers published. Outside of the famous MacArthur Awards, I know of no bestowing bodies that proactively canvass the field. Every award requires an application if the candidate is to be considered.

So when you read of a call for papers in some journal, take the time to determine if your work might lend itself to such a paper. If you find a competition for "customer service quality," explore whether you might collaborate with a client to assemble an entry. After all, that is the ultimate win-win scenario.

Other practitioners of technique 4 will probably be "advertising" their winning efforts, so you need only be on the lookout for who won what under which conditions. How can you compete in the future? And winning isn't the only salutary outcome. Merely by competing, you will be able to examine your own practices, enhance your own standards, and increase your own profile in the process. You may win an "honorable mention" or a specialty award, which can be appropriately "advertised." You can publicize the mere act of *competing* for a prestigious honor.

There is no grand arbiter who examines all companies for all practices and makes bestowals and awards based upon pure empirical evidence and absolute merit. Neither the Olympics (have you ever watched the diving or skating judges?) nor the Oscars (has a comedy ever won "best movie"?) are that impartial. You must enter, compete, and keep trying. If you're diligent and your work is worthwhile, you will eventually carry home an honor or two, and your "box office" value will be enhanced.

6. Diligently Send Out Press Releases

Press coverage of your activities is worth its weight in gold, because an independent, objective source has seen fit to comment on you or your work. Keep a separate mailing list of newspaper and magazine editors (usually the business editor, but this may vary depending on your slant) and alert them whenever:

- You are appearing as a speaker in their area
- One of your clients has completed a dramatic project with your help
- You have earned an award or honor
- You have published something of note
- You have an internal publication of relevance to their publication
- You have a finding that is of relevance to their readership
- There is a significant event in your firm's history (e.g., tenth anniversary)
- You produce a new product or offer a new service
- One of your regular client mailings goes out

Once you get to know the editors and the publications, you can begin to customize the material to better pertain to their personalities and their readership. For example, some might prefer scholarly reports, while others print business surveys,[5] and some accentuate CEOs' observations. This technique requires perseverance: most such releases don't receive careful (or any) attention at most times. But eventually, because you've hit the right combination or it's a slow news day (sometimes it's better to be lucky than good) you'll hit the print, and your profile will bask in the growth.

---

[5]*The Wall Street Journal* is forever publishing items on its front page that begin, "A survey by Acme Consultants reports that..."

7. Conduct Independent Surveys

This is a simple and grossly overlooked method to enhance repute. All you have to do is decide on an issue about which clients would appreciate some information, arrange for a suitable survey to obtain it, and disseminate it.

Let's hypothesize that your clients and prospects are concerned about turnover among newly hired college graduates, believing that there is a decline in company loyalty among this group and that they must take extraordinary measures to retain these hires. You can send out a mail survey to your client base (and, if it's not big enough, to similar organizations chosen at random) asking questions about their experience with new hires, their efforts or lack of efforts to retain them, comparisons with turnover among longer-tenured employees, and so on. This is not a scientific survey but an anecdotal one (unless you choose to use scientific rigor), and the results can be expressed as such.

In any case, you will be seen as a "leading edge" factor in your field. Organizations will usually cooperate if you offer to share results with them in return for their participation, and if you keep the survey simple, offering return mailers and professional documents. Many publications are eager to print such results, and most organizations are happy to review them, since they lend perspective to current approaches. You are the perfect intermediary to provide cross-organizational information of this type.

Surveys may cost you a few hundred dollars to create and interpret, but you are under no deadlines and the work can be accommodated as time permits. This technique is superb for establishing repute and a profile that may be far greater than your actual previous work in the area.

Intensifying Your Personal Profile

Multidimensional growth is a key component of financial success, which in turn supports the life goals that a career in consulting can sustain.[6] Since we've reached a point in the book that deals with exploiting success and capitalizing on such growth, let's spend some time examining "passive" sources of income. I call them "alternative" sources, since they are not a direct result of consulting engagements. For example, we've

---

[6]As to whether this is a career, a profession, a job, a calling, or none of the above, see "So This Is A Profession?", *Consultants News,* July/August, 1991, page 1, for an interesting discussion.

talked about the value of books and speeches, and the fact that they are lucrative in and of themselves, beyond the more immediate marketing value. These are direct or active sources of income.

One growing source of passive income is in audiocassettes. There is an enormous self-help market that gobbles up cassettes in subject areas ranging from self-motivation and personal grooming to time management and managing cultural diversity. Consultants who deal in virtually any area of management—who have their clients as practical "laboratories"—and who may be publishing their approaches in various print media, are ideally placed to create audiocassettes. We'll examine some of the traditional ways, then we'll look at what I consider the absolute best way to record your wisdom for posterity.

There are large, mail-order cassette providers that advertise prodigiously, exemplified by the Nightingale/Conant organization in Chicago. Largely through direct mail and well-targeted print advertising in airline magazines and specialty catalogs, they market "names" such as Brian Tracy and Tony Robbins. These are generally people who have achieved cult status in popular psychology, self-help, motivation, inspiration, and related fields. It is extremely difficult to break into the club, although a best-selling book will usually buy you a ticket. However, royalties are fickle things and margins in the business are razor blade–thin. The big names and big promotional efforts will create substantial earnings, but these are few and far between.

A second route in this field is the "interview" tape. There are production companies that create "management series" by interviewing authors, consultants, and executives around a unifying theme and promoting it in the area of "Managing Innovation" or "Mastering Change." These can be valuable marketing tools for you (especially if you have high-profile colleagues on the tape), but there is usually no fee and little if any royalty arrangements. Moreover, you won't get any free samples, and you might not even get yourself! One company interviewed me and *after* the interviews—which, evidently, passed muster—asked if I would agree to an actor portraying me on the actual recording, since their policy was to use professional voices for all the interviewees! I told them to hit the erase button.

A third approach is the equivalent of self-publishing. You write your material, obtain a recording studio, engineer, and editor (very easy in virtually any city), record a 2-to-12 cassette album, and have labels and artwork produced to your heart's content. I estimate that you can assemble a six-cassette album in this manner for about $5000, assuming you've used first-rate help. After that, cassettes cost less than $1 each to duplicate in bulk, labels are a few cents, and your album itself might cost you another $3; so a run of 500 will put you out about $10,000, which includes one-time start-up costs and duplication. If you sell the album for $49.95, which is the low-to-moderate part of the spectrum, 200 sales will earn back all of your production costs. If marketing requires another $2000, about half of your run (250) represents the breakeven point. When you sell out, you'll have earned about $12,000 profit, and the next run of 500 will net you about $23,000.

Self-publishing in the cassette business can be lucrative, but there are some drawbacks that cast a pall over my profit figures:

- Promotion is difficult. It is highly competitive, and direct mail is a science that can drain your time, focus, and resources.

- The creation of the cassettes is difficult and time-consuming. You have to organize your ideas in writing, then hope they translate well to recording.

- Your topics can become dated quickly, rendering the album obsolete. Today's "empowerment" can easily become yesterday's "transactional analysis."

- There is no endorsement other than your own credibility. No matter how sound your credentials, it is clear that you have published the tapes on your own behalf because you wanted to create and sell tapes.

I've seen many consultants become fascinated and enamored by cassette recording, and lose sight of their primary business because self-publishing can easily become a business unto itself.

This brings us to my special recipe. I believe in synergies among your various focuses in the consulting business, and here is an example that has worked splendidly for me. Whenever you make a speech in front of a major audience, there is a 50-50 chance that it will be recorded. Associations and conventions, for example, almost always have an agreement with a professional taping service to record all sessions (even the smaller, concurrent ones) and then sell the tapes to participants during the convention itself.[7] These firms create an excellent master even from wireless, lavaliere microphones. Even at smaller conventions or in-house management conferences, there is often a sound engineer available to make professional recordings.

In your speaking contract with the client organization, *always stipulate that you will allow your speech to be recorded at no additional fee, provided that you receive two complimentary copies of any recordings*

---

[7]I recently appeared as the general session speaker for the American Newspaper Classified Advertising Managers Association, and tapes of my speech were available for purchase in the lobby within 30 minutes of my saying, "Thank you" to the audience.

made. Many speakers prohibit the recording of their talks, and others charge stiff fees for the right to do so. Consequently, your trade-off is quite reasonable. After all, your speech is your proprietary work, and recordings have been known to wind up in other organizations and even in other speakers' materials. No organization has ever contested this clause in my contract, and many times I've stimulated them into recording the session when they themselves hadn't originally considered it!

If the client isn't considering taping your presentation, then suggest that such a tape be made to leverage the client's investment. All you want in return for your permission is a copy of the tapes.

What you will walk away with is a live recording of your work and the reactions of a live audience. You have to ensure that you do the following:

- Provide the person who introduces you with a written introduction, and ask that it be read exactly as it appears.

- Carefully prepare your material with the knowledge that it will appear on tape. (For example, if you generally use a visual aid at a key point, it won't be appreciated on tape unless you explain it or translate it into an oral example.)

- Investigate whether the audience reactions will be picked up on the recording equipment, and if not, see if you can make arrangements for better audience pickup (especially important if questions and answers are a key part of your presentation—always make sure you repeat questions before responding to them).

I've found that 15 minutes spent with the audio engineer or top manager on-site from the recording company is well spent. I tell them that a good recording will result in large-scale purchases from me and specify what I'm looking for. This always results in careful attention and excellent results.

Once the recording is made, listen to it and decide how to edit it. This might include all or some of the following:

- A professional voice-over introducing the tape, its subject matter, and the setting; for example, "You are about to hear management consultant, author, and speaker Alan Weiss deliver the keynote address to the annual convention of the National Auto Dealers Association, recorded live in Atlanta." (Omit when the speech was given, since you don't want to date the tape.)

- Editing out of the thumps and whacks that occur when you inadvertently pound the mike or drop a glass of water (or belch).

- Augmentation of the audience's applause, laughter, and/or questions, if needed.

- A professional voice-over concluding the tape, reminding the listener of who you are, and providing the means to contact you for further information.

- Background music to precede and follow the voice-overs.

On occasion, when my introducer has done a horrible job despite my preparation, I've had the introduction replaced by the professional voice-over. Also, make sure to insert an oral request to turn the tape over if the speech is continued on the other side.

I then have my graphics artist or the tape company's artist prepare a simple label with my logo, and I select an off-the-shelf album box which accommodates the number of tapes I envision for that series. (They generally hold 2-to-12 tapes.)

Operating in this manner, I chose two live speeches that complemented each other and created a small album, complete with artwork on the cover and a promotional piece on the rear (with 800 number). My total cost to create 100 as a test run, including start-up and duplication, was $900. I sell the tapes for $29.95, again in the moderate range. Thirty albums paid my costs, and the profit from the run was $2000. I don't spend any money marketing them—instead, I include mention of them in all of my promotional material, my regular mailings to clients, press kits, etc. In a run of 500, as in the example above, my profit is slightly over $13,000.

Using these live recordings greatly reduces risks. First, you have the audience reactions, which helps to shape the eventual listeners' reactions. Like the music accompanying a movie, the audience helps the listener to know when to laugh, when to "ooh" and "ahh," and when to reflect. Second, the live nature helps to maintain the staying power, despite the topic. Third, the "recorded live" promotion adds tremendous credibility to the tapes. These are not tapes done by a guru who feels that the world should pay to hear the message, but recordings of a live speech made by an expert to people who paid to hear that message. You're simply doing prospective listeners a favor by making the message available to those who happened not to be present.[8]

Finally, these live recordings are among the most powerful of all the promotional tools you'll develop (and infinitely more so than self-published tapes). You can have extras duplicated for very little (as opposed to the entire album). These "singles" provide high credibility to prospects when they appear in the mail simply as a routine part of your press kit.

I knew I was on the right track when a participant at a speech came up to me and told me he was happy to finally hear me in person. "My predecessor," he said to my glee, "left one of your tapes in his desk, and I've listened to it a half-dozen times over the past year." The best part was, he kept telling that story to everyone around him.

Becoming a Star: The Camera Calls

There is a logical progression from audio to video. For those of you who are about to skip this section because it is too far out, I would advise you to stay put. Twenty years ago it was unusual for a consultant to be on audiotape, and 20 years from now it will be common for consultants to be on a variety of compact disk media. If you can't view change as opportunity, how will you ever get your clients to do so?

Being on videotape serves several purposes, any one of which may apply to you:

- It is a marketing or "audition" device to acquire speaking engagements.
- It can be a passive income source: "Tom Jones on Leadership in the 90s."
- It can be a "leave behind" for appropriate consulting interventions.
- It can provide a skills-transfer medium for internal client consultants.
- It provides powerful credibility to refer to "my video on the subject of..."
- It can serve in place of a published book.

Convinced about the utility? If so, read on to learn how to be a star.

---

[8]Many professional speakers record their own speeches through the use of a cordless lapel microphone and a high-quality cassette recorder that operates automatically. The equipment is available under trade names such as Freedom Mike and costs about $500–$800, complete.

The best way to create a videotape is analogous to the creation of an audiotape: try to be taped in front of a live audience. I've never encountered a convention or association that routinely videotapes presenters, but many client organizations have the capacity to do so. I've been taped by three different clients with facilities ranging from a company employee with a stationary camera in the rear of the room, to a production team brought in for the purpose, to a professional stage with video shot from a projection booth.[9]

Your best bet for video is to have a client tape a presentation. As with audio, many clients are willing and able to do it, but they simply haven't thought of it. It's your job to help them understand the value of creating such a tape to show to people who couldn't attend the session, people in distant locales, people who join the organization in the future, and as a later point of reference for those who do attend. You may be able to add more reasons, given the nature of your talk and/or consulting project. These simple but accurate justifications are usually highly influential.

> ***You must prepare your presentation to take advantage of the video medium.***

Set up your talk to take advantage of the medium. This is much trickier than audio, although even there you had to make some adjustments (for example, no lengthy nonverbal demonstrations). *The absolute worst video sin is the "talking head" syndrome.* Nothing creates stupor faster than watching someone on the screen stand in one place and talk for 30 minutes or more. Closely allied to this horror is the person on video—a fairly sophisticated medium—using a flip-chart or chalkboard—fairly primitive media—to illustrate points for the audience. Similar problems arise with slides and overhead transparencies because of lighting problems.

Work with the client to best exploit the video format. Since you've suggested (or even if the client has suggested) the videotaping, invest a

---

[9]This was at what was then the Golden Nugget Casino, a client in Atlantic City, which is now known as Bally's Grand. On one such occasion I addressed casino management from the stage, and several days later Frank Sinatra sang to the high rollers from the same spot. I was told to avoid the video screens set flush with the stage, which couldn't be seen by the audience. They were installed so that the song lyrics could scroll while Mr. Sinatra sang, enabling him to glance down to find his place if needed. All I could envision was crashing through them in mid-anecdote.

few hours over the phone with the person running the equipment. Find out how many cameras will be used, where they will be placed, whether they can zoom, if there are "dead spots" in the room, what the sound system will be, and so on. Inform the operator of your plans for movement, visuals, and audience participation, and carefully work out what can be effectively covered and what cannot. Here are some guidelines for videotaping effectiveness from the speaker's perspective:

- Arrange to have your introducer included in the taping, and prepare that person carefully for the introduction you want.

- Try to move across the front of the room and use physical gestures. This means that you can't be tied to notes, which must remain on the lectern. Make sure the camera can be panned in that fashion, and that the operator is prepared to move with you, not "catch up" with you.

- Repeat any questions from the audience for the camera and sound system.

- Try to have sound pickups to capture the audience reactions.

- Don't wear white shirts or blouses or black suits. Conservative dress comes across best, since the medium somewhat exaggerates colors. Navy blue is always a safe choice.

- Practice until you are smooth, but don't worry about perfection. Correct any errors in a natural, conversational way: don't harp on them or try ad lib humor. The benefit of a video of a live presentation is that the video audience is not surprised by minor, normal errors, but they will be distracted by someone obviously playing to the camera.

- Pretend the camera isn't there during your delivery. This will enhance the natural aspects of the presentation.

- Keep the session relatively short. My bias is for a 30 to 45 minute duration. It's tough to edit these down, since later points are often dependent on earlier foundation.

- Keep the visual aids simple and sensitive to the medium. For example, holding up an item is ideal, providing it's large enough for the camera to capture. Try to stay away from slides that require lighting adjustments. (It's often possible to edit in a picture or diagram specifically for the video later if something from the session doesn't show up well on tape.)

- Review your notes to avoid making any references to timing or events that would indicate the date, and refrain from ad libs that do so.

- Offer to stay after the session to reshoot any segments that the operator feels might not have been captured well. Even with the room empty, you can deliver a 5-minute example or restate something that was garbled earlier. In most instances you'll be able to immediately view the completed tape.

Once you've obtained a master of the video, you can work with a production house to create whatever packaging you desire. I recommend the following essentials:

1. Include a voice-over at the beginning with background music.
2. Add a title graphic with the topic, your name, and client or group. Don't include the date.
3. Edit out extraneous material (picking up dropped notes, an interruption in the rear of the room) and enhance the audience reactions if needed.
4. It's often best to end the tape during the applause and/or while the host is thanking you. Fade to a final graphic.
5. Conclude with a voice-over explaining what was just seen, accompanied by a graphic showing where to write for more information. This is the place for your 800 number if you have one.
6. Package the video in a simple box with a professional label, including your name, company and logo, and title of the subject.

These tapes needn't be placed in albums; they can stand alone in their boxes. In volume (over 100) you can easily find sources that will duplicate for less than $10 per tape, and sometimes as low as about $5 per tape. Production costs for editing and voice-overs generally run less than $300, depending on how elaborate your needs are. (My advice: keep it simple and professional.) So for something around $1000 you could have 100 tapes duplicated to your specifications, and I suspect you might get that down closer to $500 if you investigate carefully. (Does the client have a production house they often use that they could recommend to you?)

I choose not to sell videotapes, and use them only for marketing and promotional purposes. But you certainly can sell them, and a price of $29.95 wouldn't be unusual for a 30- to 45-minute professional tape on a management topic (especially "recorded live"). That creates a net of conservatively $1500 on the first 100, before any marketing expense, and probably a net of about $2500 on every 100 after that.

Finally, what if your clients don't videotape? The best alternative is to seek permission to have your own production company shoot the session. You can find local firms (that is, local to your presentation—you don't want to pay for travel expenses) easily, often from the client's suggestions, who professionally tape such sessions for reasonable fees. In my experience, you can have a presentation shot with an outside group for under $1000, and that will often include the subsequent editing. Be careful about minimum time requirements, however; some firms demand you retain them for a day, since they can't do anything else but your job anyway. The advantage of an outside firm hired by you is that you know the video will be done well and coordinated with your efforts, since you are *their* client.

The only downside risk is the client's sensitivities about confidential matters, company policies, and so forth. If you want to bring in an outside firm, always offer to waive any fee you're getting for that particular speech, or grant the client *something* — a reduction in the project fee, free copies of the video for distribution, an additional presentation at another site, etc. Make it worth the client's while, since it's certainly worth a great deal to you. Often, trade associations and conventions will most readily agree to your bringing in a video outfit, particularly if you waive your speaking fee for these budget-conscious groups.

Your firm is doing well, your growth is accelerating, and your personal profile is being enhanced. Yet we've established that this is a *relationship* business. Let's turn, then, to the ultimate relationships.

13
The Ultimate Relationships

When Clients Call *You*

Long-Term Contracts

Intelligently managed growth creates its own momentum. Gradually you will find that the breaks that never came your way when you were struggling begin to turn in your favor. "Where were they when I *really* needed them?" we are prone to ask. The fact is that we make our own breaks, and the mere act of developing your business creates a force that sweeps newer and better opportunities your way. The great Brooklyn Dodgers general manager, Branch Rickey, responding to critics who said he was merely lucky in finding the best players in the game, replied that, "Luck is the residue of design." And master science fiction writer Robert Heinlein, with scores of books and awards behind him, noted that, " 'Luck' is the term used by the mediocre to explain away genius."

> *The* very act of growing *creates a momentum that generates additional opportunities which hadn't been anticipated.*

One such opportunity is that of long-term contracts. Although I've advocated finite, shorter-term projects with clear starts and finishes, I've also advocated long-term relationships, from which such projects periodically arise. Occasionally, a client will have a legitimate and attractive situation that calls for ongoing collaboration. By "long-term," I mean consulting relationships that meet these two criteria:

- The agreed-upon period is at least one year.
- The objectives are dynamic, not fixed.

The one-year provision is my own arbitrary assessment of what constitutes long-term. In most cases, this will involve two fiscal years for the client, even if all payment is made in only one of them.[1] It will involve the completion of a year's results to be compared against plan, and the creation of the next year's plan. And it will involve sufficient normal change in the operation—turnover, competitive actions, new products and services, acquired and lost customers, etc.—to provide a realistic opportunity to assess the impact of your assistance. In other words, you can tell quite clearly whether your presence is improving the client's condition.

The second criterion means that the client might say, "Let's meet twice a month to brainstorm what I should be doing to improve the operation in view of ongoing results. In the interim, wander around the business and tell me what you think I don't know or appreciate." The client isn't looking for your participation in installing a system or procedure, in delivering a workshop, or in helping to redefine reporting relationships, *although any of these activities might, in fact, occur if conditions warrant.* Your relationship is based on establishing objectives for improving the organization, not on meeting predefined ones. You are functioning as the "independent expert" on the chart of possible interventions from Chapter 1.

These types of contracts are the ultimate demonstration of trust. The client is not expecting specific tasks to be accomplished, nor is there a particular objective that needs to be met. Instead, the client is trusting you to provide the ongoing advice and assistance that will improve the organization and is trusting that it will be delivered with candor, accuracy, and pragmatism. Firing all the vice presidents doesn't usually solve anything. Establishing written statements of accountability that all officers help to write, commit to, and agree to be evaluated against usually does.

[1] In my experience, it is very difficult to secure fixed-fee consulting assignments that call for commitments from the client in more than two fiscal years. Many organizations have policies against such multiyear commitments.

1.00
170209
302044

I've been working with the Calgon Corporation's Water Management Division for three years now. After meeting the newly appointed president, we agreed on a six-month assignment, which led to a second six-month assignment, which led to a year's assignment, and a third year's assignment, which I am now in the midst of. During this extended period I've conducted workshops, facilitated meetings, shadowed the president, interviewed all the key executives and managers, visited field meetings, gone on field service calls, designed programs, recommended personnel moves, evaluated outside programs, and helped establish key accountabilities. None of these activities was specified at the outset. The need for them became apparent as the relationship continued. Most of the time the president and I agreed; sometimes we didn't. No matter. I served in the role of consultant to the management team and provided help as requested or as I thought needed to be initiated. It is one of the most rewarding consulting assignments I've ever had. Over the course of three years I've seen my recommendations implemented, observed the results in terms of the business goals of the organization, and have been able to fine-tune as needed. I know virtually every manager in the home office and the field, and there probably isn't one who would hesitate to call me if he or she thought I could be of help. I am part of the team.

After the first year, the division met (and exceeded) its plan for the first time in several years. That was when the group president noted that, "You must be very pleased to have been a part of our success this past year." And that's exactly how I felt.

Long-term contracts[2] are extremely valuable, because they provide the maximum opportunity for multidimensional growth. (See Figure 13-1 for the essentials of a long-term contract.) You are able to consistently test the envelope in a setting that is familiar, trusting, and accepting of change (or you wouldn't be there). These relationships are the exact opposite of what most people in the consulting profession seek:

> Too frequently, external consultants helped companies implement programmatic change. They designed and staffed corporate training programs, drafted corporate mission statements, designed gain-sharing programs, and implemented quality circles. Such programs are ideally suited to the role of external consultants. They are easy to describe to potential customers. Precisely because they are programmatic, they can be replicated from one company to the next. Because customers are buying a known product, they can accurately estimate the time and cost of implementing the new program. Programs that

[2]When I speak of *long-term relationships,* I mean continuing contact with a client over the years, which usually involves several fee-paying projects during that time period. By *long-term contract,* I mean a fee-paying project that lasts for at least a year.

> # A Long-Term Contract
>
> - Is usually established with the CEO or business unit head.
>
> - Requires extended time on-site and with client customers.
>
> - Should never include competitors as your clients, since extensive confidential data is usually shared.
>
> - Is usually established at the request of the client, not as a result of a proposal from you.
>
> - Requires that you establish credibility and trust with management several layers down. (If you are seen as a threat or a "hatchet," your long-term value will be nil.)
>
> - Requires a far greater amount of innovation and initiation on your part, since you must both react to and anticipate change for the client. Your attitude must be not to *fix,* but rather to *improve.*

Figure 13-1. A long-term contract has these six characteristics, in addition to the duration and dynamic objectives already cited.

do not require lasting changes in ongoing employee behavior are not usually threatening. But while such programs are easy to sell to companies, *they do not promote revitalization.*[3]

There are two basic methods of assessing fees in such contracts. The better of the two is consistent with the advice already provided in terms of fixed-fees based on value.[4] What is the value to the client of your long-term, personal help in understanding the operation and its people intimately and in providing specific assistance to improve the client's condition? How valuable is it for the client to have a priority call on your time? My preference is to establish your fee for the year (or whatever the period is) and fix the payment terms, again providing a discount for one-time payment. (This is often highly attractive in such situations, and provides you with a substantial sum of money at one time.) Alternatively, require your usual 50 percent deposit, and establish periodic, calendar-date billing times. Expenses should be billed at the end of each calendar month.

The second alternative is a monthly retainer. If this is preferred by the client, always establish in your contract one of two provisions (or both):

[3]Michael Bee, Russell A. Eisenstat, and Bert Spector, *The Critical Path to Corporate Renewal,* Harvard Business School Press, Boston, 1990, page 175. (Italics are mine.)

[4]See Chapter 8.

- The retainer is paid in advance, a quarter at a time.
- There is a contractual guarantee of six months.

In this manner you have protected yourself from unforeseen events, such as falling victim to a bad sales month.

Long-term contracts ensure that you are a going concern. They also alleviate cashflow worries and, most importantly, provide for the multidimensional growth vital to million dollar consultants.

Since the client generally calls you for such contracts, how do you help to make them happen?

Client Advisory Groups and Conferences

A friend of mine whom you met earlier, Mike Robert, personally specializes in strategy consulting, particularly in the formulation stage. He charges fees of about $100,000 per assignment at the corporate level, and less for business units within the corporation. He does virtually no advertising, doesn't exhibit at trade shows, and I've never found him in any professional listings. Yet in the first half of 1991, he booked ten strategy assignments. His only employee in this venture is a full-time secretary/administrative assistant. Otherwise, he sells, services, delivers, and follows up on everything himself.

Mike Robert is the president of Decision Processes International.[5] Although he has partners around the world, and has built a $5-million business in the training field, the strategy work is solely his personal realm. Welcome to another member of the million dollar consulting club.

How does he achieve this rate of business? Well, 1991 was his best year ever, and he began it (during the Gulf War, no less) with a client symposium. He invited some of his ongoing, satisfied strategy customers, some likely prospects, and some outside speakers to a couple of days at a posh resort. Spouses were encouraged to attend. There was no fee for the session, but everyone paid their own airfare and lodging.

The result? By June, Mike had sold a strategy formulation to all but one of the prospects who had attended the symposium.

Mike long ago learned the lesson of investing money to make money. He saw the symposium as a strategic marketing tool, and employed a

[5]He is the coauthor of my first book, *The Innovation Formula: How Successful Organizations Turn Change Into Opportunity*, HarperCollins: New York, 1988. He has also authored himself, *The Strategist CEO: How Visionary Executives Build Organizations*, Qu orum Books, Westport, CT: 1989.

tactic that is one of the most powerful in our profession: peer influence. Mike did little selling during the course of the meeting. He let his current clients sell for him during cocktails, in the halls, and on the golf course. These are examples of the ultimate relationships: clients selling to prospects through the communications channels you establish.

> *There is no greater influence, no more powerful sales stratagem, than arranging for one executive to have the opportunity and the motivation to say to another, "Use this consultant. I thank my stars that we did."*

Client conferences are an excellent method for achieving the interaction that results in peer influence. The key factor in successful client conferences is ensuring that you invite *more than just clients!* If you are running a symposium, as did Mike, or a general conference on a particular management subject, then it makes sense to have a strong mix of people—clients and prospects alike. But if you are running a client-oriented conference, most of the attendees will be clients, but some should be high priority, high-quality prospects. You might even want to pay for their transportation if their organizations don't forbid the practice. Every conference you hold is a marketing opportunity of enormous value.

Here is the checklist for successful conferences. (By "successful," I mean that the participants find the time investment well spent, and the prospects are moved closer to a buying position.)

- Attendees notified at least three months in advance, preferably more
- A ratio of at least three high-quality prospects to each six or seven clients
- One excellent outside speaker—a recognizable/prestige name in field—per day[6]
- The use of a superb facility with a wide variety of recreational opportunities
- A limited formal agenda (i.e., mornings only), with ample time for socializing

[6]Estimated cost: $5000–$7500.

- Prearranged press coverage during the conference, or publicizing via the press afterwards
- Provision of complimentary copies of books, articles, or examples of use during the conference
- Provision of a postsession report, summary materials, and offer of ongoing help after the conference

Note that these conferences are intended for present and potential *buyers* of your services. Many firms hold "user group" meetings, which encompass the internal facilitators, instructors, and others who have been instrumental in implementing your project work. These are valuable undertakings that enhance the relationship you are trying to form with clients, but they are not the significant, peer-influence marketing tool that buyer-level conferences and symposia are. Moreover, the user-group meetings can often be held internally, or regionally among several clients, using client facilities. Their goal is enhancing the technical application of your project work. The buyer-level meeting is a marketing opportunity of tremendous value, which is why a significant investment is justified. But don't confuse the two, and *never mix executives and implementors at the same conference.* Not only is their frame of reference going to be different; your intent with them will be radically different.

Client advisory groups are another technique used to build ultimate relationships. I have an insurance client, whose CEO has asked four of us—all outside consultants—to participate in an informal advisory board. We meet twice a year at resort locations for no fee, but with all expenses paid and spouses encouraged to attend. Typically, we spend one day on company business, advising the CEO on issues that are on his priority list, and often arguing among ourselves about our advice. The result is that we explore every issue thoroughly, and the consultants learn as much as the CEO. The second day is spent socializing—at the beach, on a fishing boat, or whatever.

That CEO is getting a wealth of consulting help during those few days a year. It doesn't replace what we do for him independently, working on clearly defined projects, but it augments all of our work and provides him with a valuable (and unique) sounding board unavailable within his organization. None of us holds back, and no one ever says, "Wait a minute, this issue should really be addressed on billable time!"

Commensurately, it's a good idea for you to form advisory groups from among your clients and nonclients (who may someday become clients). These informal outside advisers *should not include your attorney or financial adviser.* Those people offer advice in narrow, important fields, but should not be included in an advisory board. Keep your advisory board or group small—no more than eight members, but more than just a handful, since schedules will always interfere with some individual participation at meetings—and meet infrequently. I think that twice a year is about right. You don't have to fly everyone to Antigua, but you should foot the bill for two days at a decent place, with sufficient social time built in. This is to allow for that old peer influence to operate, among other benefits. Remember, consider including at least two or three nonclients, who are key prospects in the group. And keep the membership at executive level only.

Among the issues you can ask your advisory group to discuss and "consult" with you on are these:

- Your strategy in the marketplace
- Major moves/investments: alliances, office expansion, new hires, etc.
- Major marketing plans
- Publishing plans
- Economic trends
- Pro bono work
- Emerging management priorities
- Competition

Client advisory groups serve to cement existing client relationships by forming a collaborative effort on behalf of *your* business. They also develop potential relationships among nonclient members *and* member contacts.

Client advisory groups or boards are not boards of directors, which I would discourage you from forming. As long as you are taking the risks and providing the talent, a board of directors can serve no purpose that an advisory group cannot. Meanwhile, a board has certain significant drawbacks in terms of restrictions on your activities and divulgence of personal business affairs. The advisory board has all the supportive elements of a board of directors, and none of the disadvantages. (They are also considerably easier to form, alter, and end when necessary.)

No matter what you call your efforts in creating special relationships and forums—symposia, conferences, meetings, boards, committees, gatherings, sessions, task forces, councils, etc.—your goal should be the same: to create opportunities for peer influence to sell your services to prospects, and to create opportunities to solidify and extend the ongoing relationships you've formed with existing clients. These alternatives provide you with great leverage in those marketing pursuits.

The Value-Added Discounting Principle of Never Losing Clients

Every book needs a clever acronym. Maybe this is mine: TV-ADPONLC. On second thought, I'd probably better explain.

"The value added discounting principle of never losing clients" is simply my way of emphasizing that the longer-term the relationship, *the longer-term it is likely to be.* No, that's not a truism. At birth, an individual's life expectancy might be 73 years. However, once that individual has reached 40 successfully, the life expectancy is probably about 80 years. And once you're 79, the odds are that you have a few more years left. In other words, the longer you live, the longer you will probably live.

Client relationships follow these actuarial realities very closely. But not for the same reasons.

As you have no doubt realized by now, my path to millions of dollars in business is through the establishment of long-term relationships. The creation of those relationships is in turn based on creating and implementing the value-added qualities that enable you to improve the client's condition. The *sustaining* of those qualities and that improvement over time creates a bond that is quite difficult to break, *because your worth to the client increases geometrically as you move from project to project.* You are not merely the sum of the performance evaluation system you implemented plus the customer survey you conducted, plus the creation of educational strategies for the human resources area. As you've engaged in those projects, the *client organization has imparted information to you that has made you wise in the organization's ways and culture.* Your value-added is no longer merely the talents you bring to the client, it is also the *wisdom* you can now apply through your intimate knowledge of the client. *And wisdom is critical, because it isn't readily replaceable.*

> *Most consulting assignments begin with the gathering of information and application of knowledge. These activities are replaceable and duplicatable. The attainment and use of wisdom is an intrinsic value that is difficult and time-consuming to recreate.*

Clients can find a great many alternatives to implement succession planning systems, to design workshops on innovation, and even to assist in formulating strategy. In all of these and myriad other consulting activities, there is a joint educational process occurring. The client learns processes, methods, and skills from the consultant which improve the client's condition.[7] However, preparatory to that result, the consultant must be educated about the client's organization. The less the consultant knows about the client and the client's industry, the more education is required, the longer the process of learning, and the more the chance for early errors, misconceptions, and misjudgments. The more the consultant knows about the client's organization and industry, the less remedial education is required, the shorter the process of learning, and the less chance for errors, misconceptions, and misjudgments.

Typically, when I begin an assignment for a new client, I include what I call "roaming" time in my plans. During my roaming, I try to:

- Meet every key senior manager to learn their responsibilities and perceptions of the organization
- Meet a wide cross section of middle- and lower-level managers to learn their perceptions
- Meet a wide variety of hourly and administrative people to learn their perceptions
- Accompany field people on client calls and sales calls, and attend field sales meetings
- Observe the normal work routines, including the way complaints and crises are handled
- Immerse myself in the organization's culture, mores, beliefs (real and perceived), and attitudes toward customers

This roaming never really ends, but it's most intense in the beginning of the assignment, when I try to gather this information in as little time as possible, so that I can be as productive for the client as quickly as possible.[8] On succeeding projects for that client, my primary education

[7]That learning depends on the type of intervention, as discussed in Chapter 1.

[8]Consultants who simply enter client organizations with canned approaches and off-the-shelf interventions don't do this, and are never as potentially useful and powerful as true consultants, who design interventions based on unique client needs and conditions. No one makes $1 million delivering workshops on time management, but you can make tens of millions showing organizations how to save time and increase productivity by changing their systems and procedures.

needs have been met, my knowledge is intact (although the continuing education never ends), and I begin to become a source of wisdom for that client. That is, my consulting help now has the added dimension of a thorough understanding of my client's beliefs, goals, culture, comfort zones, and unique problems: I am a wise man.

In Australia I've had a very warm reception, as do American consultants in general. We are cordially (I like to believe) referred to as "wise men from the East." I think there's more to this quotation than meets the ear.

Data can be exchanged. Information can be exchanged and communicated. Knowledge is readily shared. All of these things are based on facts and circumstances that can easily be *instantiated* — moved from the abstract to the concrete via the written word, examples, discussions, and exchanges. That's one of the reasons why organizations hold so many meetings. They are frantically trying to share information so that their knowledge base can be increased. Information alone isn't valuable. It is only a prerequisite for knowledge, which is the application of that information to improve the workings of the organization. (See Figure 13-2).

For example, you may have data about turnover which includes the fact that it is 5 percent in marketing, 7 percent in sales, 6 percent in administration, and 22 percent in production. As you investigate and gather more data, you learn that the general manager of production has a different compensation plan which is strictly oriented toward quarterly production goals. As you combine this data, you have information which suggests that employee turnover is unimportant to production management, and that the reward system actually encourages turnover if production goals are met. If the company's objectives are to reduce the expenses of turnover and create long-term employees, your knowledge of the problem and of effective organizational interventions provides this solution: modify the reward system and educate the general manager about the organization's needs to reduce turnover *as well* as meet production goals.

So far, you've applied information to create knowledge and improve the client condition. Let's assume now that the client has asked for your advice about the reorganization of the field force to reduce unnecessary layers of management. During that process, you advise the client (given your experience with production turnover) that the reorganization must include a restructuring of the field management performance evaluation and reward criteria, since the organization has a propensity to manage task rather than result. In fact, the correct emphasis on long-term business goals for field management will be *the* key factor in the success of the sales force reorganization. The client leans back, ponders you for a moment in deepest respect, and says, "That's very wise. Tell me more."

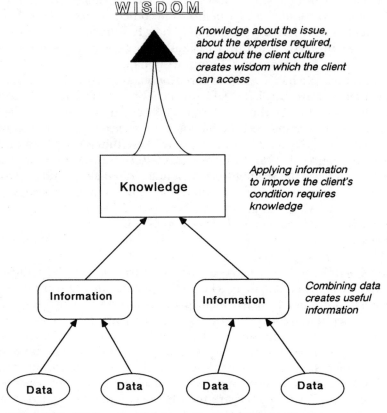

Figure 13-2. Wisdom: the ultimate contribution of the consultant.

I've heard many people sarcastically say, "Don't be so smart." But I've never heard any say, "Don't be so wise."

Once you've acquired the wisdom that comes with the successful implementation of several client projects, close relationships with key managers, exposure to the organization's "soul," and establishment of credibility and trust through your improvements, you are a wise person. *That wisdom is worth a great deal to the client, because to replace it would cost a fortune.* To replace your level of wisdom with a new consulting source would require that the new person engage in several successful projects, develop the necessary relationships, gain exposure to the inner workings of the organization, and build the credibility and trust you have already acquired. *Even if another consultant charges fees less than yours, the cost of bringing that consultant up to your current level of wisdom is prohibitive.*

So now we have arrived at the ultimate relationship. You have become so valuable to the client — so wise in the client's ways — that replacing you is far more expensive than whatever your fees may be. And if you recall our discussion (Chapter 8) on establishing fees, the best and most lucrative way to do so is to base fees on perceived value. *Your perceived value is never higher than when you have arrived at a long-term relationship in which the client sees your wisdom as irreplaceable.*

An executive at Merck told me a story about one of his most brilliant lieutenants who was clearly destined to become one of the very top people in the organization. However, one day the subordinate reported that he had made a huge error in judgment, and that his bad decision would cost over $1 million to correct. After making a candid disclosure, the subordinate tendered his resignation.

"Why on earth do you think I'd accept that?" asked my client.

"After this disaster, you have no choice but to fire me, and I wanted to make it as easy as possible for you," responded the subordinate.

"Are you crazy!" said the boss. "I've just invested a million dollars in your education. You're much too valuable to lose after that. Now get back to work!"

Your job isn't to make million dollar mistakes, of course, but to make million dollar improvements and contributions. If you consistently do that, you become much too valuable to lose — *in good times or bad* — and fees are literally not an issue. In tough economic times, it's easy to cut outside consulting expenses. If you are a little-known entity, or simply implementing "programs," your time to go has probably come. But if the executive says, "We've got some tough decisions to make. Get Alan Weiss in here for our next meeting, and tell him we'll be needing a lot of his help..." there probably isn't too much to worry about other than making plane reservations. You see, I'm not a consulting expense to my clients. I'm Alan Weiss, a *person* who has provided substantial assistance in the past and has the wisdom about the operation to continue to do so. *In tough times clients cut expenses, not wisdom.*

The ultimate client relationships are those in which you are the wise man, whose contributions are a synthesis of personal talents, organizational knowledge, and interpersonal relationships established with top management.

In these ultimate relationships you are simply too valuable to lose, and the cost of replacing you is prohibitive, because of the client's past investment in your education. Consequently:

1. You will not tend to lose clients in tough economic conditions.
2. Your fees can be value-based, and will not be an important issue.
3. The client will call you regularly for assistance.
4. You will be immune to inroads from other consultants.
5. You will develop a priceless model and reference for other work.

What I've been calling "ultimate" relationships are not purely a factor of longevity. Simply hanging around a client for a long time doesn't do it. You have to amass wisdom through continual learning about the client and the organization's business goals, and you must constantly learn about and consider new interventions. *This is why a single consulting model, limited programmatic offerings, and a "flavor of the month," fad-type approach will never result in such relationships.* They don't represent any unique synthesis between the client and yourself, and they are readily replaceable with other alternatives without great expense. I've seen consultants thrown out of client organizations after five-year relationships because the one trick in their bag had finally worn out. (Workshops and seminars are famous for this. They identify you with a single narrow intervention — decision making, say — and after you've trained everyone in the discipline, what do you do next, train them again?)

The "value-added discounting principle of never losing clients" simply means that:

1. If you become sufficiently valuable in the client's eyes you will be continually called upon for assistance.
2. That value is based on becoming wise in the ways of the client, and combining that intimate relationship with your own talents and never-ending search for new interventions and solutions to improve the client's condition.

You only need relationships like these with a few clients to make — and keep — a million dollars a year. As I wrote this last page of this chapter — honest to goodness — I was interrupted by a call from a client with whom I've worked continuously for six years. He told me to "prepare my schedule and time allotment" for 1992 accordingly, because they have just submitted a budget calling for me to conduct a

minimum of two major projects for one division alone. I never submitted a proposal, and one of the projects was totally unknown to
me. An early guess is that the two projects will *net* about $200,000. It
could be more, of course, because the fee won't be a major issue.

14
Beyond Success

Money Is Only
a Means to an End

Ethical Issues

As you achieve multidimensional growth and the firm prospers, the nature of the problems and challenges you face evolves. At the outset of your consulting career, you are typically concerned about cashflow, marketing, and developing the expertise required to complete more diverse assignments. In midcareer, during the firm's dramatic growth, the issues become those of finding the right alliance partners, developing long-term relationships, and establishing proper fee levels. Once you are a going concern, the priorities become the unique issues related to your very success.

Million dollar consulting generates some million dollar ethical challenges. How would you respond to these ten?

1. Can I simply charge the highest fee possible and not even worry about perceived value? If I'm in demand, isn't the guideline "whatever the traffic will bear"?

2. I choose to travel first class, stay on the concierge floor of the best hotels, and prefer limos over taxis. That's my travel style, and I'm worth it. As long as I'm honest about it, shouldn't the client be billed for my normal travel preferences?

3. There is nothing new under the sun, and I'm a recognized name and sought-after figure. There's nothing wrong with taking some

ideas espoused by other consultants and authors and using them in my work or writing, as long as I put my personal spin on them. You can't copyright ideas, so I can use what I wish, right?

4. I'm seeing three clients on this trip. I know that if I attempt to pro rate expenses, their accounting systems will question the charges. However, if I simply bill each one for the entire airfare and lodging, there won't be a single question. Shouldn't I make it easier on myself and on them and bill each of them for 100 percent, since I have to visit each one anyway?

5. In doing my research within a client organization, I'm told by a midlevel manager *on a strictly confidential basis* about an internal leak to competitors and an ongoing employee theft. If I divulge this to the president, it will be clear that I was the source, and my value to the client within the organization will be nil. Isn't it better—and even ethically necessary—to maintain the confidentiality and continue to be a valuable resource within the organization for the client?

6. A client offers me first-class airfare to visit its European offices. I can use my free airline mileage to take my entire family, and, by cashing in the first-class tickets, pay for all our food, lodging, and recreation. There's no reason to explain all this to the client is there, since it's my personal business?

7. A competitor of one of my largest clients wants to hire me, since my reputation has been associated with my client's success. Is there any problem with taking on competitive organizations?

8. A client asks me to conduct an anonymous employee survey by mail, but asks me to use a hidden code to differentiate by unit—though not by person—the source of the feedback. This is because the client is sincerely interested in the quality of the unit managers and wants to isolate those whose people are unhappy with their treatment. Is this a legitimate goal to justify the subterfuge?

9. I am asked to write speeches and articles for the president of the organization who is my client. He confers with me on topics and critiques the final work, but the actual writing is totally mine. The president gives no attribution whatsoever, publishes some of the articles in the trade press, and gives the speeches at business conferences to great acclaim. Is this a service that I should continue to provide?

10. Through an alliance partner, I develop a client contact with the alliance partner's blessing. After a three-month, highly successful assignment, the client asks me to take on a long-term project in place of the alliance partner, with whom the client has been unhappy for some time. Can I ethically accept this project?

Most of these situations have happened to me, and the rest have happened to colleagues. There are no magic answers to ethical dilemmas. Ernest Hemingway observed that, "What is moral is what you feel good after, and what is immoral is what you feel bad after." Of course, no one ever recorded that Hemingway tried his hand at consulting, otherwise *For Whom the Bell Tolls* might have been called *An Analytic Report on Bell Cacophony, Causation, and Demographic Probabilities.*

> ***You can't do much better than consistently try to do the right thing.***

I'd rather go with the credo that I've heard virtually all managers at Merck & Co. articulate when they are asked what to do in ambiguous situations, when policy and precedent don't apply: *do the right thing*. Here's what I consider the right thing to do in each instance:

1. Should You Charge the Highest Fees You Can Get Away With?

There is certainly no moral prohibition that I know of to discourage you from charging what the traffic will bear. If you are charging on a fee basis, and the client is aware of and accepts the fee, the client has obviously determined that the value is worth the investment. However, I would emphasize two caveats:

- It is never advisable to overpromise and underdeliver. Consequently, if you are justifying that high investment through extravagant promises and providing only marginal delivery, you are certainly not building long-term potential. Which is better: a single $150,000-project that results in no further work, or an ongoing series of $75,000-projects, the results of which send the client into fits of ecstasy?

- If you *are* charging a per diem or by some other fixed standard, despite the strictures of Chapter 8,[1] there is never an excuse to charge for anything other than actual hours performed, on-site or off-. "Padding" days goes beyond an ethical transgression—it's theft.

---

[1] Frankly, if you are charging by the day I doubt that you'll ever need the advice in Chapter 14.

2. Should You Travel First Class
and Bill the Client?

You can make a case that if the client approves of a sybaritic travel style, there is no problem. However, your primary charter is to improve the client's condition. Do you help fiscally through this kind of expense (which has nothing to do with your value or expertise), and do you help credibly, through this kind of image with the client's people? I doubt it. There are some high-flying organizations in which this mode of travel is the status quo, and in those circumstances the luxury makes sense. I've also found that most clients offer first-class transportation overseas, and many do for domestic coast-to-coast trips.

Nevertheless, my rule of thumb is simple: if the client doesn't offer it, I don't abuse it. I travel first class, use limos and the best hotels, but I charge clients for coach, taxis, and standard Marriott-type rates. And I won't use limos or other frills if their visibility causes questions about the "high-priced outside help," even if I am paying for it myself. And don't pull a fast one: take the luxury travel difference out of your pocket as a decreased margin; don't pad the fee to make up the difference.

3. Should You Borrow Others' Ideas
and Present Them as Your Own?

It's true that you cannot copyright concepts (you cannot even copyright book titles), and that there are few breakthrough ideas. Most of the really good ones are merely old ideas reapplied in new ways. But your clients are smart. People recognize ideas that were formulated by others. Since it's your *application* of the idea for your client that is novel, why not give credit where credit is due? It's the mark of a successful, self-confident consultant to say, "This is a technique developed by Sally Smith and written about in the *McGoo Review of Management*. I've developed an adaptation for your situation that I believe we should implement."

You are not expected to be a rocket scientist or an R & D factory. You are hired to provide pragmatic consulting interventions using the best ideas extant. Since that is what you are paid for, it makes sense to reveal the source of all ideas and techniques.

4. Should You Bill More Than One
Client for the Same Basic Expenses?

Never double-bill (or, in this case, triple-bill). I've seen every excuse under the sun for doing this, and none of them passes muster as "doing the right thing." Send a cover letter with your expense statement explaining why you are only charging the client one-third of the full amount on some of the receipts (i.e., airfare) and the full amount on others (i.e., meals during the days working exclusively for that client). Turn the procedure into an *opportunity* to demonstrate your fiscal responsibility toward that client.[2]

5. Should You Pass On to the Client Confidential Information Given You in the Course of Your Assignment?

Who is the client here? You were brought on board to help improve the client condition, and it's up to the client to determine what the most useful role is. In this case, you're ethically bound to inform the client about what you've discovered, and allow the client to decide whether to take action immediately or to preserve your current role by not taking action. You cannot make these moral decisions *for* the client, only in collaboration *with* the client, and only with the client reserving the decision-making prerogative.

By the way, I never ask for information in return for a promise not to reveal it, and I *never* agree to accept information on the condition of not revealing it. Once you do that, you are ethically compromised on the spot. When someone tells you, "This is confidential, but…" you are free to listen and use the information as long as you haven't acknowledged that you will respect the confidentiality. Good consultants find out what they need to through intelligent questioning and keen observation. Relying on "informants" isn't consulting. It's spying.

6. Should You Use Tickets Supplied by Your Client to Bring Your Spouse Along?

This might be *your* personal business, but the tickets are the *client's*. There's nothing wrong with this practice *if* you inform the client of your plans. You can never be too honest or err on the side of excessive honesty. I've taken my wife on many trips using the tons of free air

---

[2]I once had two clients whose accounts-payable bureaucrats both demanded the single, original receipt for the airfare. Since there was only a single original (*which I like to keep for my records*) I gave them each a choice: I would send the original to whichever wanted to pay the entire air bill, and a copy to the one who would pay a 50 percent share. Both quickly accepted copies, and I had examples to show my buyer of internal policies which, when blindly followed, create waste.

mileage we all acquire, and I tell the client what I'm doing and that I'll simply charge the equivalent of coach airfare. I also pay any difference in the room rate. I've never had a client say anything other than, "It's always a good idea to take along your spouse whenever you can; I always try to myself."

As for "it's only my personal business," here's what happened to my own personal physician who consults on medical/computer applications. The client provided a ticket to Paris on the Concorde. The doctor cashed it in to pay for two business-class tickets for a subsequent European vacation with his wife, and he booked a coach fare on Pan Am. Just before his departure, he received a fax informing him that the client's limo would meet him at the special Concorde arrivals area!

"Innocent" falsehoods can develop into complicated and unnecessary questions about your ethical standards. Either tell the client what you're doing, or don't do it. (If you're uncomfortable telling the client, the chances are strong that what you're doing is unacceptable.) As for my doctor, he had to 'fess-up, which is why he's a full-time physician and only an occasional consultant.

7. Should You Accept an Assignment from a Client's Competitor?

This is a tricky one, and I've found the following criteria to be sound in determining whether to accept or decline an assignment:

- I will not do anything that reveals confidential information, directly or indirectly. A direct revelation: "Tell us how they plan to promote in region X." An indirect revelation: "Design a succession planning process that is similar to theirs." Acceptable conditions: "Evaluate our field-force management personnel and tell us what developmental work is needed in light of our business goals." (No competitive revelation is necessary at all.)

- I will try to assign different personnel to each project. If I am personally demanded, I will make the provisions in the first criterion clear at the outset.

- I will inform my present client of the competitor's request and the tentative project, and ask if the client wishes me to decline.

- If the new assignment is accepted under the above criteria, I will not divulge anything learned to the current client, either.

There is nothing intrinsically wrong with working for several clients within the same industry. After all, many buyers use "experience in our industry" as a hiring condition. The critical, ethical consideration is this: are you being hired for your expertise and ability to improve the client's condition, or for what you happen to know about the competition? Revealing confidential data is never itself a confidential process and, once inevitably discovered, it will propel you back to a nine-to-five job very rapidly.

8. Should You Agree to Use Secret Identifying Codes on a Confidential Survey?

Sorry, but ends do not justify means. Despite the client's pure thoughts on the matter, the action is unethical. Anonymous surveys are supposed to be exactly that. You are committing an unethical act as soon as you tell people that their responses are confidential, and then provide a document which exposes them by area.

If the client's need for information makes sense, as it does in this case, there are other options. You could tell people that responses are sorted by unit. Or you could provide a place for the unit to be recorded at the respondent's option. Or you could suggest other alternatives altogether, such as focus groups or direct observations.

There are always pragmatic reasons for doing the right thing. I've found that any attempt to disclose respondents' feedback by unit or person, despite promises to the contrary, is always found out by the rank and file. There are no secrets in organizations. There are simply some facts that take longer to surface than others.

9. Should You Continue to Write for a Client Who Passes Off Your Work as His/Her Own?

No problem here. The president is paying you for your expertise, you have agreed to the arrangement, and the president is acting with your permission. (Presumably, this service is also specified in your consulting contract with the client.) The only trouble with plagiarism arises when permission is not obtained. If you don't like someone else taking credit for your pearls of wisdom, don't open the clam by accepting such assignments.

10. Should You Agree to Supplant an Alliance Partner Who Introduced You to the Client?

Well, yes and no. Improving the client condition certainly justifies the project, since the client, having worked with the partner and you, is convinced that you can better meet current needs. But you also have an obligation to anyone who has introduced you to a client that you won't "steal" his or her revenue.

In these cases, I tell the client I can accept after I speak to the partner, explaining my obligations and ethical concerns. This usually raises my esteem in the eyes of the client. I'll explain the situation to my alliance partner, encourage the partner to contact the client to talk about it, and offer assurances that this initiative was the client's not mine. *Having done all this, I will accept the assignment.* The client has made an objective choice, my expertise is deemed appropriate, and I've been honest with the partner organization. Of course, engaging in *any* action whatsoever to supplant a partner at your initiative is unqualifiedly unethical. If you feel comfortable informing your partner of the situation and inviting the partner to discuss it with the client, you have probably acted well. If you accept without providing that opportunity, you have no doubt acted badly.[3]

One of the benefits of building a successful consulting firm is the opportunity — and necessity — to ponder on, develop criteria for, and take action about ethical issues with clients and colleagues. I've described composites of ten of the more common ones that I've encountered, but you'll undoubtedly be faced with some unique quandaries of your own. So, in conclusion, here are the guidelines I find useful in determining whether I am "doing the right thing":

1. Does the activity improve the client's condition, or merely my own?

2. Is the activity something that I am comfortable explaining to the client?

3. Is the activity something I am proud of and would publicize as a trait?

4. Is there harm being done to anyone without their being able to respond?

5. Is this treatment something I would willingly subject myself to?

---

[3]I have a short list of consultants whom I would never use as subcontractors, because I have seen evidence of their theft of business from former employers or other consultants. I freely tell my partners and colleagues about them. A pox on their houses.

These are not simple yes or no answers. In fact, the very act of putting the question to the client may often be sufficient to help you avoid ethical compromise. Ultimately, the client will be thankful that you asked.

Expanding Internationally

The only reasons not to pursue foreign clients early in your career are the problems of lack of focus and lack of funds. It takes more time to develop relationships abroad, and certainly more of an investment. However, I've found that foreign organizations are very receptive to consulting help, particularly if you carefully target your efforts. Once your firm is well established, with both repute and resources in larger supply, international expansion is a logical and practical consideration. As I write this, Eastern Europe, parts of Africa and Latin America, and the Pacific Rim nations present very viable targets. (I find that Western Europe is more difficult, since there are both strong domestic consulting operations and a substantial U.S. overseas presence, but with the right alliances, even this area can present opportunities.)[4]

I believe there is a hierarchy of requirements when picking targets for foreign concentration. (See Figure 14-1.) These criteria apply, irrespective of whether you are pursuing a target of opportunity or an organization is pursuing you. I've seen many situations in which what appeared to be a lucrative overseas consulting assignment turned out to be just the opposite because funds couldn't be taken out of the country (one poor soul wound up investing his consulting fee in local baskets, which he tried to import and sell in the states); or because a key client manager demanded a bribe (they're often listed on the books as "commissions" in Latin America); or because the client, after hearing all the consultant's ideas in the proposal process, decided to "handle it internally."[5]

The best way to acquire overseas clients is through strategic alliances. I work with people in Singapore and the United Kingdom whose skills

---

[4]I do not consider Canada a "foreign" target. I don't want to do violence to anyone's belief system, but it is as easy for any U.S. consultant to do business in Canada as it is in the U.S. The key is to be certain that the client understands you are citing *U.S. funds,* and that the client draws checks payable on a U.S. bank in those funds. (Otherwise, your bank will slap you with a considerable fee for collecting the Canadian funds, you will suffer in the exchange translation, *and* you will be forced to wait four to six weeks before the check is cleared. Other than that, there's no problem!)

[5]In the Republic of China, all management ideas are considered the property of mankind, and thus belong to everyone. In Indonesia and the Philippines, plagiarism of published work from even major authors and publishers is widespread and tolerated, and copyright laws are virtually unenforceable.

Language

1. English-speaking as a first language (i.e., UK, Australia)

2. English-speaking as business language (i.e., Hong Kong, Singapore)

3. English-speaking capability common (i.e., Germany, Switzerland)

4. English spoken by elite only (i.e., Spain, Thailand)

Sophistication

1. Information-based, knowledge-oriented society (i.e., Japan, France)

2. Emerging from manufacturing base to knowledge (i.e., Brazil, Korea)

3. Labor-intensive manufacturing (i.e., Indonesia, Nigeria)

Currency Policy

1. Stable and relatively easy to convert and exchange (i.e., Germany)

2. Somewhat unstable, easy to convert and exchange (i.e., Italy)

3. Difficult to exchange (i.e., Philippines, Brazil)

4. Highly unstable (i.e., Argentina, Eastern Europe)

Figure 14-1. Priorities to bear in mind when choosing a foreign target for concentration.

and approaches are complemented by my own. They will often underwrite a trip for me, during which we make joint sales calls after I help them on a particular project. In this manner I've developed work with Shell Singapore, Citibank in Singapore, and the Singapore Straits Times, as well as Case Communications, Lucas Engineering, and the British Standards Institute in the United Kingdom. These alliances are extremely productive because they combine current, fee-paying projects with the opportunity to develop new business.

A second effective method is to pursue international work through existing multinational clients based in the United States (or based elsewhere, with a U.S. operation as your primary client). Through an international division of Merck, I've had the opportunity to work and develop a reputation in the United Kingdom, Costa Rica, Hong Kong and Brazil. (Note that when you pursue this avenue, some of the difficulties involved with the lower-priority targets are mitigated. For example, I don't worry about currency restrictions or instability in Brazil, because I'm paid in the United States by the parent company.)

Still another way to market internationally is to write for international publications. There are management journals in most developed countries, and they will usually accept articles written in English. (Many publish in English as well.) I've generated many contacts from writing for such publications in the United Kingdom, Brazil, Mexico, Singapore, Germany, and Hong Kong. As a rule, foreign clients place a much higher value on written papers and research than do Americans.

Finally, you can market overseas by seeking speaking opportunities at international conferences. This is no different from seeking domestic speaking assignments, except that you will often be asked to pay your own way. This is one reason why I only advocate such tactics after you have established yourself. The greater your reputation, the more the likelihood that your expenses and fee will be accommodated, but even if they are not, the greater your growth, the more you are able to underwrite such marketing opportunities yourself.

As I write this, I have been asked to appear as a guest speaker at a major Asian management conference in Manila. I've contacted both a client, Citicorp, and a strategic partner in Singapore, to see how we might jointly underwrite a major marketing swing attendant to my appearance. These plans are made by fax, phone, and letter, so that everything can be well established before the major expenses are incurred.

> *There may be more potential for dramatic,*
> *multidimensional growth overseas than at home in*
> *the near future.*

Given the nature of the post–Cold War world and the increasing globalization of business, there may well be more opportunity for dramatic growth abroad than at home for entrepreneurial consultants. Million dollar consulting is just as lucrative when the components are pounds, francs, yen, lire, marks, and pesos. And once you've worked internationally, you have a tremendous marketing opportunity at home for your business literature, proposals, interviews, speeches, and articles. You are now an international consultant, who has worked in X number of countries. If you don't think that carries instant credibility, try it out yourself. The first time a client asked me what I could possibly contribute to their benchmarking plans and I replied, "Let me give you an example from my work on innovation with the British Standards Institute, anticipating the advent of the European Economic Community," there wasn't a sound in the room other than the client's pen sliding out of his pocket to sign the contract.

Designing the Future

My experiences in the consulting profession have led me to establish a very simple philosophy:

1. This is a relationship business.
2. Multidimensional growth provides for high-quality, enduring relationships.
3. There is no limit to the firm's—or your own—income from those relationships.

At this point you may be asking, "How can it be that simple? After all, if everyone is trying to establish those relationships, aren't we all back in the old competitive-commodity ball game, trying to prove that a relationship with me is somehow superior to one with the other consultants? What about all the people reading this book? Won't we all look the same going out there to try doing the same thing?"

I'd like to respond to these concerns by drawing on a consulting assignment as an avatar. I've been working with a large specialty chemicals firm that finds itself a diminishing "number three" among its competitors. Whereas it once had hopes of overtaking its two much larger rivals, it found itself facing the possibility of smaller organizations chipping away at some of its traditional business. The firm's strategy was divided: do we invest the substantial resources needed to make a run at the leaders, or do we solidify our position as number three, fighting off challenges to that spot? Neither position was terribly attractive. After all, to overtake the leaders would take years, flawless performance, and a great deal of luck. But to remain number three was to manage an "also-ran," and it's hard to attract, retain, and motivate people in an acknowledged loser.

The answer, of course, was breathtakingly simple: to be number one on the company's own terms. The company redefined itself in terms of what it did better than anyone else in the industry—including the larger competitors—and established a vision and mission of being number one *in the market, and under the conditions, it had defined for itself.*

Strategically, it's quite simple. *You don't allow the competition to define the playing field or to write the rules.* When I began my own practice leading up to my current firm, I was told unequivocally that I couldn't generate over $300,000 in income, and that I would have to add people and facilities, probably using outside investors. I was also advised that I would be swallowed whole unless I specialized in some market segment as protection against "the big guys."

> ## *It's extraordinarily difficult, if not impossible, to break the paradigms when someone else is defining the paradigms.*

Now listen up: those pieces of advice were probably accurate for someone who chose to play by the existing, conventional rules. But *I defined what I wanted to become.* Under *my* rules, such as the three listed at the beginning of this section, traditional conditions didn't apply. I wasn't competing with anyone, because I was going to be numero uno as a unique, boutique-type of consulting firm that did business with Fortune 500 organizations and their brethren. The key is *not* to out-think your competitors, because to do so is unlikely and overwhelmingly tiring. The key is to *have* no competitors, because you have defined your own playing field and written your own rules. The specialty chemical firm did this, avoiding the suffering of a myriad of organizations in similar straits, which have vainly tried to play by others' rules. I did it, made a fortune, and emerged to write this book, because I determined how I would play the game. But the idea itself isn't mine. It's practiced by the most successful business people and entrepreneurs in the world.

> Don't try to be smarter than your competitors, because any competent competitor will be working just as hard to be smarter than you. The trick is to have *no* competitors.[6] —*Warren Buffet*, CEO, Berkshire Hathaway

Once you've established who you are and how you'll play, concerns about the competition and "Isn't everyone doing this?" evaporate. You'll always need to be cognizant of what the competition is doing, but you'll never need to be *concerned* about what they're doing.

A couple of weeks ago, another consultant whom I've previously mentioned, Bob Janson, and I were with the CEO of a company which is a client of both our firms. We were returning from a day-long fishing trip off Montauk, Long Island, with two of our kids. There were five

---

[6]Quoted in *Emory Business Magazine*, Emory University, Atlanta, Ga. 30322, and cited in *Boardroom Reports*, Vol. 20, No. 16, August 15, 1991, page 2.

tuna in the hold and Bob and I were very contentedly reflecting on the lives we had carved out in this business.[7] I remarked that client relationships didn't get much better than this. He pointed out something that never ceases to astonish me: "The relationship is one thing," he said, "but it's exploiting the opportunity that it presents that sets people like us apart. Most consultants I know are pretty good at scrambling around and overcoming setbacks, enabling them to survive. But very, very few know how to exploit success, and know how to prosper."

Maybe out there off the continental shelf we were suffering terminal male bonding. But Bob's observation makes just as much sense to me here on dry land.

Each of us has to transcend the mere survival reflex, and understand that surviving is not the point. "Prospering" to me is the ability to meet personal and family goals through the income, wisdom, and experiences generated by a thriving business. The multidimensional growth I've been espousing doesn't pertain only to your professional life. As you grow personally, you grow professionally, and as you grow professionally, you grow personally. That's why this business is so wonderful.

As you prosper you will begin to create what I call a "body of work."[8] By that I merely mean that the combination of the types of projects you are best known for, your publishing and/or speeches, your pro bono efforts and your general visibility will represent those facets of your business at which you have become most adept. Nearer to the beginning of your career, you will have had to deliberately establish your unique, number-one-in-the-field strategy. As your career blossoms, your body of work will speak for you. By the very nature of what you've accomplished, you will be considered the best at what you do, and your clients and prospects will see you in that distinguishing light.

The future of the firm then becomes whatever you wish it to be. What will become of Summit Consulting Group, Inc.? I'm still not sure. My teenage kids won't be going into the business, apparently, since one is headed for broadcast journalism, and one for rock 'n' roll. I don't plan to retire, since I can do what I'm doing—consulting, speaking, writing—without age constraints, although I can become more selective over the next thirty-odd years. Will a larger firm buy us out? Possibly—I'm sure there's an amount of money somewhere that constitutes an offer I can't

---

[7] For those who have been wondering, I'm 45. Bob is 52, and his firm is much larger than mine.

[8] When a different publisher expressed interest in this book, the acquisitions editor told me I had "a nice shelf." After a stunned moment, I learned she was referring to the solid sales of my previous three books. I didn't know whether to be disappointed or relieved. I'll try not to be so obscure here.

refuse. Perhaps people with whom I work, or even clients, will take over the firm. Frankly, it's a matter of no great importance.

My firm is, and always has been, a means to an end. That end has been the well-being of my family, the pursuit of our interests, and what Maslow quaintly termed, "self-actualization." You see, the future of the firm isn't so important, it's the future of the founder that's crucial! Your body of work defines more than your company's projects and positioning. It defines your values and contribution to the environment around you. I have since completely lost the source, but I remember Peter Drucker saying once that

> An organization is not like a tree or an animal, successful merely by dint of perpetuating the species. An organization is successful based on the contribution it makes to the outside environment.

For an individual to establish a consulting firm that contributes to the improvement of its clients' conditions, to the enhanced productivity and quality of their people, to the increased profitability of their operations, and therefore to the increased well-being of *their* customers and stockholders, is an ultimate contribution to the outside environment. And if, in so doing, you personally achieve success through the realization of your personal life goals, then you are in rarefied air indeed.

How many of us are in a position to meet personal and professional goals — and to amass wealth — through a constant process of helping others to meet *their* personal and professional goals, and enhance *their* wealth? Professional consulting isn't just a wonderful profession, it's a wonderful way of life. And if, in that pursuit, you make a million bucks, who can object?

Annotated Resources

This book should not be an isolated "event," but rather part of an ongoing process on the road to million dollar consulting. So, before you close the book, here are some resources to facilitate the transition from my printed pages to your bank account.

Associations

ACME—The Association of
  Management Consulting Firms
230 Park Avenue, Suite 544
New York, NY 10169

Formerly the Association of Management Consultants, ACME merged with the Institute of Management Consultants to form the Council of Consulting Organizations, of which ACME is a division (got that?). They hold annual domestic and foreign meetings, offer newsletters, directories, surveys, etc. Under CCO, individuals as well as firms are embraced, although the organization has some large and notable nonmembers and some members who are barely active. Still, it's all there is, and it has shown signs of trying to get its act together.

American Management
  Association
135 West 50th Street
New York, NY 10020

As cited repeatedly in the text, this is an important organization which has improved tremendously over the years. Membership is only $150 at this writing, and for that you get access to a first-class reference department, the monthly *Management Review,* which is a source for your publishing, invitations to conferences and local breakfasts, and a great deal more. This is one of the best values around for consultants.

American Society of Association
Executives
1575 I Street, NW
Washington, DC 20005-1168
(202/626-2723)

The society's monthly publication, *Association Management,* goes to over 23,000 association executives. It may be a good source for publicizing speaking activities, or for simply learning what this market is concerned about. You probably can't join it (nor would you want to), but you ought to keep abreast of it and its activities. It is especially useful if you tend to specialize in nonprofit organizations or intend to market through industry trade associations.

American Society for Training
and Development
1640 King Street
Alexandria, VA 22313

This is the organization that every human resource professional in existence seems to belong to. It holds an annual convention and regional workshops (at which consultants often present their wares by speaking and/or exhibiting) and publishes the monthly *Journal,* which prints consultants' articles on a regular basis. More importantly, I've found its annual *Buyer's Guide and Consultant Directory* an important place to be listed. The listing currently costs about $150, but could go up to $500 if you want your logo and some extra bells and whistles. I think it's a good deal.

Council of Consulting
Organizations
(See ACME, above.)

National Society for
Performance and Instruction
1300 L Street, NW, Suite 1250
Washington, DC 20005

This society focuses on instructional and performance technologies to improve human performance. Its orientation is heavy on training, but it is also appropriate for consultants. It offers a cross-industrial membership, journal and quarterly publications, and annual meetings, which are usually well attended. You should belong at least to the ASTD *or* NSPI, and an overlap of the two wouldn't be fatal.

National Speakers Association
1500 South Priest Drive
Tempe, AZ 85281

This is a useful organization to hone speaking skills. It is more valuable for the neophyte than for the seasoned veteran of the platform, and its conventions often resemble a tent revival, with everyone on their feet applauding despite the content and level of competence. There are local chapters that do not require national membership, although at about $250, membership is a bargain. They publish the annual *Who's Who in Professional Speaking*, which is sent to 8000 or so meeting planners, as well as a monthly magazine, *SpeakOut*.

Young Presidents' Organization
451 South Decker, #200
Irving, TX 75062

All the members of this organization are people under 50 who are presidents of firms with at least 50 employees and $5 million in sales or $100 million in total assets. The organization's major international meetings always feature outside speakers. These meetings offer a splendid opportunity to be heard by entrepreneurial, action-oriented executives. (The group's annual operating budget is over $15 million.)

Books

Consulting Technique and Practical Information

The following works are more pragmatic than classic. The entries would tend to vary depending on whom you asked, but these are as good a starting point as any. (The classics are listed in the following section.) Note that these are mostly older works.

Bellman, Geoffrey M., *The Consultant's Calling: Bringing Who You Are to What You Do*, Jossey-Bash, San Francisco, 1990.

Bellman discusses the merging of personal values and work, and offers his insights from 25 years of consulting, with a focus on balancing your lifestyle and work style. This may be consulting as Sartre would view it, but it's worth adding to the library.

Bennis, Warren, *The Unconscious Conspiracy: Why Leaders Can't Lead*, AMACOM, New York, 1975.

This is the one popular work which is a must-read about leadership. Note that it's his first treatment of the topic. Nothing he's written since on the subject can compare, and you're better served looking for this early version.

Blake, Robert R., and Mouton, Jane Srygley, *Consultation,* Addison-Wesley, Reading, Mass., 1976.

These authors are the famous "management grid" folks, adjusting their work to consulting. It's a difficult book to read (and pseudoscientific in my opinion), but it will provide a diagnostic exegesis of the consulting process (and it contains a wealth of useful references, despite its age). This is a good counterbalance to Block's highly people-sensitive approach (see below).

Block, Peter, *Flawless Consulting: A Guide to Getting Your Expertise Used,* Learning Concepts, Austin, Tex., 1981.

Block tackles every aspect of the consulting process and provides techniques—both process and interpersonal—to hone the skills necessary to successful consulting engagements. This work is best for those just entering the profession or considering it. It's a vastly different approach from Blake's rigorous science (see above).

Drucker, Peter F., *The Changing World of the Executive,* Times Books, New York, 1982.

Any consultant worth his or her business card ought to be intimately familiar with friend Drucker. He isn't always right, but he's always provocative. His older works (written before he was quite so cantankerous) are better than his newer ones, and in addition to the one above, I recommend these others: *Managing in Turbulent Times,* 1980, *The Effective Executive,* 1966, and *The Age of Discontinuity,* 1968, all from Harper & Row, New York. Read any two of these four and you'll be a better person for it.

Mager, Robert F., *The Mager Library,* Pitman Learning, Inc., Belmont, Calif., 1984.

Mager is *the* guru of competency-based instructional design, and he's a helluva guy to spend some time with at his home in the desert, as well. This library contains his classic paperbacks: *Developing Attitude Toward Learning, Preparing Instructional Objectives, Measuring Instructional Results, Goal Analysis,* and *Analyzing Performance Problems.* If you want to undertake large learning design projects, these works are a must. Mager's a card (one of his famous questions to determine skill versus attitude problems is, "Could he do it if his life depended on it?")

and the back cover of his library contains a photo of the back of his head. Don't miss it.

Schein, Edgar H., *Process Consultation: Its Role in Organization Development*, Addison-Wesley, Reading, Mass., 1969.

If you read Schein and nothing else, you'll know more than most about consulting from the standpoint of working within organizational contexts. Note the date; some things never change. Schein once said, "If you really want to understand something, try to change it."

Schrello, Don M., *The Complete Marketing Handbook for Consultants*, University Associates, San Diego, Calif. (updated periodically).

I've known Don for a decade, and he's the only person I've found who has specialized in marketing techniques for consultants, although his approach is skewed toward the training end of the business. This is a loose-leaf set taken from his seminars on the topic, issued through (what else?) a consulting firm.

Shenson, Howard L., *Shenson on Consulting: Success Strategies from the "Consultant's Consultant,"* John Wiley and Sons, New York, 1990.

The late Mr. Shenson was an enigma to me. Apparently he wrote extensively on consulting and billed himself as the "consultant's consultant," yet I never heard him mentioned by colleagues, and none of my clients ever used him. I'm listing this because otherwise you might wonder why I didn't. It does contain the nuts and bolts of contracts, proposals, billing, etc. It focuses on how to begin in the business, not how to develop a business.

Tregoe, Benjamin B., and Zimmerman, John W., *Top Management Strategy: What It Is and How To Make It Work*, Simon and Schuster, New York, 1980.

This is also a case of the original being better than anything that has followed it. It's a concise, process viewpoint of strategy that will provide an orientation toward the discipline for clients *and* toward your own strategic goals.

Consulting Classics, History, and Philosophy

If you need a formal education in the history and genesis of our profession, I suggest you read each of the following classics. If you do so, you will be more knowledgeable than 99 percent of your colleagues (and every obscure reference to a model or historical design you're ever likely to encounter will be accounted for). While these are all older works, they are all readily available.

Argyris, Chris, *Integrating the Individual and the Organization,* John Wiley and Sons, New York, 1964.

Argyris is one of the leading proponents of positive team relationships resulting in individual well-being and, consequently, in enhanced performance.

Fiedler, Frederick, *A Theory of Leadership Effectiveness,* McGraw-Hill, New York, 1967.

Fiedler is the champion of the contingency leadership approach, as opposed to normative and path-goal theory. (See Vroom, below.)

Herzberg, Fred, *Work and the Nature of Man,* World, Cleveland, 1966.

This is the origin of the so-called hygiene theory, which includes the position that the absence of dissatisfaction does not lead to the presence of satisfaction, which is, in my opinion, a fundamental reason why money is not an automatic motivator.

Likert, Rensis, *New Patterns of Management,* McGraw-Hill, New York, 1961.

I find Likert a tough author to comprehend, but his studies on leadership and achieving desired levels of performance led to groundbreaking work at the University of Michigan, with some of the best brains in the business beginning their careers as his disciples.

Maslow, Abraham, *Motivation and Personality,* Harper & Row, New York, 1970.

Maslow is the originator of the "hierarchy of needs" theory, which postulated that we are motivated by increasingly sophisticated needs, from basic security through self-actualization. He is forever being cited by managers who know only the buzz words, but the practical application of his work is questionable.

McClelland, David, *The Achieving Society,* Free Press, New York, 1961.

This is an early work on leadership and power needs—including leaders' conflicting need to influence others and be liked by others—and the ramifications of such conflicts on leaders' effectiveness.

McGregor, Douglas, *The Human Side of Enterprise,* McGraw-Hill, New York, 1960.

The source of the famed "Theory X and Theory Y" management styles, according to which the manager is either task-driven or people-driven.

Rogers, Carl, *On Personal Power: Inner Strength and Its Revolutionary Impact,* Delacorte, New York, 1977.

As opposed to Skinner (see below), Rogers emphasizes the humanistic and inner-driven nature of behavior in a concept similar to Maslow's theory of the need for self-actualization.

Skinner, B. F., *Beyond Freedom and Dignity,* Knopf, New York, 1971.

Skinner is the father of "operant conditioning" and the influence of the environment on behaviors. If you manage the environment, claims Skinner, you should be able to manage behaviors (irrespective of Rogers' "inner needs").

Taylor, Frederick Winslow, *Scientific Management,* Harper, New York, 1911.

By all means read Taylor, whose "Taylorism" was the first real management consulting approach, giving rise to time-and-motion studies and later to the efficiency experts who began our modern profession.

Vroom, Victor, and Yetton, Phil, *Leadership and Decision Making,* University of Pittsburgh Press, 1973.

Vroom has done the seminal work on normative leadership factors, and his original work and research with Yetton still constitutes his best stuff. He provides a fascinating and practical approach to demonstrating the *options* available to the leader, as opposed to dictating some "perfect style." (See Fiedler, above, for another approach.)

Computer Software

These applications are primarily for Apple Computers, since I use Macs and can personally vouch for their user-friendliness and business applications. The reader is advised to check for the latest editions of any software issue.

Business Finances/Check Writing

MacMoney, Survivor Software
11222 La Cienega Boulevard
Inglewood, CA 90304
(213/410-9527)

Quicken, Intuit Software
Box 3014
Menlo Pike, CA 94026
(415/322-0573)

Word Processing

Microsoft Word, Microsoft
One Microsoft Way
Redmond, WA 98052
(206/882-8080)

The best user support in the business.

Spreadsheet

Microsoft Excel, as above.

Periodicals and Reference Works

ASTD Journal

See the American Society for Training and Development under "Associations."

Boardroom Reports
330 W. 43rd Street
New York, NY 10036

Brief articles and paragraph excerpts from current works provide a monthly source of new ideas or reaffirmation of old ones. This is a high-visibility source for you to be cited in, almost always from a book or article published elsewhere. Interviews with the same old board of contributors become hackneyed and self-serving, but each issue usually provides one useful idea, and that's more than sufficient payback. (There is a similar sister publication, *Bottom Line,* oriented toward personal applications. In fact, both are useful in consulting, and they often overlap. A subscription to both is worthwhile.)

Consultants News
Kennedy Publications
Templeton Road
Fitzwilliam, NH 03447

Jim Kennedy has established himself as a combination gadfly and moral conscience of the consulting profession (and executive search business). But he's right more often than not, and he's always on top of relevant issues. He manages to embrace the humongous firms and the sole practitioners with equal zeal and lack of mercy. It's a good monthly read and you shouldn't be without it. I'd rate it a must.

Management Review

See the American Management Association under "Associations."

The National Directory of Addresses and Telephone Numbers
General Information, Inc.
Box 3299
Kirkland, WA 98083
(206/483-4555)

Every major public company is provided with address, telephone number, and fax number, alphabetically and by SIC code. This is an invaluable reference resource, issued annually.

National Trade and Professional Associations of the United States
Columbia Books, Inc.
1212 New York Avenue,
Suite 330
Washington, DC 20005

This is an extremely useful resource that includes every imaginable association, its officers, conventions, themes, membership, and other goodies. Ideal for targeted mailings, marketing strategy, speaking opportunities, and so on. Issued annually.

News Media Yellow Book (of
Washington and New York)
Monitor Publishing Co.
104 Fifth Avenue
New York, NY 10011
(212/627-4140)

This is a who's who in the print and broadcast market. It can be useful for press releases and targeted publicity. Direct phone numbers are provided.

Training Magazine
Lakewood Publications
50 South Ninth Street
Minneapolis, MN 55402

Although training-oriented, articles in this periodical tend to be pithy and more candid than in ASTD's *Journal.* (Neither has ever printed anything that might antagonize an advertiser.) The magazine often publishes consultants' articles in a variety of formats, and will also report on consultant research. It publishes an annual *Marketplace Directory,* in which you can be listed free. It also hosts annual and regional conferences at which you may apply for speaking opportunities. The conferences are similar to the American Society for Training and Development conferences.

Resources for Building Skills in Public Speaking

Communispond
485 Lexington Avenue
New York, NY 10017
(212/687-8040)

Provides seminars and workshops in public speaking. It has offices around the country. Your best bet is to enroll in something geared toward executives with as much individualized attention as possible.

The Executive Speaker
891 Mayfield Avenue
Winter Park, FL 32789
(407/664-5256)

Similar to Communispond above. Offers individual sessions.

The Executive Technique
716 North Rush Street
Chicago, IL 60611
(312/266-0001)

Similar to Communispond and Executive Speaker, with somewhat more emphasis on the executive speaker.

Publishing Resources

Herman, Jeff, *The Insider's Guide to Book Editors and Publishers,* Prima
   Publishing, Rockland, Calif., 1990.

This reference work provides the name of virtually every publisher and key editor in this country and Canada, as well as candid tips on how to get their attention, how to get your manuscript in order, and what mistakes to avoid. Jeff Herman is one of the exceptions-to-agents rule; he's very honest and very effective. If you have a manuscript or an idea for one, you can do a lot worse than the Jeff Herman Agency, 500 Greenwich Street, New York, NY 10013.

Writer's Digest, Writer's Digest Books, 9933 Alliance Road, Cincinnati, Ohio, 45242

This is a monthly magazine oriented toward the beginning writer. It provides tips for getting published, advice on style, and examples of successful editing. Its focus is primarily on articles and the magazine market. This company also publishes an annual reference work, *Writer's Market,* which includes every publisher of consequence and all pertinent information — including preferred style, audience, and payment schedules — for every major market, including the business market.

Index

Advertising, 10, 106, 214–215
Alliances, 118–119, 123, 244, 250–252
Answering service, 49
Arbitrator, 7
Article publishing, 101–102, 162–164
Audiocassettes, 106–107, 218–222
Awards, 18, 19n., 215–216

Bank, choosing of, 196–197
Barker, Joel, 59–60
Behavior consultation, 7, 8
Bid requests, 38, 41–44
Bill paying, 203–205, 207–208
Book publishing, 104–105, 164–165
Bookkeeper, 193, 194
Breakthrough positioning, 64–66
Brochure, corporate, 50
Business card, 108, 112
Business decline, 173–176
Business goals, 32–36, 55
Business growth, 28–30, 41–57, 254–257
  business goals and, 35–36
  challenges, 110–114
  considerations in, 85
  models, 50–54
Business logo, 47
Business name, 46

C corporation, 47
Capital, 85–90, 191–208
  cashflow, 197–198
  credit lines, 191–197
  expense management, 202–208
  receivables collection, 198–202

Cartoons, 157–158
Cashflow, 197–198
Chamber of commerce referral service, 39
Client:
  abandoning of, 29–32
  advisory groups, 233–234
  communications, 155–160
  competitor of, 244, 248–249
  conferences, 231–233
  mailings, 100–101
Collaboration fees, 126–129
Commissions, 30n., 68
Commodity consulting approach, 61–62
Conference presentations, 213
Consultant, 3–8
  income of, 18, 32
  learning and, 25–27, 55
  number of, 8n., 18n.
  work habits of, 23–28
Consulting:
  consulting value, 5–8
  principles, 90–92
  trends in, 17–21, 53–54
Contacts consultation, 7–8
Content consultation, 5–6, 8, 113
Contingency contracts, 200, 201
Contracts (interventions), 13–17, 51
Contrarian consulting, 180–184
Controllable rejection, 41–42
Corporate brochure, 50
Cox, Allan, 183
Credit accounts, 203
Credit lines, 191–197

*Index note: An *f.* after a page number refers to a figure; an *n.* refers to a note.

Darien, Steve, 26–27
Debt financing, 87–90
Direct mail, 29, 100–101
Directory listings, 105
Diversification, 178
Double-bill, 187, 244, 246–247
Down times (*see* Transition period)

Employees, 115–116, 136
Equity financing, 87–88
Ethics, 69–70, 179–180,
    243–251
Expense management, 184–187, 202–208
Expertise consultation, 6, 8, 15, 24
External consultant, 4

"Failure trap," 187
Fees, 135–153, 243, 245
    below value, 135
    discount, 96, 198–199
    evaluation of, 73
    fee-commitment dynamic, 73–75, 138
    for long-term contracts, 230–231
    market demand, 140–143
    per diem, 132*n*., 135–140
    raising of, 29, 82, 150–153
    ranges for various activities, 141*f*.
    for speeches, 26, 152*n*., 200*n*.
    staff, 124–129
    during transition period, 82
    value-based, 143–150
Finances, 193–195
Financial advisor, 193–194
Financial growth, 72–73
Finder's fee, 30*n*., 68, 125–126
Ford, Gerald, 7–8
Foster, Richard, 44, 45*f*.

Geographic diversification, 178,
    212*n*., 251–254
Gift giving, 69–70
Goals, business, 32–36, 55
Government consulting, 9
Growth (*see* Business growth)

Herman, Jeff, 161*n*.
Home telephone number, 67

Image consultant, 7
Image (*see* Professional image)
Imprudent risk, 56
Income of consultants, 18, 32

Indirect marketing, 95–96
Information service, 67
Internal consultant, 4
International consulting, 212*n*., 251–254
Interventions (contracts), 13–17, 51
Interviews, 104, 218

Janson, Bob, 24–25, 255–256

"Keepers," 97
Knowledge consultation, 6, 8

Leads (*see* Selection process)
Legal issues, 47–48, 85, 86
Logo, 47
Long-term contract, 174, 227–231

Mailing list, 10, 67
Market demand fees, 140–143
Marketing, 100–108, 209–226
    advertising, 10, 106, 214–215
    audiocassettes, 106–107, 218–222
    awards, 18, 19*n*., 215–216
    business card, 108, 112
    clients and, 69, 100–101, 155–160
    conference presentations, 213
    corporate brochure, 50
    direct mail, 29, 100–101
    directory listings, 105
    indirect, 95–96
    interviews, 104, 218
    mailing list, 10, 67
    networking, 39, 98–100, 107, 159
    options checklist, 101*f*.
    passive, 9, 217–222
    press releases, 216
    pro bono work, 102, 169–172
    prospect mailings, 101
    publicist, 107–108
    referrals, 9, 68, 103–104
    surveys, 42, 55–56, 217, 244, 249
    talk shows, 213–214
    timing, 36–40, 156
    trade association memberships, 107
    trade show exhibits, 103
    video tapes, 222–226
    visibility, 48, 106
    Yellow Pages, 106
    (*See also* Publishing; Speeches)
Mediator, 7
Meetings, 42, 146*n*.
Mentor relationship, 30

Meyers-Briggs Type Indicator, 51–52
Multidimensional growth, 71–72, 217, 229

Name of business, 46
Networking, 39, 98–100, 107, 159
Never worked in the industry challenge, 110–111
Never worked on particular assignment challenge, 112–113
Nine-dot problem, 60, 61*f*.
Number sequence problem, 60–61

Office requirements, 48–50, 205–206

Paradigm, 59
Paradigm shift, 59–75
  breakthrough positioning, 64–66
  fee-commitment dynamic, 73–75, 138
  products, 61–65
  relationships, 62–71, 227–241
  services, 61–65
Partners, 117–118, 123
Passive marketing, 9, 217–222
Payroll service, 193, 194
Per diem fees, 132*n*., 135–140
Personal conduct, 108–110
Personality assessment, 51–52
Peters, Thomas J., 18
Pipeline, 173–176
Press kit for speeches, 167–168
Press releases, 216
Principles of consulting, 90–92
Print solution, 47
Pro bono work, 102, 169–172
Process consultation, 6
Products, 61–65
Professional image, 45–50, 95–114, 209–222
  business logo, 47
  business name, 46
  corporate brochure, 50
  errors in, 11*f*.
  growth challenges, 110–114
  "keepers," 97
  legal entity, 47–48
  networking, 98–100
  office requirements, 48–50
  personal conduct, 108–110
  professional organizations, 95–98
  reference library, 99
  visibility, 48, 106
  (*See also* Marketing)

Professional organizations, 10, 95–98, 259–261
Profile (*see* Marketing; Professional image)
Profits, 136
Promotion (*see* Marketing)
Prospects, 42, 101, 175
Protégés, 30
Prudent risk, 56
Publicist, 107–108
Publicity (*see* Marketing)
Publishing, 159–165, 211–212
  articles, 101–102, 162–164
  books, 104–105, 164–165
  international, 253
  resources for, 268–269
  staircase approach, 161*f*.

Receivables, collecting of, 198–202
Reference library, 99
References, 9, 113, 123
Referrals, 9, 68, 103–104
Rejection, 41–44
Relationships, 62–71, 227–241
  client advisory groups, 233–234
  client as partner, 71
  client conferences, 231–233
  client publicity, 69
  with clients' subordinates, 70
  fee-commitment dynamic, 73–75, 138
  gift giving, 69–70
  ideal, 66
  information service, 67
  issue raising, 67–68, 70–71, 244, 247
  long-term contracts, 174, 227–231
  resources, 68
  telephone numbers, 67
  value-added principle, 235–241
Report writing, responsibility of, 24–25
Reputation, 9
Resource centers, 38–39
Revenue-sharing fee formula, 126–129
Reversal, 39–40
Risk taking, 54–57, 137
Robert, Michel, 28–29, 231–232

S corporation, 47
S-curve theory (Foster), 44, 45*f*.
Scholarly research, 211–212
Selection process, 8–13, 64, 66, 106
  advertising, 10, 106, 214–215
  business image and, 11*f*.

Selection process (*Cont.*):
  internal data, 10
  personal contact, 10
  professional affiliations, 9–10
  reputation, 9
  timing, 36–40
  word-of-mouth, 9
Services, 61–65
Shenson, Howard, 18*n.*
Slide projector, 50
Sogomi, 113–114
Speakers' bureaus, 103, 168–169
Speeches, 102–103, 165–169
  fees for, 96, 152*n.*, 200*n.*
  international, 253
  press kit, 167–168
  recordings of, 106–107, 219–222
  resources for, 268
Special skills consultation, 7, 8
Staff, 111–112, 115–133
  alliances, 118–119, 123, 244,
    250–252
  characteristics of, 115
  delegation of duties, 129–133
  employees, 115–116, 136
  expense policy, 208
  fees, 124–129
  hiring of, 115–116, 121–124
  partners, 117–118, 123
  subcontractors, 118–121, 123, 124
Strategic planning, 6
Subcontractors, 118–121, 123, 124
Success trap, 41–45, 78
Surveys, 42, 55–56, 217, 244, 249

Talk shows, 213–214
Telephone, 49, 67
"Thinking blinders," 60
Timing, 36–40, 156
  bid requests, 38
  chamber of commerce referral, 39
  networking, 39
  resource center, 38–49

Timing (*Cont.*):
  during transition period, 84
  want ads, 39
Toll-free telephone number, 48, 67
Trade association memberships, 107
Trade show exhibits, 103
Training, 4–5, 10
Transition period, 77–85
  business decline, 173–176
  client participation, 81–83
  contrarian consulting, 180–184
  expense cutting, 184–187
  fee changes, 82
  feedback, 82–83
  intractable client, 84–85
  plan, 77–79
  service phaseout, 83–84
  timing, 84
  triage system, 79–81
  "up-time" rules, 176–180
Travel, 204–206, 243, 244, 246–248
Tregoe, Ben, 137*n.*
Trends, 17–21, 53–54

Uncontrollable rejection, 41
Unlimited meetings, 146*n.*
"Up-time" rules, 188–181

Vagelos, Roy, 69*n.*
Value-based fees, 143–150
Velocity sales, 125, 130–131
Vendor quality, 46
Video tapes, 222–226
Visibility of business, 48, 106

Want ads, 39
Waterman, Robert H., Jr., 18
White-collar moonlighting, 18
Wisdom, 235–241
Working capital, 86–87
Workshops, 10

Yellow Pages, 106